THE
CRUISING GUIDE
TO
CUBA

FIRST EDITION

HAVANA
CABO SAN ANTONIO
ISLA DE JUVENTUD
CAYO LARGO
CASILDA
TRINIDAD
MANZANILLO
CABO CRUZ
GUANTANAMO
SANTIAGO DE CUBA
BARACOA
PUNTA MAISI
VARADERO
THE CAYS

Published by:
Simon Charles & Cruising Guide Publications, Inc.
1-800-330-9542

Distributed by:
Cruising Guide Publications, Inc.
Phone: (800) 330-9542 • (813) 733-5322 • Fax: (813) 734-8179

Author:
SIMON CHARLES

Editing & Art Direction:
ALLEN CONRAD

Illustrations by:
SALLY ERDLE

Photography by:
GEORGE HALLORAN
SIMON CHARLES

This guide is intended for use with official navigational charts. Every effort has
been made to describe conditions accurately, however, the publisher makes no
warranty, expressed or implied, for any errors or for any omissions in this
publication. The skipper must use this guide only in conjunction with
charts and other navigational aids and not place undue credence in the
accuracy of this guide. This guide is not to be used for navigational
purposes. NOTE: All sketch chart depths are in feet and
compass courses are magnetic unless otherwise indicated.
Views and opinions expressed are the author's, based
on personal experience while cruising Cuba.

1st Edition

Printed in the United States of America

ISBN 0-944428-26-6

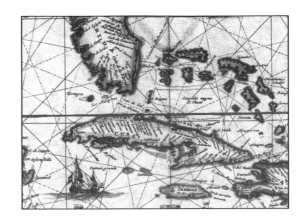

I went to Cuba because I was curious; because no one agrees on its strengths; because I'd read so much about it; because it is forbidden; because it's heartbreakingly lovely; because so many people have championed it while so many others have abandoned it; because Cubans make great music and aromatic cigars; because they've thumbed their nose at their former patron for more than three decades; because I'd grown weary of writing about Latin American "democracies" where forlorn illiterate campesinas sit on city street corners selling combs, nail clippers, and undervalued handicrafts while their malnourished barefoot youngsters turn their palms up and say "gimme" instead of learning how to hold a pencil or read a sentence; because of its rich literary tradition; because my favorite players on the Washington Senators in the 1950's were Cuban; because I'm an incurable romantic; because we still have a navy base there; because Cuban women are astute and alluring; because in the last five hundred years of travel writing few cities in the world have been so effusively praised as Havana; because Teddy Roosevelt led the charge up San Juan Hill; because I liked *Our Man in Havana* and *The Old Man and the Sea*; because I got a kick out of Desi Arnaz; because I was distrustful of Cuba's bashers and its cheerleaders; because I liked the twinkle in Fidel's eyes; because I'd never been to a Communist country; because I wanted to learn to rumba; because Columbus landed there; because it has hundreds of miles of unspoiled beaches; because of its mystique.

Tom Miller, 1992
Trading With
the Enemy

TABLE OF CONTENTS

Morro Castle: One of Havana's most recognizable landmarks from land and sea. (Photo by George Halloran)

INTRODUCTION

This book has been a year in preparation since it first suggested itself one sunny morning during the hurricane season in Santiago de Cuba. It has entailed much investigation, both in the form of quietly nosing into secluded bays at dusk, and endless seemingly casual inquiries of anyone who could offer advice on local conditions.

Here it is, and I hope it results in many more cruisers making what will almost certainly be the trip of a lifetime, to the most fantastic island in the Caribbean.

I have no other motive for this book. Indeed, to avoid charges of bias or influence it was deliberately written and researched without the aid or knowledge of any form of authority in Cuba, the U.S., or anywhere else. Further, I have reported things as I alone have seen them. No other opinion is represented, nor do I seek to encourage anyone to break any applicable laws.

A few other people have assisted me, indirectly or unconsciously, and it is only fitting that I mention them.

There were the crews of the *Charmill* and the *Tanac*, small vessels which plied the South American coastline of British Guiana where I spent parts of my youth. Beginning at age eight they took me down dark, mysterious butterflied rivers where silent Indians paddled dugout canoes filled with turtle eggs, macaws, and—deliciously to this boy—feathered bows and arrows. Perhaps it was they who planted the germs of adventure in my mind.

My uncle Mark recultivated those germs with occasional damp, North Sea cruises in my later school years. An author himself, maybe he too had something to do with this.

Regarding the present, I should like to thank the team at Cruising Guide Publications, notably my editor/art director Allen Conrad who unfailingly put up with my ill-humor during the production process. It was he who laid this book out in present form and I thank him for it.

Finally, I would like to dedicate this book to Fiona, without whom it could not have been done, and to the people of Cuba, without whom it would not have been worth doing.

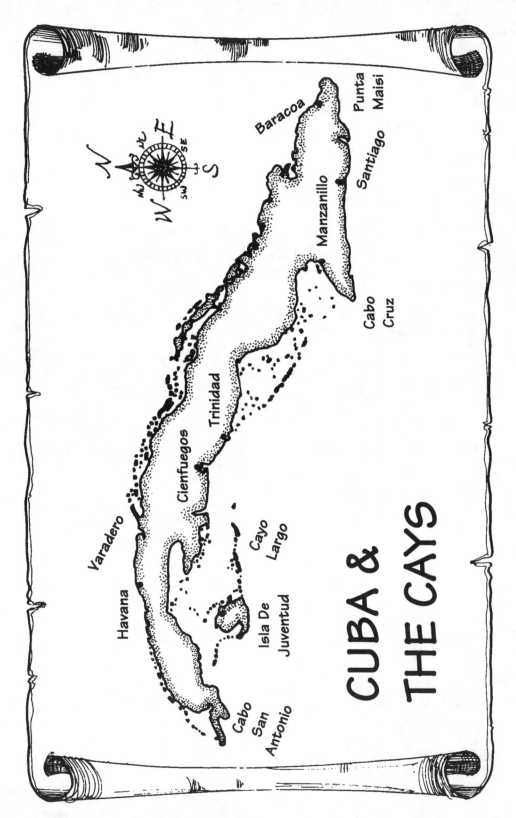

CUBA &
THE CAYS

CUBA AND THE YACHTSMAN

To most of us, Cuba is a strange, fascinating mixture of images. On the one hand we have our old sepia-tinted memories, culled from half-forgotten movies and curling magazine photos; while on the other, we have the more recent bombardment of new, politically tailored messages. The Cuban system is, after all, only one of many wildly opposed systems operating in the world today; and yet if we look past the obvious differences, one finds that there are more similarities than we sometimes care to admit.

This is a cruising guide, and one that strives to remain politically neutral. Recognizing that wide extremes of opinion presently exist on the subject of Cuba, please forgive me if I take great pains to avoid consciously projecting one particular point of view. I seek only to ensure the safe passage of all who would use the seas to travel where they will.

Nevertheless, I would say this: If you have the slightest interest in what's going on there, you really ought to see for yourself rather than through the eyes of the popular media; and if, as a sailor, you desire the best cruising in the hemisphere, then call on the coast of Cuba.

So why don't I just tell you the truth; I mean, Cuba's not some rinky-dink little island offering the same sort of thing you get in Florida only in a different setting. It's not a series of identical resort areas, each purporting to be different. Each somehow, more *Caribbean* than its neighbor a half-mile up the coast. It's not a place where a secluded bay means you're only sharing the anchorage with six other yachts; and where you get that panhandling little threat you ignore at your peril, "Hey, mon... Watch your boat?".

No, Cuba isn't about mooring alongside a series of full-service docks for the duration of your holiday. And it's certainly not about lounging on deck gossiping with your neighbor about the weather, or the price of stainless fittings.

It's about ancient cities, whose historic centers may be crumbling, but still nevertheless, retain the old charm. Cities, not yet raped by identikit offices, and screaming burger joints in the service of the fast buck. Cities rather, where decaying colonial facades house genuine families; and children play on that selfsame balcony a blushing Spanish girl once graced with fluttering fan.

And then too, like anywhere else, it's about suburban mistakes. Those poured concrete monstrosities so beloved of eastern-bloc architects, where the awful central committee just plain screwed-up again.

But no, it's not just about cities; it's about people too.

In Cuba, overcrowded, rattling buses may belch diesel, but they'll always stop for just one more passenger; and hitchhiking is a way of life (just how it used to be), not an invitation to violence.

It's where a stranger's approach is greeted with a smile, not doubt; and conversations, so easy to start yet so difficult to stop, revolve around literature, politics, religion, the latest fads in your country; and what are you doing later on?

Those very conversations, sometimes abruptly dropping to conspiratorial whisper and theatrical sideways-glances. After all, perhaps, those walls might indeed have ears.

Your cruise is about these things and more. Bays, so narrowly guarded by ruined fortresses perched among the creeping vines, and yet so wide, so sheltered, and so hospitable inside.

The cays too; still pristine, isolated and echoing to the cry of bird and beast rather than bulldozer, and boom-box. Ashore, that path you made through the trees will likely be the only sign of human presence for years to come; and there's only one boat at anchor in the turquoise bay.... Your boat.

The beaches along those cays too, with sand white enough to melt a snowbird's heart; and whilst there are plenty of those along the northeast coast, they're absolutely deserted elsewhere.

No, none of those stylish coconut-branch beach-bars, so artfully contrived to look sort of "local", and selling beer that costs five dollars a shot to the Jimmy Buffet wanabees.

Instead, it's where the last yacht you saw was Thierry's (you *always* know their names), 400 miles back on the south coast near Casilda.

Yes, Cuba is for serious cruisers.

INTERNATIONAL PASSAGES

For a North American based cruiser planning a journey further afield towards the West Indies or Mexico, the island of Cuba just cannot be ignored.

As the largest land mass in the Caribbean, Cuba stands along the direct route from South Florida down through the chain of islands which stretch as far as South America, and only a few miles off the direct route to Mexico. A glance at an overall chart of the Caribbean will confirm its strategic position. Any trip along one of those routes can only profit from using the shelter provided along the way, and either of its extreme ends are only a few miles from the nearest landfall. For example, Havana is approximately 90 miles from Key West in the U.S.

Using the Cuban coastline, a trip from the Dominican Republic to the U.S. would only require about 170 miles of open sea passage from Manzanillo in the northwest. Landfall could be made at Baracoa at the eastern tip of Cuba. The next 350 miles could be made along a coastline offering shelter every few miles as far as Varadero (itself also only 90 miles from the U.S.), while were you to have braved the traumas of Haiti, the city of Santiago would be even closer along the route.

Jamaican cruisers (longtime visitors, albeit in small numbers), find Santiago only 120 miles to the north of Kingston, and there are other Cuban ports not 90 miles from Montego Bay.

The closest international port in Cuba is about 180 miles from the Isla de Mujeres in Mexico, or approximately halfway the direct distance to Key West. This makes for an easy run across to Havana, then westwards along the coast, and on to Mexico.

Were you to plan a trip north from the Cayman Islands, then the distance between Cayo Largo and Georgetown is around 140 miles. Departure could be even more easily accomplished from Cayman Brac, making it another alternative were you travelling northwest from Jamaica.

And, of course, the Cuban coast runs parallel to the Bahamas, whose shoal waters might dissuade many.

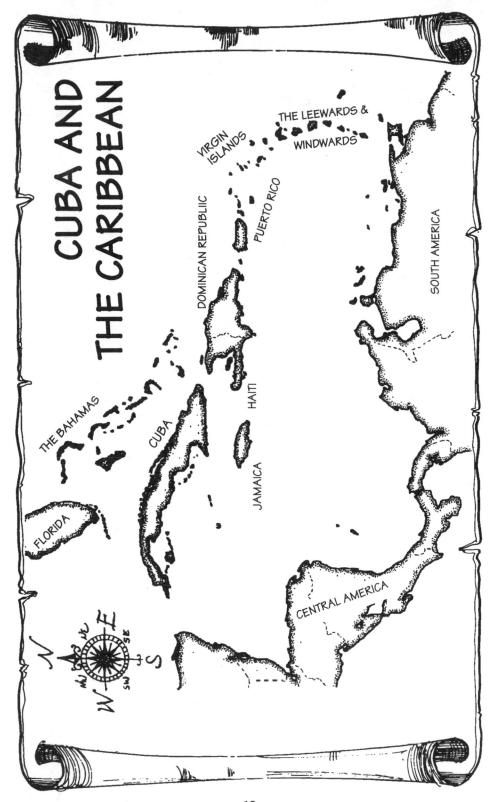

CUBA AND THE CARIBBEAN

THE LEEWARDS & WINDWARDS

VIRGIN ISLANDS

PUERTO RICO

DOMINICAN REPUBLIIC

SOUTH AMERICA

HAITI

JAMAICA

THE BAHAMAS

CUBA

FLORIDA

CENTRAL AMERICA

CUBA
A BASIC OVERVIEW: AS MUDDLED AS THE COUNTRY ITSELF

Over 750 miles long and covering some 44,200 square miles, Cuba is the largest island in the Caribbean, comprising over half of the total land-area of the West Indies!

Its median width is about 60 miles, ranging from only 5 miles in the extreme west to over 120 miles in the east.

Lying along the Tropic of Cancer at the entrance to the Gulf of Mexico, it is positioned only 90 miles from the Florida Keys at the northwest end of the Caribbean chain of islands. It is made up of one large and numerous smaller islands, islets, and cays.

Cuba is as large as England.

The terrain is varied, 60 percent of which is lowland plains, basins and foothills. There are three major mountain systems.

1. **Oriental:** The Sierra Madre in the eastern part of the country, containing such notable peaks as Turquino (over 6,000 feet).

2. **Central:** A number of lower hills and ranges, such as the Escambray Mountains.

3. **Occidental:** Along the western quarter of the country, the Cordillera de Guaniguanico and the Sierras de los Organos; a most spectacular formation of Karst topography where the limestone mountains have been severely affected by underwater erosion.

The river Cauto (160 miles) in the southeast is the largest in the island and is the island's principal inland waterway.

The climate is semi-tropical, officially averaging 79° F.

Seasonal temperatures range from 77° F in January to 87° F in August, but do not trust these figures too much. I have recorded over 100° F during the daytime inside my vessel (with all windows open), dropping only as far as 86° F at night in the summer.

Water temperatures average out less, but vary considerably depending on where you are, being hotter by some 4-5° F on the southern side of the island.

There are two seasons simply called "wet" (May-October) and "dry" (November-April), with most of the rain falling in the form of tropical rainstorms and averaging 54 inches per year.

The hurricane season runs June-November, but in spite of popular mythology they are rare.

Apart from the mountains in the east, the island is covered by lush vegetation encouraged by the balmy climate and the abundant rainfall. There are tropical pine and mahogany forests, and a profusion of other trees such as kapok and the stately royal palm (the national tree).

Fruit also features prominently, consisting mainly of lime, lemon, papaya, and most significantly, grapefruit and orange. The agriculture is based on the cultivation of sugar-cane, coffee and rice.

There are only modest mineral resources in Cuba, with a little oil being extracted around the Cardenas Bay in the north, but there are substantial deposits of nickel further east.

The original Indians having been rendered nearly extinct, the population (estimated 11-million) is composed of three main racial groups; mulattoes, blacks and whites.

During the last century there was a majority of mulattoes and blacks, the descendants of some 750,000 slaves imported in the 18th and 19th centuries, but now it is estimated that about two-thirds of the population is of white descent.

Traditionally power has been mainly vested in the white population, but strenuous efforts have been made during the last thirty years to broaden the base of political and social influence, and as a result racial conflict is rare. Although there is still undeniably an economic underclass, it is refreshing to be able to walk freely without feeling threatened by one race or another.

Marxist-Leninist ideology is the dominant force in secular life; all other political parties being proscribed.

In spite of official disavowal of religion in the 1960s and 1970s there has been a certain accommodation recently so that now some 40 percent of the population consider themselves to be vaguely Roman Catholic or similarly Christian. There is too, a small practicing Jewish community.

Increasing efforts by non-denominational humanitarian organizations, like the group Pastors For Peace, have also obtained some (if presently limited) successes in local involvement.

All over Havana and other cities, houses of worship still stand unoccupied while awaiting the future, and even though there is continuing tension between state and church those buildings have remained largely unmolested... Whatever that signifies.

There is also some unacknowledged influence derived from traditional Afro/Spanish religions, such as Santeria.

Following the revolution in the 1960s, there was heavy migration from the rural areas, but since the 1970s this has been ended by the government. Nevertheless, some 70 percent of the population is now urban, concentrated in the city and province of Havana.

Education and health have received much attention over the last thirty years (fully 25 percent of the government budget goes on this) and within the limits of available funds could be said to be the envy of most countries.

Social security programs offer a wide range of benefits, including sickness benefits, old-age pensions, maternity leave and benefits, workers injury compensation, disability and survivors' pensions.

In spite of the chronic shortages affecting the country, the population's health is generally good, and in spite of what I read elsewhere I would venture to say that I have never seen any other nation looking so fit (See Brendan's comment later under Manzanillo).

The Cuban capital building in Havana houses a one-party system. The handsome building is along a tree-lined thoroughfare. (Photo by George Halloran)

Hospitals are open to all, and in spite of the economic difficulties are modern and certainly well-staffed, especially when compared with the abysmal facilities only grudgingly offered in the rest of Latin America and the Caribbean.

Life expectancy is 74 years, infant mortality is the lowest in Latin America, and all sections of society have easy access to medical facilities in the workplace, schools and the neighborhood.

There are more doctors per capita in Cuba than any other country, and while they may not have access to the most sophisticated drugs available elsewhere, there is no doubt that the system makes efficient use of what it does have.

Having abolished private and religious institutions, the government is in charge of all education, which is free at all levels up to and including degree courses. Based on Marxist/Leninist principals, it combines study with manual labor, but unfortunately political considerations still affect entry into the universities. Nevertheless, in addition to the University of Havana, there are 40 other institutes of advanced training.

You see a lot of people reading.

The media is rigidly controlled by the state, which issues its edicts and disseminates blatant propaganda through the radio, television, and the newspapers, of which Granma is the main culprit. There is much reporting of North American, European, and other foreign hard-news, but little comment which has not been passed by the party hacks as being favorable to the present system of government.

Personally, the radio stinks.

Strangely, the cinema offers some respite being an odd mix of art and trash, and I have been astounded by queues to see Sylvester Stallone deal death and destruction.

Artistic endeavor is to a large extent controlled by the state, with political criteria being a major factor. The official view must be expressed if one wishes to succeed, and in addition there are many other more subtle forms of censorship. Many Cuban artists have left under this burden and more will continue to do so for the foreseeable future.

Musical traditions in Cuba have been formed by combining African rhythms and instruments, such as conga-drums, maracas, claves with the Spanish guitar; leading in the 1920s to the development of Son, its more formal neighbor Danzon, and the Rhumba.

Perhaps due to the former influence of Eastern Bloc countries, classical music and ballet still strongly survives amidst the other more traditional forms of entertainment.

Cuba is a one-party state, and the Communist Party of Cuba (PCC), with a membership of some 475,000, rigidly controls all formal government institutions. The party's Political Bureau is the highest policy making body on the island.

The constitution of 1976 confirmed the Communist Party's supremacy in law and government, and established the electoral systems in use today.

The People's Supreme Court exercises the functions of the judiciary.

Legislative power is vested in the National Assembly of People's Power whose members are elected by the municipalities, but the party still oversees its work.

The powers-that-be favor grandiose titles.

The economy is centrally-planned, and until the collapse of the former Communist Bloc was heavily subsidized by the U.S.S.R. There are frequent and growing shortages of consumer goods, despite gross national product (GNP) estimates placing Cuba among the leading nations of Latin America.

The continuing economic embargo placed by the U.S. government has lead to increasing problems in the economy as traditional trading partners have been pressured to abandon further commerce with Cuba. Even foreign firms are threatened now by U.S. economic sanctions designed to force economic and social collapse.

Within Cuba this action is called the "Blockade".

The agricultural economy (one-seventh of the GNP) of the island is in a shambles, and not solely due to the embargo. Just one example of what passes for careful forward planning is that the main agricultural exports are based on sugar and tobacco!

Sugar may be the principal source of foreign exchange (presently 80-90 percent) but it can hardly be said to have a secure future in the light of current health concerns.

And what can one say about tobacco.

Citrus fruit, such as grapefruit, is an increasing source of export earnings, but presently the production of staples such as rice and beans does not meet the demand.

Private agricultural holdings are apparently limited to 160 acres.

Nickel is the principal ore extracted, with Cuba holding the fourth largest deposits of the mineral in the world. There are also smaller quantities of iron, copper, and chrome being mined.

Despite the above, manufacturing is still limited, being confined to light industry, foodstuff processing and textiles.

Ghastly fashion-shows are seen as an integral part of entertaining tourists.

Tourism is increasingly seen as a means of earning foreign exchange ($400-million in 1991 and a reported $900-million in 1993), but it is unlikely that this can stem the tide of a huge balance of payments deficit, mainly to Russia, but also to many capitalist countries.

The government is seeking to expand trade with the rest of Latin America, Asia and former members of the Communist Bloc, but unfortunately due to the historic stigma surrounding actually earning a living, if you've ever tried to do business with the Cuban government you'll know just how difficult they can make it.

Cuba is the "Land of the Committee".

HISTORY

Modern Cuban history could be said to have started when Christopher Columbus discovered the island on his first trip to the New World on Oct 27th, 1492, but prior to that the island was inhabited by several small Indian groups, the Ciboney, the Guanahatabey, and later the Arawaks from other Caribbean islands.

The Spanish quickly took control, conquering the Indians, and in 1511 Diego Velasquez established the first permanent settlement at Baracoa. The island was soon divided into seven Villas (or Garrisons) to defend it against pirates and later it became a base for expeditions further afield. One such expedition was that of Hernan Cortes, who left from the city of Santiago on his way to conquer Mexico in 1519.

Unbelievably, the British (who used to just love this sort of thing) captured and held Cuba from 1762-1763, then swapped it with Spain (again) for Florida!

During the 18-19th centuries the island's economy prospered, and owing to the rapid expansion of the sugar trade some 750,000 African slaves were imported until the practice was halted in 1865, and legally abolished in 1886. By the mid-19th century, the sugar industry was the most highly mechanized in the world, and produced one third of its sugar.

Towards the middle of the 19th century various nationalist movements tried without success to cede from the Spanish colonial empire, and there were occasional bloody rebellions, notably the Ten Years War between 1868-78.

Prominent figures in the liberation struggles were Máximo Gómez and Antonio Maceo, along with the poet philosopher, José Martí. Their names are still invoked today, by both sides.

By the late 19th century, the U.S. had become the largest trading partner, and the delay in Spain's granting political autonomy to Cuba was seen as a pretext for the Spanish-American war in 1898, which eventually led to U.S. occupation of the island.

In 1901, the U.S. was granted the right to oversee Cuban internal and foreign affairs, reserving the right to intervene militarily in domestic matters and turning the island into a protectorate after independence. The U.S. also obtained Guantánamo Bay.

Various presidents came and went but unrest continued, leading to further military occupation in 1906, 1912 and 1917, while North American capital invested heavily in sugar, tourism, and gambling.

In 1958, the nationalist popular revolution of Fidel Castro finally triumphed over the dictator Fulgencio Batista, but rapidly converted to communism in the face of increasing U.S. hostility in the early 1960s, leading to the state-appropriation of industry and agriculture.

The low point in U.S. Cuban relations came in 1961 with the abortive Bay of Pigs invasion, which was actively supported by the CIA, and the Missile Crisis in 1962.

In return for the withdrawal of U.S.S.R. missiles from Cuban soil, the U.S. pledged that it would not seek to overthrow the government of Fidel Castro. Unfortunately, public records in the U.S. show that several attempts have since been made by CIA agents on the life of the president.

Over the following 20-30 years, Cuba allied itself more and more closely with the Soviet Bloc, leading to a complete suspension of all economic and cultural ties by the U.S. government, and degenerating into a total economic embargo designed to force the existing regime from power.

The later collapse of Soviet economies have placed additional strain on the island's economy and infrastructure, and it is likely that some sort of accommodation will have to be made with the U.S. if the island is not to disintegrate into chaos over the next few years.

As you read this, Cuba's history is still being written.

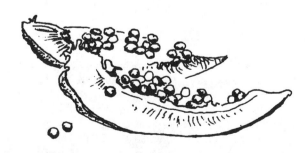

THE YACHTSMAN

Vague talk of visas and other nearly impossible-to-satisfy criteria is just that; merely talk.

For the yachtsman to enter Cuba he will need a boat, its papers, a passport and nothing else, apart from funds. And unlike many-another country, no one in Cuba has ever asked me if we had sufficient funds for our projected stay.

The emphasis being presently placed on tourism by the Cuban government has led to a considerable opening-up over the last few years, but not long ago popular opinion amongst foreign boaters was that you only had to stray close to the 12-mile limit to be strafed by jets or boarded by gunboats.

This view is slowly losing ground, but nevertheless still does command a considerable following, and in idle conversation we are routinely commented upon as being somehow blessed not to have been detained by the Cuban authorities.

West Indian Customs and Immigration officers always remark, "So they let you out, eh?", when we clear our papers, and usually seem a bit skeptical when we say, quite truthfully, that we have never had the slightest hint of trouble in our dealings with the Cuban authorities, nor have we ever had a request denied unnecessarily.

On our travels we have met many nationalities in a variety of boats, and not one of them has shown any reluctance to return. In fact, I would say that the average yachtsman encountered in Cuba, is on his second, third, or fourth visit.

It cannot be denied that the continuing strained relationship between the U.S. government and Cuba has restrained many U.S. yachtsmen from venturing over to their closest and certainly most fascinating neighbor. In spite of this, what is clear is that the existing tension between the governments is confined solely to that level, and every American I have met who took the plunge has remarked that they have encountered absolutely no hostility from anyone at all. Indeed, it is probable that nowhere else in the world will a U.S. citizen receive a greater welcome. If you don't believe me, ask any Cuban, anywhere.

Unfortunately, there are mechanisms in place to prevent free travel between the two countries, and one of these mechanisms is the existing trade and economic embargo, whose provisions as yet are imperfectly understood and just as imperfectly applied.

The Official U.S. Position:

Cuba - Consular Information Sheet May 27, 1993

Country Description:
Cuba is a developing country under the communist rule of Fidel Castro. The United States has no direct diplomatic relations with Cuba.

Entry Requirements/Travel Transaction Limitations: The Cuban Assets Control Regulations of the U.S. Treasury Department require that persons subject to U.S. jurisdiction be licensed to engage in any transactions related to travel to, from and within Cuba. Transactions related to tourist and business travel are not licensable. This restriction includes tourist or business travel from or through a third country such as Mexico or Canada. Visitors who attempt to enter Cuba without the proper documentation are subject to detention and arrest. Transactions are authorized by general license for the following categories of travelers: U.S. and foreign government officials, including representatives of international organizations of which the United States is

continued on next page

continued from preceding page

a member, traveling on official business; persons gathering news or making news or documentary films; persons visiting close relatives residing in Cuba; and, full-time professionals engaging in full-time research in their professional areas where the research is specifically related to Cuba, is largely academic in nature, and there is substantial likelihood the product of research will be disseminated. Additional information may be obtained by contacting the Licensing Division, Office of Foreign Assets Control at the U.S. Department of the Treasury (202/622-2480). Failure to comply with these regulations could result in prosecution upon return to the United States.

Should a traveler receive a license, a passport and visa are required for entry to Cuba. For current information on Cuban entry and customs requirements, travelers may contact the Cuban Interests Section, an office of the Cuban government located at 2630 and 2639 16th Street W., Washington, D.C. 20009, tel: (202) 797-8518.

Currency Regulations (U.S.): U.S. Treasury Department regulations permit travelers whose transactions are licensed to spend no more than $100 per day for their living expenses in Cuba. There is also a limit of $500 on funds U.S. citizens and residents may pay to Cuba relating to fees imposed by the Cuban government. A limit of $300 per three-month period has been placed on family remittances sent from the U.S. to close relatives in Cuba. The Treasury Department also limits to $500 the amount of funds a person may transfer to Cuba to pay travel expenses for a Cuban national who has been granted a visa by the State Department to visit the United States. For further information, travelers may contact the Office of Foreign Assets Control.

Dual Nationality: The government of Cuba considers all Cuban-born U.S. citizens to be solely Cuban citizens. The Cuban government does not recognize the right or obligation of the U.S. government to protect dual U.S./Cuban citizens and has consistently denied U.S. consular officers the right to visit incarcerated dual U.S./Cuban nationals to ascertain their welfare and proper treatment under Cuban law. Dual U.S./Cuban nationals are required by Cuban law to enter and depart Cuba using Cuban passports. Using a Cuban passport for this purpose does not jeopardize one's U.S. citizenship; however, such persons must use their U.S. passports to enter and depart the U.S. and to transit any countries en route. Dual U.S./Cuban nationals may be subject to a range of restrictions and obligations, including military service, in Cuba.

U.S. Representation/Registration: The United States does not maintain an Embassy in Cuba.

U.S. citizens who travel to Cuba may contact and register with the U.S. Interests Section of the Swiss Embassy, located in Havana at Calzada between L & M, Vedado; telephone 33-3550 through 33-3559. There is no access to the U.S. Naval Base at Guantanamo from within Cuba. U.S. citizens who register at the U.S. Interests Section in Havana may obtain updated information on travel and security within the country.

This replaces the Consular Information Sheet dated October 27, 1993 to add information concerning entry requirements, travel transaction limitations, currency regulations and reporting the loss or theft abroad of a U.S. passport.

Despite the mention of arrests and the like in the above statement, reports which I have received state that unless you have been an extremely silly boy, no fuss is made over your journey. So although the majority of cruisers are from Europe and Canada, one still does encounter U.S.-flagged vessels.

Incidentally, the vast majority of foreign boats cruising Cuban waters have transited from Florida, and many still winter there yearly.

Note: Apart from U.S. citizens, there are no restrictions on the travel of other nationalities to Cuba. It is not in fact even against the U.S. law for a citizen to travel to Cuba, but rather against Treasury Department regulations to *spend* money there. To this end, U.S. Customs can occasionally look for evidence of this in the form of Cuban receipts among a returning boat's papers.

PLANNING YOUR CRUISE

WHAT YOU NEED TO KNOW ABOUT OR TAKE

Okay, so you're beginning to think about it, and you're wondering...

Do I have the right gear? Is the boat going to be okay? And in any case, I've just pottered about in the old girl for the last few years, so am I going to be okay?

Of course you are. Just read the following chapter carefully. There's a lot in it that you already know, have, could borrow, or do without.

And there's a lot you could usefully know before arrival in Cuba.

Do you have a modicum of common sense? Can you sail?

Yeah, you'll be okay.

What do we need then? Let's see.

THE IDEAL BOAT

This one's easy. A trip of this nature is not going to be the sort of thing that requires transatlantic capability, so as long as it's not a patently unsuitable boat and it fulfills a few basic criteria, the choice will be wide indeed. Just remember it's got to arrive safely, you've got to live on it for as long as your projected cruise, and it's got to stay on the right side of the surface.

So to start off, you'll need to have a serious look at your boat.

Is it safe enough? Is it large enough?

I've seen people arrive in Havana in outboard-powered open fishing boats, which looked more suitable for a swift midnight run to and from some matt black freighter. And I've seen the sort of craft that had three masts, 900 h.p. below decks and a paid crew in white duck trousers and enough braid to rewind an alternator.

Somewhere between these two extremes will be where most of us fall.

Your vessel at minimum must be capable of crossing open water where winds and waves

A crew prepares their sailboat for a crossing to Cuba from the Truman Annex Docks at Key West. (Photo by George Halloran)

can rise without warning. If coming in from Florida, the Gulf Stream is a fast-running current which can increase your navigational problems, as well as your approximately 90-mile planned distance. While, were you to be coming in from say, the Dominican Republic, you would be facing a journey of perhaps, 120 miles with only the uncertain welcome of Haiti as a refuge.

Regarding size, I'm a great believer in having room to go and sulk in, so if it's going to be a long cruise we'll need couples in one cabin, and the kids or your friends in another. Very good friends may only need one bed in the other cabin, but that still makes for a complete cabin for them. One thing you'll not really want, unless it's going to be a very short cruise, is to have snoring bodies sprawled all over the main salon. As a matter of fact, we have a rule on board that no one dozes-off there either. That way there's at least one neutral room. And if you keep it clear of personal items like clothes, that will make it even more habitable for all aboard.

Of course, there will be exceptions too, so don't become too much of a dictator over this.

We'd like our boat to be as autonomous as possible too, so if you're planning a longer cruise you'll want a sailboat or as economical a motor boat as possible. It is possible to purchase diesel or gasoline fuel in all of the major ports, but as of 1993 the diesel price was hitting 90 cents a liter in places, and that is $3.42 a gallon to you and me! Additionally, fuel may not be available everywhere you want to go. It's important to note that Cuba has more than 1,500 miles of navigable coastline, so if you want to go all the way around, the cruising range of your craft is a necessary consideration.

Draft can be a small factor too if you are going to be exploring the cays. I once met a yacht in Santiago Harbour (don't worry, it was one of only 10 boats I met in a complete circumnavigation that time around) which drew 9 feet! This did, in fact, rule out a few areas for them, but in general if you're pulling 6 feet or less you will be okay for most places. Mind you a swinging keel would be really neat.

Although they are still relatively rare (I have only heard of one in Cuba), I would reckon a cat or trimaran is best all-round. There are not many marinas in Cuba with the limits this places on boat width in so many places, and their shallow draft can make even the most tricky passage a piece of cake.

In the end, what you really want is a boat you are comfortable with, and a boat that's comfortable with you. Far better you do your cruising in a boat you can handle by yourself in a pinch, than something that offers more features, but is less handy coming in through a tricky entrance or going alongside a couple of rafted tugboats in a current.

Maybe a few words about what we use wouldn't go amiss here.

Our boat is a 34-foot trawler. It's 19 years old with a single engine of 120 h.p. In spite of its relatively small size, it has an aft cabin, a main salon and a forward vee-berth, so when we cruise with guests it's not too much like a madhouse aboard. What is important is we're comfortable with it, and it has good sea-keeping qualities along with a handy draft of just 3 feet 9 inches.

I'd love to have twin screws and an extra couple of feet all round, but at the end of the day you go with what you can afford, and it's more important to go than to sit around dreaming.

But then, life's like that in so many ways.

FLAGS

So now you've got your boat, you'll need to dress it up a bit for international travel. Simple really; it's yours, theirs and a quarantine flag.

You'll need a flag showing the nationality of your boat. This should be flown at the stern or in the case of a sailboat with no stern flagpole, up in the shrouds.

You'll need a Cuban flag, which you fly upon entering Cuban national waters. These are actually readily available in the U.S. Pick one up in any of the chandlers or marine shops along the coast in Florida. They are more difficult to come by in the islands, but never mind, the Cuban authorities won't get too upset if you don't have one upon arrival. You can pick one up there.

They fly a lot of them from balconies. You fly yours in the shrouds.

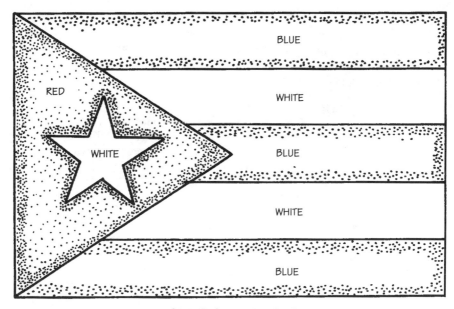

CUBAN FLAG

Incidentally, if there's a chance of continuing on down through the islands or going someplace after Cuba, then buy those flags too in advance.

You'll need a yellow quarantine flag for entering foreign waters, and a nice touch would be to take a few pennants along. These might be those of your yacht club/association or any nautical design, and make nice gifts.

DOCUMENTS

To enter any country, you need your personal travel documents. By and large, this means a passport for every member of the crew. I have heard it said that a U.S. citizen can enter on a driver's license or voter's registration card, for up to 72 hours. On a boat, I wouldn't try it. Take your passport. If you're a U.S. or E.E.C. citizen, you won't need a visa when entering by yacht. In spite of what I've read elsewhere, you don't need to inform the Cubatur organization in advance with all kinds of details about crew and vessel. Just show up.

By the way, Cuban immigration officers **never stamp your passports.**

YOUR VESSEL'S TRAVEL DOCUMENTS

The vessel too needs its own travel documents. These will consist of your ownership papers, the title, and registration documents. Reacting to what I've heard about other places, I've even taken along all my old bills of sale and so on, but no one's ever shown the slightest interest in those.

It will on occasion be helpful if you have on board photocopies of all your vessel's documents, and in all cases you should leave copies at home with friends or relatives who may have to act for you in any unforeseeable instance.

If you're borrowing someone else's boat, then you'll need to show proof in the form of a signed and notarized document giving permission. Make it out in Spanish too.

You'll definitely need your clearance out of the country you've just left, and it should list Cuba as your destination. It's called a "Zarpe" in Spanish, and they **will** want to see it upon entry.

A few passport sized photos might come in handy too. Even though I've never needed them here, you never can tell when you might need some extra document. I always carry some, no matter what part of the world I'm in.

YOUR FOLDER IS YOUR TRUMP CARD

All of these documents and all the passports will need to be accessed frequently while you are there, so keep them safe in one place. Some sort of a cheap vinyl folder with a zipper is the most convenient thing for this purpose. As soon as your papers have been dealt with, put them all back in it along with all the extra bits you've just been issued and sling the whole caboodle onto the book-shelf in one lot. The vinyl will also keep them dry when you dinghy ashore to some out of the way outpost.

Along with courtesy, having these documents ready and easily accessible will be the single most important part of dealing with officials who might otherwise become somewhat tetchy. So do it right!

In addition, you may want to carry a few sheets of carbon paper, some paper-clips, a pen and maybe a small paper stapler. These can also go into the folder ready for instant use.

You can throw your wallet with credit cards, drivers licence and the like into the back of a drawer for when you need them. And don't forget your address book. Your friends in Seattle or Utah will be tickled pink to get a card from you.

LOG BOOKS ARE IMPORTANT

This brings up to another type of document you might not have been maintaining, namely your log-books.

We keep two types of book aboard, and have found extensive use for them both. They consist of the ship's log, and a separate mechanics log-book which records in detail every occasion we do any sort of maintenance on the vessel.

The ship's log is written up almost unfailingly every hour, and chore though it might seem, this has enabled us to retrace our steps or to find our way back into some strange cove two years later.

Incidentally, this book would not be written without our ship's log either.

The mechanics log notes for example, oil changes, fuel fills, prices for same, breakdowns and repairs of charging equipment, wiring-diagrams, new navigation instrument purchases, and perhaps most important of all, the next scheduled oil changes.

We keep it in a file along with all the old receipts and instruction manuals for all the equipment aboard, including that of the engine, so all that's in the same place too.

MONEY

Yeah, isn't it a bitch.

You need U.S. dollars here; period.

Perhaps you've used Bhats in Thailand, Quetzales in Guatemala, and Cruzeiros in Brazil, handling the black-market like a champ. Here it's going to be different for the foreseeable future, or until the regulation of the so-called parallel economy is liberalized. Increasingly it has become more difficult for a foreigner to spend Cuban pesos in the streets or to use them in any form of exchange. Now I know there are those who will say they've managed to do so, but by and large on a boat you're going to be limited to where you can spend only hard currency. I won't go on except to say that it's just the way it is.

Theoretically you might be able to pay in hard currencies like British pounds, Swiss francs, and the like. That's fine if you want to pay in theories, if not, just use dollars.

First and foremost, the easiest form of payment will be cold hard cash, which will not cause the same alarm it increasingly causes in the U.S. (as a matter of fact the U.S. is the only place that views cash with such paranoia). Just make sure you take it in small denomination bills.

Fresh fish are a saleable commodity for street vendors along many of Havana and other city's streets. (Photo by George Halloran)

There is, in common with most Latin countries, a problem with making change. So aside from major purchases of fuel and so on you might have a problem breaking anything larger than a twenty.

On this note, you may be surprised to receive what looks rather like play-money in your change, namely cheaply printed notes or aluminium coins.

Don't worry, these are merely issued in lieu of American dollars by the Cuban government to make up for the shortage of change in circulation. At first you may be somewhat reluctant to receive them but never fear, you can use them quite freely in place of genuine dollar bills and may also exchange them upon departure if you haven't spent them already.

Finally regarding cash, certain hotels issue little interlocking plastic beads to their guests for use in place of currency! This phenomenon occurs mainly in package-tour hotels along the northern cays and supposedly allows half-naked guests to string their cash around their necks. Not a totally unpleasing effect if you're into red, yellow, or blue plastic beaded necklaces and little else. Incidentally, these are usually given names like Coquitos, or something similar in an attempt at cuteness.

You may use them freely only in the resort issuing them. I use them only at the bar.

Next, in the major metropolitan or tourist areas you may use credit cards as long as they are not American Express. If using others, just be sure the cards aren't actually issued in the U.S., and in your outrage please remember it's not their fault. The Cubans have in the past accepted U.S. cards in good faith only to have payment denied later on.

Of course you might have problems using plastic in some of the smaller towns.

Travellers Cheques are also acceptable, however, there can be problems here too.

I've travelled some miles along the coast before finding a major hotel which would exchange them for cash, and you may need to use them sooner than this. In Havana even, I once had to go all the way to the Central Bank downtown to cash some, and they were to pay for a flight to Dublin via Aeroflot who wouldn't accept cheques!

Please note that even if you've arrived from some West Indian island, and have a pocket full of Barclays or some such European bank's cheques, the drawing bank might well be their New York branch. Be careful to scrutinize the face of your cheques for this aspect.

A NECESSARY PRECAUTION ANYWHERE

You may have to make a stash somewhere down in the bowels of your boat to safeguard all this, but fortunately there's not a whole lot of crime against boats and you'd have to take these sort of precautions in Miami too.

In fact, apart from the parallel tourist economy most if not all of the above is more or less what goes for travelling anywhere else apart from Europe so don't be disheartened.

FOOD, WATER & THAT SORT OF THING

You've already heard of the chronic shortages affecting the Cuban economy, so it won't come as any great surprise when I say STOCK THE BOAT WELL in advance of arrival.

In the previous chapter you ought to have read about the supply of goods, but if you skipped it you should know that as a tourist, and thus spending hard currency, you will be permitted to enter any of the many so-called Diplo-Tiendas or hard-currency shops. These shops, situated in all of the hotel lobbies, and major metropolitan or tourism areas were originally only for foreigners, and Cubans even holding their own U.S. dollars could not enter. Well, since July 26, 1993, anyone can buy produce there, and this has led to both a lessening in the embarrassment factor, and a lessening in the quantity of goods available as Cuban nationals holding once illegal dollars rushed to buy foreign products.

In Havana there are a couple of these shops which are rather like poor-quality general stores cum supermarkets. Pretty well anything you need will be available, but there will be

few bargains, and don't necessarily expect to get your favorite brand.
Expect to pay two or three times what you might in the U.S. and maybe twice as much
as in any of the islands. The selection of foodstuffs will probably surprise
you if you are only accustomed to U.S. style supermarkets, in
that they will have been sourced from different markets to
those you're familiar with. There will, in fact be a
much higher percentage of Argentinian, Italian, or
French foodstuffs, for example, and the products may indeed be different too.

There will usually be complete ranges
missing, e.g. no tinned tuna and such for a
week or two, and you may find there are
three complete shelves taken up with the
likes of olives or salted peanuts, all of which
depends on the latest trade deal or the arrival
of the latest ship in port.

DAIRY PRODUCTS EXPENSIVE

Especially expensive, or sometimes hard
to find will be the old sailors staples like
corned-beef or ham, while you may
expect to part with an arm and a leg
for cheese of any acceptable flavor
or similar dairy products.

Do not buy the rip-off stuff like vastly
over-priced lobster. Instead bargain for it
in the cays later on down the way.

Potatoes, rice and greens can usually
be found, but at no time can this be
guaranteed and the only thing you can
count on is that the item you so desperately need will not have been seen that
week. If shopping there, buy what you
can expect to use, even if not that
week, and look for substitutes, you
may be surprised to acquire a new
taste!

Cuban rum is always available however, and according to my not inexperienced palate is right up there among
the best in the world. This at least is
usually a great bargain, so shop
around for the brand that suits you
best. Try Matusalem Anejo.

The Cuban beers are not great deals
compared to the wide range of foreign
beers available, but by and large all
spirits (and there will be lots of imported
brands) being tax-free are going to be
cheaper than you remember. Take lots of
aspirin.

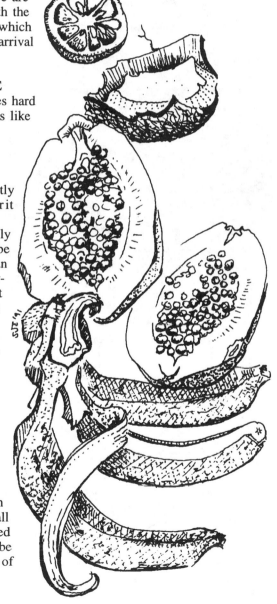

A butcher prepares meat with an onlooker. Because of chronic shortages affecting the Cuban economy, it is advisable to stock your boat well for any voyage. (Photo by George Halloran)

So, this all leads back to your stocking up the galley before arrival and maintaining the levels as and when you can.

Oh, buy bread whenever you see it. It will not be there when you return.

In the diplotiendas and such stores, you will also find general products like brake-pads for Russian automobiles, strange faucets, Chinese bicycles and ghastly lampshades. You will not find batteries to fit your particular radio, but you will find batteries for everyone else's. And if I were you, I'd be taking along all the sanitary and paper products you may have become used to elsewhere.

Another handy thing to know about is the existence of "Provedores" which are establishments set up specially to deal with ships in any of the more major ports. These will usually consist of a sort of discount bulk store, dimly lit, with piles of dusty tins, bags, sacks, rope and assorted items. The harbor master will advise you about them, and if he doesn't, ask.

You may be taken around from pile to heap, followed by a solicitous clerk with a price list and an order form. Your purchases will be recorded, packed and delivered to your boat.

And you might even be able to get eggs there!

A small token of appreciation may or may not be donated to the clerk, who will have sat in spectral gloom to record everything in longhand and in triplicate, without the aid of carbon paper.

Sometimes this service is provided by boats directly alongside, and sometimes there might be a visit from a mini-van which departs with many promises of delivery and little hope of the same.

It will be difficult to give many hard and fast rules about the prices of products as the situation changes from day-to-day. There was a 100 percent rise in prices in the diplotiendas in the week following the relaxation in the rules governing the holding and spending of foreign currency. In the weeks following that, the prices rose still more until there was some indication of a levelling out, and even a slight drop as the unspent dollars held by the population at large was used up. Nevertheless, things are still in flux and will continue to be so. This is all part of the experience of travelling in some parts of the world, and should not deter you too much. You should have tried doing your shopping in Bolivia when inflation there was in the thousands of percentage points. Now that was a lark.

PREPARATION OF MEALS IN ADVANCE

Of course, you may be thinking of preparing a lot of your meals in advance. Give due thought to the actual capacity of your freezer if you're thinking of freezing meal-sized portions. Given the actual capacity and power of most 12 v. fridges fitted to the average yacht, you may if fact find there's not a lot of advantage to this. Especially if, like us you do not have a generator aboard. We prefer to keep the little freezer compartment as full of ice as possible for those rum and cokes at the end of the day, restricting the opening of the flap to when necessary, and refilling the trays just before we go to bed at night when there isn't going to be any more loss of cold air.

And of course this leaves room for those little treats you'll pick up along the way, like fresh fish, shrimp and lobster.

If you're among the hardier sailors who don't have a fridge, but rather an ice-box, then you'll be able to pick up ice in the ports along the way, provided the ice-plants are working that day. Just don't count on it. Salt your fish or meats, and hang it in the rigging to dry in the sun during the day. Bring it in away from the dew at night. It really does work, and adds that touch of authenticity to the craft and crew. The Cuban fishermen will love you for it.

Mind you, if you have a generator aboard to power a 110 v. fridge/freezer, all bets are off.

You may, depending on the humor of the agricultural officer who boards you upon entry be permitted to enter with fresh meats and the like in the fridge. Then again, you may not, so don't depend on it. The sandwiches you packed for the journey across, but didn't eat, will probably be okay though, and similarly those vacuum packed things you're going to do without later on.

That same agricultural officer will probably scratch his head somewhat over your fruit and those hanging nets of onions, but if there isn't any evidence of weevils, you'll probably be able to keep them.

On board our boat, we have as much food as possible stashed in drawers and under the bunks, paying as much attention as possible to those items that can be kept indefinitely, like tinned or dried meats, pastas, packages of rice and dried beans. Protected from vermin and moisture of course. And La Fiona the kitchen goddess, who's mad keen on paper towels and that sort of thing, keeps a dozen rolls or more miraculously hidden too.

We've also started to carry more of our own flour, yeast and baking powder, as a reaction against the shortage of such products, and the sometimes musty taste of the breads we occasionally can obtain.

Incidentally, you can stock up too with those tinned or otherwise packaged doughs which turn into buns, muffins and the like at the drop of an oven door. You'll love them in some deserted misty cove at 6 a.m. in the morning with a steaming cup of black Cuban coffee. And won't your boat smell nice.

Cuban cigars are still recognized as one of the ultimate smoking experiences. Workers above unload bales of tobacco that will ultimately become cigars. (Photo by George Halloran)

Here's an item the average shoreside household should never be without in any case; a **pressure-cooker**. This conveniently sized and sturdy pot will cook enough for the crew without the need for another container. Properly used, it will do so efficiently on less than a quarter of the gas you might otherwise burn, and will do so in less than quarter the time.

Buy one, read the instructions, and use it ashore for a few days. You'll never be without one again, and it'll eliminate at least one other pot from your cupboard.

Filled early with a tasty stew, or soup, your pressure-cooker will fit handily in the sink where it will stay safely through wave and wind with the top fastened on, ready for a quick warm-up later on when the need is greatest. The graveyard shift will thank you again and again.

A CIGAR SMOKER'S HEAVEN

And speaking of graveyards. If you're a smoker, and especially if you smoke cigars, you're going to be in hog-heaven.

Even though Fidel Castro gave them up after a valiant struggle, the Cuban cigar is still recognized as the ultimate smoking experience. Just the sight of them in those air-conditioned cabinets is going to have you in the grip of an uncontrollable desire.

American brands of cigarettes are cheaper in Cuba than in the U.S., but on occasion you might not be able to get your favorite brand, so be prepared to sometimes smoke Winston instead of Marlboro. Buy by the 10-pack carton in Cuba and don't bother to stock up.

Cuban cigarettes are readily available, but they are for hardened addicts only. Cubans love to offer you one just to laugh at your face when you first inhale. Send some to your ex-boss.

CONSIDER WATER CONSERVATION

Water and it's conservation should be thought about too.

We have two tanks holding some 120 gallons in all, but admittedly this will be more than many yachts are equipped to carry. The point though is that on occasion we've been a week or more away from shoreside supplies, and upon dipping the tanks later on prior to refilling we find we've only used less than a third.

First, you'll want to make sure you don't have any dripping joints below decks, or taps above. This can be taken care of during the preparation stages, but you can also reduce any unseen losses by turning off the water-pump switch if fitted whenever you're not using the sink or showers, thus eliminating any pressure in the system when you don't want it.

If you forget, and late at night hear the pump occasionally cycling on and off, then this may be a clue as to the existence of a small leak somewhere, or even a tap dripping.

When washing dishes and pots, use only a couple of drops of detergent, fill the bowl a few inches deep and wash the plates, cutlery, and pots therein. We've never rinsed them prior to draining nor have we ever suffered for not so doing. You may in stubborn or serious cases prior-clean in a bucket of sea water, or even do all your washing in salt-water if you like. We use fresh 'cause we've got it.

A swim at dusk is one of the real pleasures of Cuban cruising, when you know you're the only human being for miles around, and having saltwater dry on your body is not at all disagreeable once you've gotten used to it. If you do find it so, then keep a dedicated towel for drying off the seawater so the other towels will stay dry, and you won't notice any salt crystals irritating your skin. Hey, we used to be fish, they say.

If you used swim suits, let them dry on the aft deck, they'll be okay.

If you must use fresh water to shower after a swim, then turn the taps off while soaping down and you'll not use much. In any case, rinse off from the top down.

We do our best to ensure our water doesn't get contaminated or stale by putting a tablespoon of any household bleach, like Clorox, in with every full tank or so, and it's never happened yet, nor have we ever tasted it. If you'd prefer, there are also proprietary products that do the same for more.

You will of course, also need to take a longish hose which you can keep down in the lazarette for use when filling the water tanks. It may help if it's one of those flat rolled jobs, but we've never used one. They just look neat. Take along an adapter to fit the end to strange taps which you may run into even at places where foreign yachts are commonplace (yes, they do exist). And perhaps one of those do-hickies to repair the hose when it gets cut as it inevitably will one day. Usually though, wherever you can get water it'll come in it's own hose.

There will perhaps be the occasion when through misadventure, or perhaps indeed through adventure, you need to dinghy water out or just lug it down some awful wharf to your yacht. Well, in any case, you ought to have aboard a couple of emergency plastic 5-gallon containers on the aft deck ready to deploy in a hurry. This is as good an emergency as any, and they are useful to carry your supplies out. And as an aside here, when storing emergency water supplies tied to the dinghy or escape raft leave a little air-gap inside the containers so they'll float if chucked over the side in haste.

FUEL

While on the subject of liquids, we might as well get on to fuel.

Firstly, while there is fuel available in most, if not all of the major ports, it is expensive compared to the prices you'll have been paying prior to arriving, and availability may well change from day-to-day given the changing conditions existing at time of going to press.

This should not be taken to mean that you won't be able to obtain supplies, but it does mean you should be prepared for the odd occasion when you may have to continue on to the next stop.

It goes without saying, also, that you won't find anything in an 80-mile sretch of cays where you're the only person around.

Fuel prices will continue to be in flux, but in late 1993, the price of diesel fuel ranged from 45-to-90 cents (U.S.) per liter, depending on where you got it and how firm you were with your position over the cost. Low octane petrol was more expensive still, and don't ask me about the high octane stuff. As a norm the fuel is of reasonable quality, but this should never be taken for granted. There isn't much you can do about the quality when you're desperate, but a few precautions like visual inspection, funnel filters and a regular (if not increased) schedule of filter changes will keep you going.

Our vessel, as mentioned before, is a 34-foot trawler, and as such we are absolutely dependent on our engine, so perhaps our approach to the question of fuel may be of some help.

The engine, which incidentally is 19 years old and with an uncertain history, pumps out 120 h.p. at 2,200 rpm, at which eyeball-buzzing speed the vessel scrapes 8.5 knots. A quick call to the boat's original manufacturers revealed that the theoretical hull speed could be attained on only 90 h.p., and according to one of the design team, wild claims from some owners about speeds of 10 knots couldn't be attained even if it went down Niagara Falls.

So we run our boat at a gentle 1,600 rpm, at which speed it attains 7 knots. A reduction in speed of 1.5 knots for a reduction in fuel consumption of 40 percent. And incidentally, a glance at the power curve shown in the engine's manual shows that the motor is giving 80 h.p. at these revolutions, and is right on the torque curve peak, which is the point at which it is most efficient.

The engine appreciates it, my pocket appreciates it, and our cruising range is greatly increased.

As I write this, I am looking back at our mechanics log (remember that one?), where I find a recalculation, which confirms figures we arrived at a year or two ago showing our consumption to be around 2 1/3 gph. A range of about 654 nautical miles under all cruising conditions. This includes straight lines, wandering about looking for entrances and reefs, and easing into sheltered bays.

You could quite easily do similar calculations for your own boat, and perhaps gain a similar increase in economy and range.

THOUGHTS ON CARRYING EXTRA FUEL

When we first travelled to Cuba, we were merely en route to the Cayman Islands, and uncertain about the availability of fuel, we investigated the idea of carrying a bag-tank somewhere aboard with an extra few gallons to get us there. A little shopping about showed this to be out of the range of our pockets, but 5-gallon plastic jerry-cans proved to be a lot cheaper and were much easier to store. That trip, I remember we carried 105 gallons stashed in the forward cabin and under our bunks in the rear. This gave us a conservatively calculated total range of about 900 miles. It wasn't so difficult to find places to put them once we really thought about it, and we probably could have carried 20 gallons more without any difficulty.

The thing is, we found fuel available both in Havana and along the way.

Nevertheless, we still carry at least 50-60 gallons under the bunks just in case.

We've always carried a large funnel for decanting fuel, and it has it's own gauze strainer in the bottom. I respect the warnings I've received over the years, but this setup has proved adequate when combined with a couple of extra wall-mounted fuel filters on the engine supply lines.

The only time we've had a problem with fuel was when it was decanted directly from a dubious tank into buckets and then into our vessel. This in fact is where a large funnel shows it's worth. That time, the fuel was grey, with only God knows what mixed in, but it got us to Havana and the wall filters intercepted the muck.

However, I do intend to carry a more sophisticated filter in our funnel in the future as I'd prefer to intercept sand, and small beetles (yes, I found both of those items in the filters) before they get into my tanks.

There are products available to treat your diesel's fuel, but on a cruise such as this you'll be using it at a rate that doesn't allow microbes to grow in the tanks. However, if you do leave your boat sitting around for a long while, or if you have a sailboat and only use the motor occasionally, then you should treat your fuel to prevent it becoming black and slimy.

STOVE GAS

The vapor you burn in your stove, is also a fuel so we should mention it here.

Remember that the restrictions on supply of hydrocarbons in Cuba also extend to gas, so why not sidetrack the issue and take your own?

A full 20-pound bottle should last you a month or so, and if you are going to bake a lot then it's not hard to find somewhere on deck (always on deck, never below decks) to store another. We securely bungy-corded an extra bottle under cover, inside the coaming on the flybridge.

If you do get a bit low, ask around wherever you're moored. Someone will help.

Once, we got our bottle filled from another larger one in Cayo Guillermo, for which I'd like to thank the dockmaster again.

It's handy to have the bottles with fitted contents-gauges so you know what's going on.

Construction workers pause for a photo while working on a hotel project on the Malecon in Havana. In the background is a new hotel. (Photo by George Halloran)

everything before departure. You can get oil in the major ports without much problems, but (call me old-fashioned) I prefer to use the same brand I've always used. In any case I've also run out of oil and twice had to use locally purchased oil for changes. We carry lots of oil-filters too.

To change the oil in a boat you need a pump. That way you suck it out of the sump through the dipstick and into an old oil container or two, which you can then discard properly. They're available in both hand-operation and electrical modes.

Remember you need to change oil in the transmission too, and that may well be different.

We have a very sophisticated fuel filter setup, but still change them more frequently than usually recommended, and have enough for at least four changes. Dirty fuel might cause unscheduled replacements, so provide for that. I once flew out of Havana, but made sure I brought back more filters to replace those I'd used already.

There are impellers for the raw-water pump, and a whole spare engine water pump with a thermostat too. And while I think about it, the cooling system sometimes requires a zinc anode too. Change it frequently until you get a feel for its schedule.

We have on board four or five extra engine water-pump belts, and I check daily the condition of the one in use. (See, maintenance.)

Remember that the engine has what seems like a dozen hoses. Take the more obvious ones, but you can sometimes use flexible corrugated-hose which can be cut to length and bent. This makes it truly multi-use, and you might be able to eliminate a couple of similar diameter hoses with one spare length of this.

We once had trouble with the charging system, and I replaced the whole setup with a more manly alternator and wiring system. I had the old one repaired, and it remains aboard always ready for re-use.

There's the odd fuel injection line, and because I was a bit short of funds at the time, the innards of an injector nozzle rather than a whole new one.

A head gasket was contemplated, but I reckon if the head needed lifting there would be more that needed fixing inside it, so I held off. I do, however, carry a rocker-cover gasket.

For the boat's systems you'd like a couple of toilet (head) repair kits, simple to fit and the thought of not being able to fix a head is too, too horrible to contemplate. Bucket and chuckit.

There's the main pressure pump in the fresh water supply to the faucets and shower which need spare diaphragms. And having fixed that leaking tap, did you get an extra washer too?

All those bulbs which the family leaves on need spares and while getting them, pick up a couple for the navigation lights, which always seem to live half-submerged in salt water.

SAILBOATS REQUIRE ADDITIONAL SPARES

A sailboat needs other spares in addition to those above; shackles, trunions, stainless steel cable, and all manner of cleats. Just look at your boat and ask what might disable you in some unlikely event, or even ask yourself what bits you've always been a bit sceptical about.

Epoxy resin and cloth may well be needed, and don't be caught out without a bit of that epoxy putty, which you knead together and it sets rock hard even under water. We once sprang a leak in one of our water tanks while in the southern cays near Cienfuegos and repaired it in 10 minutes flat! To this day it's still holding fine. Paint, varnish, and that sort of thing might only be needed on more extended cruises, but we carry it all and have used it all.

You never know what might suddenly let go, or what you might discover, so try to be flexible in the way you look at spares, tools, and bits and pieces.

We always make a point of keeping odd bits of steel, wood, pipe, and even plexiglass scrap, tucked away in the gaps under drawers where it's out of the way and they've come in more than useful in emergencies.

CHECK POTENTIAL PROBLEMS BEFORE SETTING OUT

On our first visit to Havana, when we were headed down to the Cayman Islands, we discovered by chance that a concealed portion of the anchor post had completely rotted through below decks in the soaking lazarette, where all manner of evil lurked unseen under the anchor rope. I won't go into why we'd not discovered this before, but for now the anchor post was only loosely attached to the boat by the friction of that portion which passed through the deck. We temporarily repaired the damaged foot of the post using old scrap steel strips of what used to serve as rub-rail edging. Drilling through the straps and cutting them into one-foot lengths allowed me to screw a lattice of them around the rotten portion and down to a more solid piece still further below. The repair held through many a night at anchor until months later when we replaced the whole post. But, I should have discovered the problem before setting out in the first place.

And in that vein, there is no handier product in a wider range of repairs than an old-fashioned wire coat hanger. We carry loads, both to hang clothes on, and to fix whatever needs fixing. Below decks, I suspect most of the boat's held together with the stuff.

INVENTORY YOUR TOOLS AND SKILLS

For all of this you'll need tools and testers. Depending on your skill with them, you may opt for a full range of mechanics tools, or at the other extreme, a tupperware box with a couple of adjustable wrenches and a screwdriver. I used to be a professional auto mechanic and may be somewhat biased, but these are what's going to get you out of trouble if anything really does let fly, so I lean towards the extreme of every type and size. Whatever, you definitely need more than the average car carries in the back. I won't go on about it. You know it makes sense.

You'll need at least an electrical test light too, which even if you don't know much about electric circuits, will tell you how far the current reached before it got interrupted.

Throw in a couple of rolls of good strong tape, some wire, a couple of connectors, a positive attitude and you'll muddle through.

Where all this fits may seem daunting at first, but in fact, it all disappears pretty soon if you look for storage. Remember the oil, filters, hoses, and assorted engine spares may well fit quite conveniently down below in the engine compartment, just don't block routine access.

Keep your tools up in the dry, and where you can get them without necessarily having to go into the engine compartment.

Finally, keep all the manuals for all the equipment you have on board, and purchase a couple of those books which deal with maintenance and repair of marine systems.

It goes without saying that you should read the materials whenever you're bored.

If all else fails and you can't fix a problem on your own, remember that years of making do have raised that skill to an elevated level among the multitude of Cuban mechanics who throng the ports. And even if it really is some exotic machine, it's unlikely that anything you can bring in hasn't been seen before, so don't worry, someone will be able to get you going again.

MEDICINE

You should, as a responsible adult and as a good skipper, know a certain amount about first-aid and CPR. In addition to this, your first-aid kit should be as comprehensive as you can afford and simple enough for you to use. If you look after yourself properly then there's no good reason it should ever come out of its drawer, except for the patent hangover cure and the insect bite stuff.

The Cuban medical system is one of their proudest achievements of the past few years, but aboard a yacht miles away from help you're on your own. There is an excellent book I would wholeheartedly recommend you have aboard called *"Where There Is No Doctor."* While it is primarily written for third-world villagers, you're one of those when you're out there by yourself in the cays. It's published by the Hesperian Foundation, P.O. Box 1692 Palo Alto, California, and is available on bookshelves in places like Bluewater Books in Ft. Lauderdale, Florida.

There are also other books dedicated solely to boating accidents too and whichever you get, you should read it before you really need to.

If, however, you do have a problem in Cuba, there are more doctors and hospitals than you could ever have imagined. There are medical posts in all the hotels, and there certainly will be medical help available anywhere ashore at a moments notice, usually only a few hundred yards away from wherever you're moored.

The service will usually be free for most minor ailments or accidents, although you might have to pay for the medication, which you acquire from the nearby pharmacies. I've had only good experiences with it and I know where I'd prefer to be involved in emergency treatment without insurance.

If like me, you have a chronic bad back, then it too will be seen to most efficiently at the Frank Pais Orthopedic Hospital while you're moored in Havana, although you may be expected to pay for this.

Remember the shortages have also affected the supply of medication, so take what you might regularly need, and remember that any of the clinics near your dock will be overjoyed to receive any extra medicines you may have brought. Anything at all.

CHARTS

I have encountered occasional yachts making their way with nothing more than a single large scale chart covering the entire island, but for serious cruising with peace of mind you need a bit more than this.

No doubt about it, your best bet will be the excellent charts published by the Instituto Cubano de Hydrografia (ICH). These charts, to a scale of 1: 150,000 cover the coastline and cays in sufficient detail for all practical purposes, and include the most up-to-date information available about buoys and marks. Originally published in 1975, they receive yearly updates at the ICH offices in Havana, and I would use them in preference to all others. To get a rough idea of the coverage offered by these, 26 charts would take you safely around the island, but you could easily stock another ten or more if you wanted even more detail.

A cruise from Havana to the western tip of the island would require four, and the trip from Havana to the eastern tip would require ten. Similar quantities cover the southern side of the island.

For serious cruising in the cays they are unsurpassed, and allow you to search out the most unlikely holes to rest up at night. The color versions are only available in Havana through the following:

Centro de Produccion de Cartas y Publication Nauticas (CPCPN)
Carretera de Berroa Km 2.5 Havana del Este
Ciudad de Havana, Cuba
Tel: 65-0324

Or more conveniently in Old Havana at:
La tienda "El Navigante"
Mercaderes 115, entre Obispo y Obrapia
Havana Colonial, Cuba:
Tel: 61-3625

At any of the above they cost around $15 each in 1993, but supplies are limited, and you may find it advisable to obtain black and white photocopies of these same charts in the U.S. before leaving. I don't know where they are available elsewhere, but perhaps you might find some. In the U.S. they are available through Bluewater Books; at a price of $17 each.

That wonderful stop for all serious sailors, Sailorman in Ft. Lauderdale, also sells a chart kit but unfortunately this kit comprises a set of photocopies haphazardly cut to a size a bit larger than 14" x 17" and stapled together. For serious chart work you really need the full sized versions.

LARGER SCALE U.S. CHARTS AVAILABLE

The U.S. government, has long had available a larger scale series of charts to a scale of 1:300,000, which in spite of being twice the ICH scale and containing some notable inaccuracies surrounding reef positions, I have also used cautiously without problems.

Rumor has it that they have recently released some previously restricted charts covering the coastline in greater detail too, so it may well be wise to investigate which are available in your area if time is limited.

British Admiralty charts are also sold widely, and while they may be somewhat old, they do contain quite sufficient information if used wisely.

A couple of charts showing whatever further passages you might be contemplating will also be required. If for example, you're going on to the Dominican Republic, or the Bahamas, then you must purchase these charts before arrival in Cuba.

If you have not managed to get hold of all you require, then a couple of sheets of tracing paper and a friendly yacht with the requisite charts will see you further along your way. I once gave tracings to a French yacht in Casilda on the south coast, and encountered them safely again in Havana some three months later.

It's nice to have a large scale chart of the West Indies too, as you can use it to plan your route further along, or back via a different route.

There is a wonderful book of charts put out by the DMA called Pilot Charts. These show the climatic conditions for every area of the Caribbean for each month of the year. They are used to plan your journey by giving you a statistical probability of wind directions, strength, and currents for each month and are published in a set of 12 monthly charts.

These charts used to be available in a Caribbean-only version up to 1993, but have now been amalgamated into a larger collection of 37 pages, which contain North Atlantic information. The price has gone up commensurately to about $25, but it's still good value and may well help you avoid travelling in certain areas when the winds aren't going to be favorable. Great for avoiding the hurricane season too, or for showing the statistically normal path they take during the season.

I am not aware of any electronic charts out there, but I'm sure they exist somewhere on some databank, perhaps held by the U.S. government, so we may expect them to become available in the future as and when relations thaw.

Of course, in addition to all this you will require plotting instruments for laying off your course. There are many and varied, but in the end it boils down, like so many things, to what you're comfortable with. You can make do with surprisingly few, and we only use a divider, a triangle, and a simple course plotter in one-piece plastic available anywhere for a couple of dollars. That way when they get lost we won't weep. Do not leave your instruments out in the sun on deck or they will warp like pretzels after an hour or two. Incidentally, our dividers are over a hundred years old and still work fine! A simple speed/distance calculator is nice to have sometimes, but by no means necessary except for predicting when you're going to need course-changes and the like.

In farming centers oxen may play as important of a role in working the fields as tractors do in other parts of the world. (Photo by George Halloran)

WIND, CURRENTS AND TIDES

Once again, if passage making, the pilot chart will be of use for currents over the whole area of the West Indies, but locally in any case, here's a sketch which shows the major influences you're going to encounter around the coast. You may use the counter-currents to your advantage at certain times so have a good look at it.

As you can see, the major influences are going to be the Gulf Stream along the northwest, the Old Bahamas Current along the north east, the Yuccutan Current at the western tip, the westerly current between Haiti and the southeast coast. There are a few easterly counter-currents along the southern Keys depending on the time of the year.

Winds and currents can help you along your way, or you can allow them to dominate you. The logical way round the island may well be counter-clockwise, but what if you have other reasons for going clockwise? Well, you're just going to have to search out the dead areas inside the drop-off along the reef, trying not to tack out too far while beating against the prevailing east winds. At least this will have the effect of giving some shelter from the swells, but be prepared to really slog it out. I've met yachts in Varadero some 60 miles east of Havana that didn't, and had to take detours using the Gulf Stream northeast over towards the Bahamas to obtain favorable wind direction later.

Along the southern coasts or the Florida Keys, you'll have the seas broken up and the winds will to some extent be more variable. You'll certainly be receiving a lot more shelter from the prevailing easterlies, while you meander about the Cuban cays and the current is negligible inside the reef there.

As regards to tides, there isn't a lot to worry about along most of the coast. The only places I've encountered anything which could call for notice are around the northeastern coast, and even there we're only talking about a foot or two.

NAVIGATION EQUIPMENT

The most important instrument aboard is without doubt, the ship's compass. For centuries, vessels of all kinds have navigated their way about the world with only rudimentary charts and hearsay to guide or point them along that way. It goes without saying that you should have it where you can see it. Move it if you can't tell exactly where you're headed from your normal and most comfortable position at the wheel. It isn't difficult, and in any case you've probably fitted a few items to the boat since you last had it swung.

Huh, swung?

All compasses are calibrated upon leaving the factory, but they don't know what old iron you've got next to it in your boat. When I got my present boat the compass was at least 15 degrees out, and it wasn't just a case of twisting it in its mounts a bit. It's a black art involving sun sights, peloruses, compensating magnets, and grizzled old men who mutter. Have it done whether you decide to cruise further afield of Maine or not. That new depth sounder you fitted last year's probably put it out a couple of degrees in any case.

By the way, does it's bulb work?

And speaking of depth-sounders, this is probably the next most important instrument you've got aboard. Those old craft did in fact swing the lead regularly in its place.

We've got three fitted, and have been grateful for each and every one.

Down below, there's the old flasher unit which still hums away above the wheel where anyone can see it. Because it's inside the cabin, the relative dimness of its light doesn't make too much of a difference, but up topsides it was all but unreadable in the sun.

On the flybridge we have two more. A bright orange digital LED unit, which due to accidents of history, is now only good at less than 120 feet, but is absolutely inch-accurate when we're in shallow waters and can be seen clearly in all conditions due to a sunshade.

We also have alongside it a LCD fishfinder affair, which shows the bottom contours on a small screen. We acquired this mainly for use searching out proper dive sites where we might want ravines and narrow gorges, but it also gives an indication about the bottom composition. In fact, a major drawback to this unit, which was not evident at the time of purchase, was the fact that the LCD display which thrives on sunlight, is all but unreadable if you're wearing polarized sunglasses! Nevertheless it has its uses along the wall and reef.

If I had to pick one and stick with it, it would be the little digital LED unit with its squealing alarm.

Incidentally, we know to within an inch the exact depth we draw, and this figure is written large alongside the instruments. With our sounders we are accustomed to trickling about with only a couple of inches below the keel while feeling out anchorages or passages.

GPS/LORAN

The argument rages as to what constitutes a good sailor. Well, I've had my share of harassment from the traditionalists who ask rhetorically what I'd do without my electronic aids. My reply is, I'd go right back to using dead-reckoning like I used to.

But seeing as I've got those aids, by gum I'm going to use them. As far as I'm concerned, the prudent skipper carries two! That really get's the old salts going.

I like to know where I am at any given time, even if I haven't been paying attention over the last hour or so, and with my GPS receiver it takes only 30 seconds now for me to have a neat cross on my chart, instead of laborious calculation while the boat lies dead in the water.

A year or so ago, most boats used in the U.S. carried Loran C receivers and this still is a cheap and accurate instrument. It's perfectly good for the U.S. and even the northern Bahamas. You may absolutely rely on it if you're only planning to cruise the north coast of Cuba, but its accuracy does begin to go off as you get out of range. Believe it or not, ours was usually spot on as far as the Cayman Islands, but there were times when it did give false readings of up to 15 miles. At that point, it needed turning off then firing up again, and the trick was to make sure it was right before leaving harbor, at which point it was generally okay all day, so don't give up on them. We still carry ours in a drawer as a spare.

GPS has given us faithful service and accuracy down to 50 feet all over the Caribbean, and the old salts aren't going to make me give it up for traditions sake. All the coordinates given in this book are from GPS.

With regards to the traditionalists, I do also have a marvelous alloy Zeiss sextant aboard, with all the books. When taking into consideration the price I paid for it, the cost of the various almanacs, books of selected star sights, and the cost of the course I attended in Southampton to learn its use, it cost me as much as my GPS did, and now you can buy a GPS like mine for half of what I paid! And of course, a sextant is accurate only to about five miles on average, and twice a day at unsociable hours.

Best get a GPS unit that can be wired into your boat's power and has an external antenna for better reception, or at least one that can be slipped into an adapter, which does that for the GPS unit.

We'll need a hand-bearing compass too, for taking bearings along tricky courses and getting other fixes on exits which you might need to record for later use. I would recommend one which you can see in the dark, or at least in the dusk, as that always seems to be the time.

Some really well-funded boats carry radar, but to be frank, although I would love to have one, it's not necessary. You won't be making more than a couple of night passages and someone can always stay awake for those. There's not going to be a lot of night traffic about, and this should go for you as well.

Then there are binoculars, the lighter the better. Not much to say here, except that there are some really pricey ones on the market, gyro-stabilized and all that. But simple and cheap is good. I use the pocket ones which are really a bit low-powered, but they do the business and fit in my pocket when I'm ashore. Mine have crossed the Andes, and climbed the Himalayas with me.

Lights are essential too. We have aboard a large Q-beam, which connected via the cigar lighter is operated by the boat's batteries. It is powerful enough to give you a good tan, and can be operated for a couple of hours at a time. But here too, we've found more day-to-day (night-to-night) convenience in a large, eight-battery, pistol-type divers light. As a matter of fact we carry a couple of dive lights. Handy for the dinghy when you might well be occasionally soaked, handy for the engine room, handy for the boat, and handy for diving.

The big Q-beam hardly gets used now.

Absolutely indispensable for those long straight runs is your auto-pilot. Well, I suppose it is a bit of a luxury, but once you've had one, you'll recognize its advantages. Having said that, it's lack shouldn't restrain you from this sort of trip. An experienced sailor can always balance his boat on sail and lashed rudder while he goes about his business.

Strictly speaking, the next item shouldn't be classed a navigation aid, but I will. It consists of a set of passage notes, perhaps jotted into some sort of a spiral bound notebook, and prepared in advance so they can be consulted at a moments notice. The items recorded could include plans for the day's passage, with projected courses, alternate harbors, and so on. The whole lot could be recorded while poring over the charts at the beginning of the run, or while waiting for the morning's coffee to cool. It's much handier than screaming at your mate because you've forgotten what the next leg should be.

BOAT PREPARATION & MAINTENANCE

Before leaving your home port, it only makes sense to have all aboard as shipshape as possible. As mentioned in the previous sections, facilities for repair are few and far between, while the supply of spares is uncertain. So it only makes sense to spend a day or two going over the boat making right those little items you've been meaning to sort out for the last year or so. And this makes just as much sense, if not more, when the engine has only been recently serviced.

Were you to find yourself unable to start your engine when necessary, somewhere in the Virgin Islands, you might be no more inconvenienced than the time it took for some Good Samaritan passing by to answer your VHF and arrive waving a set of jumper cables. This same problem might be considerably more serious were it to occur out in the southern cays, so let's make sure your batteries can start your engine, even though the lights have long since dimmed and the refrigerator is leaking. When I rationalized the electronics on our boat following our experience along those lines, I knew there wasn't room below for a generator nor funds available for same. We were able, however, to set up a system which allocated two batteries for the circuit covering the lights, fridge and electronics, and also a separate battery dedicated solely to starting the main engine. This has enabled us to start our main engine no matter the state of our other electrics. The individual batteries are always isolated when the main engine is off, so there can be no mistake. We also took the opportunity to upgrade our alternator from a wimpy 55 amps to a more capable 125-amp unit. This is perhaps the bottom limit, but in fact we've never had any more problems and the set up is now able to run all the main electric systems for three days before we need to run the main engine.

We are, to be honest, apart from running a refrigerator at all times, frugal in our uses of power, turning off all lights when not needed. There are larger vessels which run electrical generators, and they can utilize much more power quite freely at the expense of only a couple of gallons a week. And there are simpler craft than ours, who happily use much less power than we do. We've come across yachts which utilize none at all, keeping strips of "Boucan" or dried meats in the rigging, and using kerosene lanterns and stoves. They have as much fun as us, while eating and drinking at least as well. Well, red wine after all doesn't need chilling.

Get a good book on marine electrics, and check out your requirements properly, or go by what your experience tells you.

Of course, there is shore power available for hook-up at the marinas in Havana, Santiago, Cienfuegos and other major ports.

CHECK FLUIDS AND BELTS DAILY

Daily before each run, when checking the engine oil and water, I also inspect the water pump belt. Do not overtighten, or you run the risk of ruining the bearings in the alternator.

On some engines, including our own, one needs to remove a water hose to get the belt around the pulley. We temporarily removed the hose in port, fitted three or four spare belts in place behind it and fastened them up and away from the pulley with plastic ties. A belt which breaks in service can now be easily replaced in two minutes, instead of having to struggle to fit a new one, while pressurized boiling water sprays from a disconnected hose and the boat drifts towards the reef. Believe me this strategy is a saviour at those times when the engine's temperature alarm (which you've previously checked) sounds.

Have a look at the hoses, squeezing them and replacing those which show signs of cracking or otherwise giving cause for concern, and to round off the cooling system, change the impeller on the raw-water pump and the zinc (if fitted) in the cooling system.

When changing your oil and filters, remember that there may be an oil change required for the injector-pump too. Forget this one at your peril.

Once again, if you aren't up to doing all the engine work yourself, you should have a service done by a competent mechanic, but make sure you personally check-out the items afterwards

The bilge pumps can be run a few times, and maybe the wires looked at. There are some excellent water-proofing compounds or sprays which can seal off the connections on those old repairs done to the wiring by who knows whom. If they can't stand a tug, they can't be trusted.

The sails may be inspected both before your cruise and at regular intervals while on the water. It would hardly do for a sail to blow out just when you're beating into a fresh northeaster with daylight fading. Of course the runners and other rigging come in for the same treatment too, and the shrouds may have corroded during the lay-up. Sort them out in advance.

And remembering my tale of the rotted anchor post, slimy things lurk down in damp lazarettes, if left unchecked. Inspect yours thoroughly.

The auto-pilot, while largely maintenance-free, might benefit from a check on both its mountings and its connection into the steering system. If it's hydraulically operated, then the hoses and connections need inspection with a dry rag and a bright light, while if it's chain connected, you'll not want slack links riding up on the sprocket in a heavy following sea when the servo motor is whizzing around from port to starboard and back like a demented thing.

Air scoops for cabins need a bit of thought. It's going to be hot if you travel in the summer months between March and September. You may be able to purchase a designer scoop, or with a little skill you could improvise using some canvas in the same shape which may be tied into place facing into the wind. I remember when we had a large scoop into the front cabin which totally blocked the rest of the scoops to the main and after cabins. When the door to the front was closed for privacy, the remainder of the boat became stifling hot, and more scoops had to be fitted to the sides to compensate. Remember that you also need to get the heated air out too, so try to maintain a complete through-flow along the length of the vessel and out the back.

SOME THOUGHTS ON REFRIGERATION

Refrigeration may benefit from a word here for the neophyte cruiser. There are several types of units now available. The first is a plain, simple ice-box into which you put blocks of ice and rely on the insulation to preserve the ice for as long as possible, depending on how much food you put in, and how often you open it to take that food out.

And there are the electric refrigerators which run off your batteries, a separate generator unit, or even an engine linked compressor. They are generally either water or air cooled, and even though it is beyond this book to describe all these in detail, if your choice hasn't already been made by the boat's manufacturers, then the most efficient units are water-cooled. Your choice should be governed by space considerations, but if you can in fact fit a water-cooled 'fridge, then it will use anything up to 50 percent less power (with consequently less wear) than an air-cooled job.

Having said that, if you are forced to use one of the more readily available, economical (at least as far as initial purchase price goes), and smaller overall air-cooled units, then increase the through-flow of cooling air from outside. On our vessel we have had to cut four cooling vents behind the compressor to allow in twice as much air as recommended by the manufacturers. The unit still runs acceptably, in spite of temperatures far in excess of those it might normally experience in the U.S. where it was purchased.

A note of caution, we once took so much green water over the bows that it squirted in through the side vents, shorting out the power-pack. We've now fitted baffles to prevent this occurring again and have had no further problems in spite of equal seas. (See sketch.)

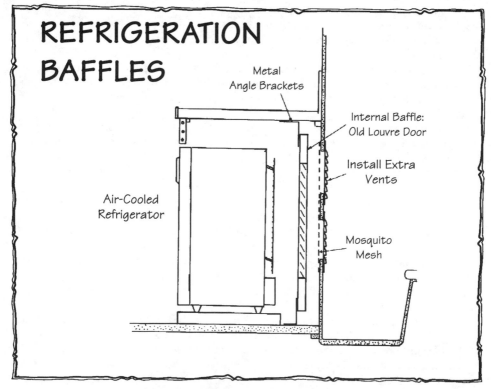

REFRIGERATION BAFFLES

Metal Angle Brackets

Internal Baffle: Old Louvre Door

Install Extra Vents

Air-Cooled Refrigerator

Mosquito Mesh

Anchoring in Cuban waters overnight will likely be inside the reefs, and in turtle-grass or similar vegetation. The bottom characteristics are a factor in determining your best choice of an anchor. (Photo by Simon Charles)

ANCHORS & ANCHORING

There are many publications which deal with the skills of sailing. Most of them discuss at some length anchors and anchoring, so I am torn between the desire to get on with the rest of the book, feeling that anyone cruising in Cuba will have some knowledge, and a sneaking feeling that the subject is still worthy of some discussion here. However, making the assumption that there will at least be some readers who make this their first cruise abroad, I shall err on the side of caution.

The bottom composition has a major effect on the efficiency of the anchor's holding power. The right choice of anchor tackle combined with the correct method of deploying it may result in an anchor which is capable of holding fast under any conditions, whereas the reverse is also possible if things are not done right.

There are in the main, four types of bottom which will be encountered. Grass, mud, sand, and coral. Of these, inside the reef, where the majority of us will spend our nights, the most likely is turtle-grass or some similar vegetation.

This is not to say that one will not spend long periods of time anchoring over say, sand or coral, but at first glance it might appear that in an ideal world your primary anchor should be the most suitable for turtle-grass or the like, perhaps with a sharp point for penetrating through the mat of rotted vegetation on which it grows, and into the sand below. The best type for this is the old-fashioned kedge anchor such as you see tattooed onto sailors forearms, but unfortunately, it is little used nowadays as it can be bulky and difficult to store. As it requires a heavier weight for a similar performance in other bottoms, it has been largely superseded by newer designs, and you may even find it difficult to obtain one nowadays.

Almost all anchor-manufacturers produce figures which show the theoretical holding power of their anchors in various ground conditions, but I note that they are universally reticent on the subject of penetration into turtle-grass. However, all is not lost, as the multitude of boats which safely anchor over this sort of terrain daily attest, and they all seem to use different anchors!

In any case, we would not really wish our main anchor to be too dedicated as it were to one type of bottom, given that we will almost certainly anchor over a different type the day after tomorrow. In fact, it might well be argued that when anchoring in turtle-grass, we are already in some sort of shelter, and more often than not are in a position of leisure, whereas sand and coral bottoms might be found closer to dangers. Be that as it may, we do need multi-bottom capabilities in our anchors, with ultimate strength a high priority for emergency conditions.

I won't enter into the conflict between the various manufacturers over which anchor is better, except to say that whichever you choose it should be matched by your anchor rode, and that anchoring technique will be more important than the arguable superiority of one type over another.

On the next page I list the various anchors available, and their suggested maximum holding powers. Were I setting out on a long cruise, I might well be tempted to renew my anchor rode, saving the old one whole for use in cases of hurricane or storm mooring.

Many of the boats happily pottering about the U.S. coasts are equipped with minimal anchors. I remember when my own vessel was purchased, it came with an anchor that looked increasingly piddly with every degree south we travelled. I have survived with underweight anchors, but it's extremely unwise. In fact, I have brought an anchor back to the U.S. as hand-luggage on a commercial airline to part-exchange at Sailorman for a heavier one when I had the chance.

There is some controversy about whether or not an all-chain rode is superior to a 3-strand nylon rope, but what is not in doubt is that some sort of chain is required at the business end to prevent the actual rode chafing through on sharp bits of coral. It also has the function of both providing the required weight to cause the angle of the anchor to as closely approach horizontal as possible, and providing enough weight to act as a shock-absorber preventing the rise and fall of the bows in a turbulent sea from working the anchor loose. As an **absolute minimum**, I'd go for 15 feet of chain.

Indeed, if you do go to an all-chain rode you are likely to be faced with a considerable weight requiring a sturdy windlass to raise the anchor rather than mere muscle-power. Failing this you may be faced with acquiring a sturdier anchor wench!

On our boat we have often experimented with La Fiona handling the helm and controls,while I do the raising/lowering, but this has invariably led to arguments. You need to do better than us in this aspect.

Diving the anchor is better than any other method for acquiring peace of mind and a secure fastening of boat to ground. Snorkeling above and watching an anchor tear loose while the crew backs the motor will give an unforgettable image of just what goes on below the surface.

Remember that in among otherwise impenetrable turtle-grass, there are usually gullies every so often. The diver can swim down and physically shift the anchor over into one of these where it will dig into the walls rather than slide over the surface.

ANCHOR SELECTION CHART

Boat Length in Feet	16	18	20	22	24	26	28	30	32	34	36	38	40	42	44	46	48	50	52	54	56	58	60
Economy Fluke	Fluke 8		Fluke 13			Fluke 18		Fluke 22															
West Marine Traditional	TRAD-4	TRAD-8				TRAD-13				TRAD-22			TRAD-40										
West Marine Performance		PERF-5					PERF-12				PERF-20				PERF-35			PERF-70					
Nav-X Fortress		FX-7						FX-11		FX-16			FX-23			FX-37		FX-55					FX-85>
Nav-X Guardian	Com	G-7			G-11		G-16			G-23													
Bruce	4.4		BR11			BR16.5		BR22		BR33			BR44				BR66					BR110	
Simpson Lawrence CQR			CQR25									CQR35					CQR45					60, 75	
Simpson Lawrence Delta		DEL14				DEL22				DEL35						DEL55							
Paul Luke 3-Piece Yachtsman		Luke 40					Luke 50				Luke 70												
Anchorline dia x length		3/8" x 200'(28)						7/16" x 200'(28)		1/2" x 200' (28)			5/8" x 250' (36)				3/4" x 300' (43)			7/8" x 300 (40)			
Proof Coil Chain, size x length		3/16"PC					1/4"PC						5/16"PC				3/8"PC			7/16"PC			
Hi Test Chain, size x length		1/4"HT													5/16"HT					3/8"HI			

- Chart based on a sand bottom: call for mud anchor suggestions.
- Suggested sizes are for boats of average windage and proportions.
- Anchor sizes for other than Bruce anchors based on windspeeds up to 30 knots.
- Bruce anchor suggestions based on wind speeds of 42 knots by request by Peter Bruce.
- Delta suggestions based on light displacement craft; heavier types would be from 10-20% shorter re: to Simpson Larwence.
- For storm conditions, use one or two sizes larger.
- Recommended scope: 7:1 for rope/chain and all-chain in shallow water, 4:1 for all-chain in deep water (over 30').
- Chart based primarily on anchor manufacturer's suggestions.
- Numbers in () parentheses are maximum water depths for anchor line shown at 7:1 scope.
- We suggest between one-third and one boat length of chain.
- High test chain recommendations revised downward due to the lack of high-strength shackles to attach to them.
- Suggestions revised 10/6/1993 according to 1994 catalogs.

Chart and data courtesy of West Marine

The above chart has been reproduced with the kind permission of West Marine, a large retailer and mail order supplier of anchors and other marine products, with branches across the USA. As with other similar businesses in the industry they produce a large Master Catalogue which, as well as showcasing their products, includes many pages dealing with all aspects of the art of sailing and cruising. The large section dealing with anchors, rodes, and anchoring techniques (some seven pages of good advice!) is especially well written and I would advise any cruiser to have one or another of these types of catalogues aboard, not just for the information, but additionally in case you need to order a much-needed item.

COMMUNICATIONS

For those of you leaving from North America, why not remove your VHF unit and take the opportunity to have it looked at by a competent technician in any one of the dozens of radio retailers who offer service facilities. You may find that it has drifted off-frequency in the years since you've installed it, and you might be surprised at the increase in performance acquired for only a small sum.

We've also replaced the old antennae on both our units. A 9 db antenna gives the best range, but it puts out a flatter signal beam, which can limit its use on yachts which are heeled over. Far better is the theoretically shorter-range 6 db unit mounted atop the mast. On our trawler, which does not heel except in stormy conditions, we have still obtained better all-round performance from this set up on one of our radios compared to the 9 db antenna on the other unit, because we've been able to get it up higher.

The popularity of hand-held units has made them an alternative, but their range is less than a properly wired-in permanent set, and of course they cannot be left on all the time which limits their use somewhat. In spite of only rarely having heard a radio conversation between boats in Cuba, and even more rarely been called-up, we always leave our sets on 16 all day while on passage.

Along the north coast of Cuba between Varadero, and almost to the western tip, you may also use your VHF to pick up the U.S. weather stations on the Wx frequencies, but further afield you may need to go to short wave for your reports. There are the normal Cuban AM radio stations on the medium wave, however, if like mine, your Spanish is less than perfect, you might prefer to receive your forecasts in your native language on short-wave.

If you feel the need to communicate over long distances independently of the telephone system, then you will have to go to short-wave transmitters requiring complex antennae and licences. But this is by no means necessary if you merely need to receive the long-range weather reports, which can be perfectly picked up on any good portable single sideband short-wave receiver. This unit will also pick up all the local AM/FM radio stations for your daily dose of local news and music, while you lounge on some beach.

You will want to listen for the Offshore North Atlantic and Caribbean forecasts which are broadcast on a regular schedule from various North American shortwave stations on the upper sideband. Below and on the adjoining page you will find a list of the times and a map of the sea areas to which they refer.

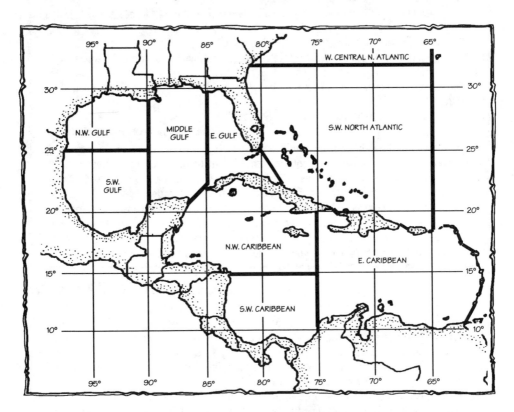

SHORT WAVE WEATHER FORECAST SCHEDULE

Local Time								
EDT	EST	GMT	Stn.	Location	Broadcast Frequency in Khz.			
6am	5am	1000	NMN	Norfolk	4426	6501	8764	13089
7am	6am	1100	WLO	Mobile	4369	8806	13152	17362
8am	7am	1200	WLO	Mobile	4369	8806	13152	17362
			WOO	New Jersey	4387	8749		
9am	8am	1300	WOM	Miami	4363	8722	13092	17242
Noon	11am	1600	NMN	Norfolk	4426	6501	8764	13089
1pm	Noon	1700	WLO	Mobile	4369	8806	13152	17362
2pm	1pm	1800	WLO	Mobile	4369	8806	13152	17362
6pm	5pm	2200	NMN	Norfolk	4426	6501	8764	13089
			WOO	New Jersey	4387	8749		
7pm	6pm	0000	WOM	Miami	4363	8722	13092	17242
			WLO	Mobile	4369	8806	13152	17362
8pm	7pm	0200	WLO	Mobile	4369	8806	13152	17362
Midnight	11pm	0400	NMN	Norfolk	4426	6501	8764	13089
1am	Midnight	0500	WLO	Mobile	4369	8806	13152	17362
2am	1am	0600	WLO	Mobile	4369	8806	13152	17362

Note:
1. Your radio must be capable of Upper Side Band reception.
2. Experiment with higher frequencies during the day and lower frequencies at night.
3. Sometimes stations will delay broadcasts if busy with telephone relay traffic.
4. WLO broadcasts on Mobile local time only (not GMT), so schedule will vary as shown during winter or summer.

I have always found the best of these to be station NMN from Norfolk, Virginia., while WLO out of Mobile, Alabama comes in clearly all over Cuba too. I have found on occasion that I cannot receive the Florida Station WOM, but I have never received station WAH out of St. Thomas.

If listening to NMN from Virginia, you will have to wait for them to wade through 10-15 minutes of forecasts for the northern U.S. coastline before getting down to what concerns you. Stick with it, and don't worry if you tune in late, they probably haven't reached your areas yet.

On the other hand, the Alabama and Florida stations start off with a bang, and their announcers don't hang about, so be ready with pencil poised at the hour appointed.

It will be well if you have a sheet of paper already laid out with the sea-areas already written in, so all you have to do is note the figures and directions as they spew forth. Believe me, you won't have time for much more, and you can then analyze what's going on at your leisure.

We keep a small dedicated notebook for the purpose, so we can look back over the last day or two to see how systems may be developing. Listen daily, to get a feel for the language used before you need it for real.

Finally, all the stations will begin and end their broadcasts with any hurricane-warnings, so if fright has frozen your pencil finger, you'll get a second chance. In the event of this sort of thing, note the position, direction and speed of movement, then plot the system onto your large scale chart of the West Indies to see if you're in the danger zone, and you can make arrangements well in advance for your safety.

WEATHER

Cruising the Cuban coast may present the occasional drawbacks for the inexperienced, but one of the advantages you will find here is that all journeys are short, and shelter is near.

Use common sense, and you are unlikely to find yourself caught out in a major blow, unless it is one of those that springs up from nowhere. Only a sixth sense developed from years of observation and experience will warn you of those.

Once again, there are many books dealing with how you can predict the weather over the next couple of days. This particular book does not pretend to teach you how you may do much more than normal daily passage-planning, and for more than that I would urge you to read one of those books while avoiding becoming too bogged down.

I have even come across formulae which predict storm velocities and paths from the length and frequencies of the waves, but none of these have I ever remembered to use, and consequently master. My methods are considerably simpler, and while they may not make me an expert, they have worked adequately for me wherever I have sailed, and they should certainly work on a cruise around Cuba, remembering that you'll never be lost on the high seas for weeks on end.

A few clues...
• Pay attention to the radio.
• Be aware of the Kabatic effect around the coastline.
• Look out of the window in the morning.
• Finally, remember what it was like yesterday.

The radio reports will tell you what's setting up over there towards Africa, or the Lesser Antilles, where the trouble starts brewing. By and large, you will have a few days warning if you're listening to the short-wave stations, and as you plot the storm system's approach, you must at this point make arrangements for fight or flight.

If it's a hurricane, then there is no question. It is flight.

Anyone who has been in a hurricane will confirm that the fury of the winds are beyond anything one can imagine. The hurricane that wiped out a portion of Miami in 1992 should have shown many prospective Cuban cruisers just what is entailed in survival ashore, and they at any rate can imagine what it would be like aboard a boat. Then there are the survivors of Hugo, and its predecessors, some of whom indeed may have been boat owners. There aren't many boats, large or small, which are going to survive a direct hit from a hurricane out at sea, and precious few which will survive one inshore at anchor either, no matter what the shelter or what you have arranged in the line of tethers. The only thing you can do is get the boat as far inland as possible so that the force of the wind has to some extent been dissipated by the land by the time it strikes you. Then there's the storm-surge to be considered, where the river may well rise by 20 feet or so! It would not be uncommon to find your boat up to a mile or more inland from the banks of your refuge upon your return. And your boat is going to be a low priority in the eyes of any rescue or rebuilding effort by the authorities who will be coping with far, far greater problems. This goes for all parts of the world which might be affected and not just Cuba.

So, to lessen your chance of that direct hit, you need to get out fast from the projected path. If that is not possible, then move the vessel to whatever shelter is available, tether it as best you can, and remove yourself to a place of safety. You can get another boat, after all.

Having said that, there are hurricane-holes, flats, and the like, which will provide shelter in the more likely event of a glancing blow or just a strong gale, so use your head, and make your own value judgement as to which refuge you seek. A complete discourse on boat survival is beyond the premise of this book, but there is an abundance of literature on the subject, and all competent skippers should be familiar with their options.

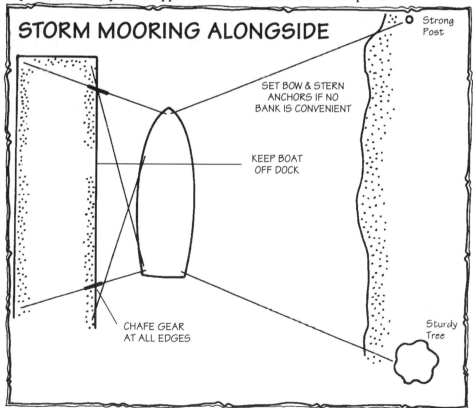

Remember all that line you saved when you changed the anchor rode? Well this is the time to use it, with all chocks fitted with anti-chafe protection.

You will also have to remember that in any sort of a blow you need to double or triple the length of the anchor line played out.

THE KABATIC EFFECT

This is the name of the phenomena which causes the wind to blow towards the land during the day, the wind to blow away from it at night, and the lull we experience at dawn and dusk.

If you think of the land mass as something which might heat up during the day under the influence of the sun, then you can understand that the air directly above it might be also heated in turn by the land. That air will have a tendency to rise as it expands, and consequently cooler unheated air will rush in from the sea to fill the void left under that warm air which having risen to its maximum height will spread out away from the land. Again, this incoming cooler air will also be heated, and the whole process will continue in a loop until sundown. Then the land will cool and the air above it will become cooler than the air over the sea. Now, the air above the land will contract and become denser, causing it to fall towards the land at which point it will spread out away from the land and over the sea.

So you might see that during the day, the incoming air will come from the sea towards the land, and at night the breezes will take the opposite path, with calmer periods at daybreak and nightfall when the two features are equally balanced.

Of course this effect is rarely strong enough to counteract the prevailing winds head on, but it certainly has an effect along the Cuban coast, which in the main lies along the direction of those winds, and thus it has a distinct influence on passage-making strategy and anchoring.

As an example of passage-making strategy, we can use the early calms for rounding capes which might otherwise be potentially rough and difficult passages. Then we could rest up later on when those winds have started to heap the seas over the bows and into our faces.

An example of how it influences anchoring techniques might be that in the cays we could well expect a wind-shift later on at night, forcing the boat towards the shoreline rather the opposite direction you anchored in a few hours earlier.

It is my personal impression that these influences are more readily felt in the southeast and southwest cays, and along the southern coastlines, rather than the north. Perhaps this is because of the prevailing winds being too strong to be too much affected along the northeast coastline, which to some extent faces into the wind, but it nevertheless still does have some effect there.

USE YOUR OWN SENSES TO JUDGE WEATHER

Look out the window in the morning; does it look grey and stormy? Has the boat acquired a coating of spray rather than the usual dew? Or does the light just look a bit odd?

Why bother to leave just then? Assuming your radio has not given any indication of stormy weather or gales (and to be honest, in spite of everything they are still not that common), then make a leisurely cup of tea and wait. If the weather has been steady for the last couple of days, and unless conditions have markedly changed, it may only be a minor cold front passing through. Your barometer will give some indication of just what you can expect later on. Is it falling rapidly? Uh, oh, better get out the foul weather gear and look to your ground tackle.

If, however, it's steady then you may well assume it's temporary, and a minor delay in your departure could be all that's called for.

Here perhaps, I could say something about barometers. Mount yours where it's not subject to too much in the way of vibration i.e., not on the engine-room wall or any wall that picks up engine vibrations. We've had nothing but trouble from this. And it has rendered two separate and increasingly expensive instruments useless. We used to keep a graph tracking the barometric pressure's rise and fall, but after a couple of weeks the vibration affected it so much that the needle gradually showed we were in the middle of a permanent hurricane! At that point we ignored it, having looked out the window.

There are always the occasional longshoremen or fishermen with whom you can exchange gossip and speculation over the state of the weather, but in my experience you usually get a sage nod and the words "frente frio" (cold front) are bandied about. Treat advice with caution unless he looks as though he obviously knows more about it than you. Yesterday he may have been a photographer.

Trust your own nose.

How you can carry your dinghy may determine your best choice in a dinghy type. (Photo by Simon Charles)

YOUR DINGHY

What can I say about them? There are so many prides and prejudices governing the choice, but in any case a word or two cannot go amiss.

It is indisputable that a rigid craft like a small skiff rows more easily but this may present storage problems when compared with a deflatable which is sold on its potential for storage. The ubiquitous inflatable however is not all that easily broken down and reinflated on a daily basis, and I've never come across anyone who routinely did this.

Nevertheless, on occasion, it is necessary to do so for packing below or vehicle transport, and this capacity just cannot be ignored unless you have ample room on deck, or perhaps davits fitted which store the auxiliary craft out of the water securely. So in spite of the availability of strange folding boats, I shall confine my remarks in the main to the inflatable.

Your mind may well have been made up for you some time hence, but if considering a purchase you will wisely be governed by size and weight, as much as price.

Be guided by what you can comfortably lift into place aboard, rather than other considerations like total size or other factors. You may find that to heft a 10-foot inflatable is just too much if there are only two elderly crew aboard. Go to a smaller size and reduce your expectations of what it will carry. After all, you will have to lug it aboard every time you make a passage. A 10-foot inflatable will comfortably carry four persons through most of the seas you will be using it in, and if you need that sort of capacity you will likely have extra labor to bring it aboard or up into its cruising position. Of course, the size of your vessel will have its say governing the dinghy's size too, so think of where it will be stored when the boat is under way.

The same goes for the outboard engine if you are using one. There are those who see no point in the extra bulk and the other considerations surrounding an outboard, preferring to row, but you may find this somewhat limiting in the huge area of the Cuban cays, or when moving about bays and harbors which may be a mile or more wide.

There is a limit, generally set by the dinghy's manufacturer governing the amount of allowable horsepower you may fit to an inflatable. If you exceed this it may void any insurance or warranty claims, as well as causing an occasionally uncontrollable craft, but within these limits I would go for the maximum power which you can find in an easily liftable package. It can be a bit uninspiring to spend an hour slogging along with wavelets sending spray over the bow when you could have planed over them a lot faster and more smoothly using say a 15 h.p. motor weighing exactly the same as your 10 h.p. engine, from the same manufacturer, and costing only $100 more. The same might also go for the 5 and 8-h.p. motors.

The various engine manufacturers give the weights in their catalogues, so look at this factor closely before buying.

We have never regretted getting the more powerful engine fitted to our inflatable, especially as we use it so often.

While on the subject of weight, you may be tempted to tow your dinghy rather than bring it into the cruising position. I would recommend against this practice, as on the rare occasion we have done so, we have invariably reversed onto it having forgotten its presence in the wake. If however, you opt to do this, then please take note of the time when crossing a bumpy Harwich Harbour in England, my uncle Mark looked back at the dinghy, and turning with a suddenly white face demanded, "Did *we* take the outboard off the dinghy?"

We hadn't; the waves had.

If you are moored in Havana's Marina Hemingway, you may be asked by security guards to bring the dinghy aboard at night, or to chain it up. At first I thought this was mainly on account of a reluctance to allow free and unrestricted immigration, but later on another visit, I discovered it was not merely that.

A tale: Last year, I became friendly with a couple in a yacht who were able to tell me about their dinghy, which had been stolen while they were in supposedly secure docks in Havana the year before. Apparently someone had distracted the guards while their dinghy was stolen from right under their noses. Later, they received full compensation from the marina offices, who were understandably embarrassed over this incident. I could not bring myself to tell anyone, that some days before hearing the tale, I had been asked by some Cubans to repair a dinghy for them. I declined, because as visitors our position was tenuous, and in any case I had no means of knowing if in fact they were genuine. However, offering advice regarding using it for fishing purposes, I did get a glimpse of the craft. It had the name of the stolen dinghy all over its bows.

There is no need for undue alarm in most places, but occasionlly it may be wise to retain your dinghy securely by means of a stainless steel cable, such as you may find in any ship's chandler. This may be fitted with eyelets swaged on at both ends, such that a lock may pass through and the whole rig fastened at one end to the outboard. The other end may be fastened to your vessel having first passed the line through the towing ring at the bow. There are many locking devices which in turn fasten the outboard to the transom securely, making it impossible to steal the whole show.

If you have recently overhauled your yacht, you may well have a length of old stainless steel rigging, and in lengths of over 20 feet this is ideal. You will also find it second hand in many dealer's yards. It's a lot lighter and friendlier than chain. We have only felt the need to use this setup on three occasions in Cuba, and I am sure that in any other country we would have lost the dinghy a long ago.

I must note that increasing problems in Cuba may make for an increased vigilance on your part, but always less than in the rest of the West Indies.

THE BICYCLE

There are millions of bicycles on Cuban roads, and you'll be glad you had one aboard so often it hardly merits discussion. We acquired an ancient rusty second hand model before our first trip, and it saw constant use even two up with Fiona perched crosswise on the centre-bar in the West Indian fashion, as opposed to the more unstable Cuban method of transporting passengers on the rear carrier-rack. The saddle was a sorry mess of protruding wire springs covered with a torn plastic bag, but we loved it and mourned its eventual loss (in another part of the world, I should add) to a casual thief. It lived on deck, and consumed huge quantities of WD40 oil to hold the salt at bay. Even hardened officials, having a bad day, were softened by the sight.

The usual bike in Cuba is a sturdy old-fashioned Chinese model the sort you'll see all over the world, and if you wish to blend in then this is the sort to have. No gears, an upright handle-bar, and a pictur-esque name ("Flying Pigeon"). However, this may be somewhat difficult to transport in a small inflatable, so you might be tempted along the lines of any of the folding bicycles available, and you should in any case invest in a sturdy locking chain as you would any-where else.

Personally, I do not think a ten-speed racing bicycle would be strong enough for

Fiona cleaning our bicycle during a passage. (Photo by Simon Charles)

the sort of work it might be called upon to perform, and along with its cousin the mountain bike, might be a bit flashy if that sort of thing matters to you.

You will need to take a patch-kit and a pump just in case, but the pump can also be used to inflate the boat's fenders and even pump up the accumulator tank on the water-system! Leave it in the engine room, and do not carry it around on the bike.

LOCAL TRANSPORT

Firstly, buy yourself a good map before leaving home if possible. Order one if you have to, as supplies in Cuba are not certain. Get one with the city maps included if you can, as even if you do obtain a city map from a car-rental agency it will be close to useless. We have an old photocopy of a Freytag Berndt map.

When in port, it will not be uncommon for your dock to be situated some distance away from whatever attractions the city has to offer, as in Santiago de Cuba where your dock will be some 5 or 6 miles outside the city proper. So let's consider the options here.

You can obtain taxis merely by contacting any of the management of whichever dock you find yourself moored at, and at night the watchman will happily do the telephoning for you. Prices will usually be in U.S., and there will be a meter showing the charges. It used to be possible to get fares in pesos, but this is becoming more difficult if you don't look or act Cuban, and anyway the amount of taxis on the road are rapidly diminishing due to shortages.

A bicyclist enters a bike lot, similar in function to parking lots found in the U.S. (Photo by George Halloran)

Sometimes you may even obtain private citizens who will act as your personal chauffeur in their own cars (yes they exist), and you can obtain their services for a whole day for much less than you would ordinarily pay for a taxi. Pay in dollars, and he will obtain petrol from his own sources. You will need to ask around on the sly for this service.

There are city buses (called gua-guas, or "wah-wahs"), which you board having firstly joined the wrong queue, unless you asked someone in the line. They only stop at designated halts, so don't expect to hail one as you normally would in the rest of Latin America. Having no name up front you would be hard pressed to know the destination if they did. You pay on entrance, or if boarding from the rear, just send your coin up to the driver via other passengers. Things change, so find out locally what the routes and standard fares are when you arrive in Cuba. Use local currency which you can easily obtain.

Intercity buses are available at the main terminals, but you will have to work hard to get a reservation. They will be full normally, so if the management of your marina has obtained a seat for you, show up early and be prepared for anything.

Trains can be also used to get about, but as with buses it will be best to get the management of the docks to sort it out for you.

Aero-taxis will take you between major resorts, and I still remember my wonder at the quaint radial-engined Russian biplane bringing in tourists to the airstrip only a few hundred yards away from my dock in Cayo Largo in the south. These, and other more conventional aircraft may be your best bet if you want to leave your boat at one place, while you see a bit more of the country than your schedule might otherwise allow.

Wonderful large, Russian hydrofoil boats rise out of the water on extended struts with wings underneath, and can cheaply and easily transport you at tremendous speeds between Batabano and the Isla de Juventud. You'll love them, but stay out of their way if sailing in the area!

Rental cars are theoretically available almost anywhere, although sometimes outside the larger towns, you may find that they're all mysteriously under repair or out on hire.

The phrase "rental car" is synonymous with "rip-off" in my mind, so be warned. You will find the prices absolutely exorbitant (expect over $50 per day for a cheapy, plus more for insurance), and can expect to pay about 90 cents a litre of gasoline with limited refueling facilities. Plan your itinerary well, however, and you will be able to take in a lot more than you might otherwise.

You'll be stunned by the amount of gaily decorated horse-drawn carriages all over the countryside, especially in the south with passengers being picked up on an ad hoc basis. Good fun and you can be assured of a long conversation with all and sundry aboard, and perhaps, even more fun afterwards as someone's guest.

And finally, there are both mopeds and bicycles available for rent at most of the tourist resorts near which you might be docked. Just ask around at the dock.

MOSQUITOS

At certain times you will swear that these little critters have it in solely for you. Never fear, they go for everyone. It's just that you probably haven't got whatever antibodies Cubans normally carry in their blood, to lessen the effects.

At the calm which occurs dawn and dusk, as you sit on deck listening to the BBC World Service news on short-wave, watching fish jump and sipping your carefully crafted rum cocktail, you will feel a sharp nip. Look around, announce calmly that you are just going below for a short while, and get out of the way of the stampede to follow in less than 20 seconds. That's how long it takes for the real onslaught to begin.

Take heart, this is the time you can use to prepare supper, and perhaps, get the forecast for the next day, because in an hour it will likely be all over as the wind picks up. This will send them back to shore, and you can come out again.

Before leaving home you will be wise to fit mesh screens to all including the tiniest openings. Velcro will suffice for some, but the main cabin door (okay, companionway) will really need a sturdy plastic zipper all the way round. Search out each and every gap and put mesh there (including refrigerator vents), because if you don't the mosquitos will find them.

At the height of the assault, you will see them clustered on the window or doorway mesh waving their stings at you and drooling hungrily. Mosquito-coils, which smolder for up to 8 hours seem to keep them at bay, or at least hiding in nooks. They are cheaply obtainable anywhere in the southern U.S. or the West Indies. They're not so accessible in Cuba, so plan to pack enough to burn an average of two per night. You might find that citronella candles, equally unavailable in Cuba, also have some effect, so by all means try them.

We have heard from more than one source that vitamin-B has a repellant effect, as it is exuded from the skin, but I personally have no experience of this, so please let me know if it really works.

No matter how careful you have been, there always seem to be a couple of mosquitos which get in during the day, and we always carry out an organized slaughter some time before retiring, as just one of them on the prowl will keep you awake all night with its whining threat. The Cuban variety seem faster than any I've come across, with reactions quicker than a wielded towel, so the ultimate answer is a purpose built fly-swat. And a damp tissue to clean up before what was originally *your* blood dries.

If in spite of repeated hunts there still remain a stubborn two survivors in the sleeping compartments, your only recourse if you wish a peaceful night may be to remember that their bite is infinitely easier to bear than their bark, and you can always wear earplugs!

There are also various preparations available over the counter to both repel them and to lessen the sting after failing. One of the hardest things to do is to avoid incessant scratching at your bites, but this only serves to intensify the itching a minute later and leads to open wounds eventually, so no matter what, resist.

Then there are the "no-see-ums" already familiar to many. They seem to be especially prevalent in certain parts, and like the mosquitos are active at dawn and dusk. Plan for them too, with your own favorite chemical weapons. These little buggers get right through to your scalp so if you're spraying yourself spray your hair too.

READING MATERIALS

At last we're getting to the end of things you should take, ending with reading materials you might wish you had aboard at some time or another.

Absolutely essential, even if you are a skipper with lots of hard won experience of your own, are those reference books you might need for safety, engine or electrical manuals, and literature which might be relied on in a medical emergency. A less experienced skipper might see fit to have aboard a couple of the multitude of "how-to" books with a nautical theme and a book treating with the skills of sailing e.g., Nigel Calder's excellent *Boatowner's Mechanical & Electrical Manual*, or *Chapman's Piloting*.

Then there are the various guides to inland Cuba and its history, which might be best purchased in Cuba. If you're coming in from North America, there seems to be some reluctance on the part of stockists there to exhibit politically neutral books for whatever reason.

Ernest Hemingway wrote many of his books in Cuba where he is still idealized, and some have Cuban themes. One or two would not go amiss to while away some quiet hours, and I think that any of the increasing quantities of good Latin American authors should find space on your shelves. They really do have a distinct style and will serve to get you into a Latin frame of mind. You will now be after all, in Latin America.

You might like to take a few books in Spanish too, with American or European authors.

Although Cubans are well-educated, with an education system (and lack of television saturation) which has made them highly literate compared to North Americans, supplies of foreign books are severely limited. This is not solely due to censorship, but more by the economic straits the country finds itself in, so any books will find enormous favor as gifts which will be read and passed on. If you can, then you too can read them, but by no means do you need to have this level of Spanish to get around comfortably.

SPANISH

Lets get this clear, you will enjoy yourself a lot more if you can do more than point hopefully at an object and rub your fingers together to enquire its price. Nevertheless, we have encountered many cruisers whose command of the language was limited to this, and it didn't seem to have tremendously curtailed their travel or their appreciation of the country.

In fact, although my Spanish was learned in the streets of Bogotá at age 26, it is by no means great. What I do have is a desire to gabble on with all and sundry, which is much appreciated. Cubans are delighted to talk with anyone, even if your grammar isn't too hot.

Fiona, the Anchor-Wench, speaks little or no Spanish, and I don't think she's too lonely when I'm not around. I usually come back to the boat to find someone or the other trying

his English out against her limited vocabulary of Spanish words. She does, however, understand most of what's said because she's heard so much. Everyone talks all the time, and she loves it.

In all tourist areas, especially those where there are large hotels which cater to the Canadian tourists, you will find that there are people who can assist you in English. And as those same tourist areas receive most of their clientele from Europe, there is usually someone there too who speaks Italian, French, or German. Indeed, you may find that they go so far out of their way as to be almost embarrassing to one not accustomed to it.

In spite of the above, there will be times when you have no choice but to understand an idea or to get your own idea across, so carry a dictionary.

Remember that even though you may be dealing with some official in a little coastal village, one of his primary tasks is to assist you, and unlike those in supposedly more developed countries, he understands that! If the official who requires some document or the other cannot understand you, he will get someone who does speak English to translate. It will help if you can offer the translator a dictionary and perhaps a notepad.

Finally, there is at the back of this book a small section dealing with Cuban-Spanish nautical terms.

TELEPHONES & THE LIKE

Within the confines of any of the marinas in Cuba, you will find the staff only too willing to contact any Cuban destination for you over the telephone. They'll even make calls to search out information for you, such as embassies or airlines, but for long distance there will probably be some delay, as the system is not the world's best.

Out in the streets if you need a taxi, you'll be welcome at any office building to ask them to call you one, but they'll probably draw the line at that.

Telephones are available inside any of the hotels for use by anyone, and this may well be your best bet. If trying to place an overseas call, ask at the desk.

There are also many dedicated telephone (and postage) offices who will arrange calls for you, but remember that the cost is generally quite astronomical, and connection quality uncertain at best. As an example a call to England will knock you down $3.50 per minute!

While calls to Europe, Canada and around the Caribbean are not difficult to arrange, calls to the U.S. will be. But, those are still not impossible, so try.

Faxes and so on can be arranged through any of the larger hotels.

In the streets, you need a few 5 centavo coins for use in the old telephones, and they only call locally. With the newer models you can use 20 centavo coins too, and these handle long distance as well. Put in more than you need, and get your change back on completion.

CUBAN HOSPITALITY

The Cuban government is presently making strenuous efforts to change the emphasis in language teaching from Russian and German to English. I'm not sure just how many Cuban students really did end up learning Russian fluently, but it seems that they're all learning English now.

Be that as it may, few in fact, actually speak English fluently as yet, with those that do confined to industry and tourism. Those who are still at school will only be too delighted to practice with you, and it's hard sometimes to take a simple walk in certain cities without being engaged in some sort of conversation. Usually this takes the form of a request for the opportunity to practice English, but after a short while, the conversation invariably gets round to how things are outside Cuba. If your Spanish is better than their English, then be prepared to spend anything up to an hour, and in occasional cases, much more discussing the state of the economy, religion, external politics, cars, and a neverfailing subject... how much you earn.

And Cubans love to invite you back home.

If visiting a Cuban household, you shouldn't think you have to shower gifts all round just because you are a rich foreigner. On occasion this might even cause embarrassment, so by no means don't go overboard here. Your main attraction is merely being you, so there really is no great need to spoil the effect. Cubans are proud people, and you can easily understand how you might feel if a visitor to your house felt it was incumbent on him to pay for the hospitality you have extended to him. Don't go overboard, and try to be sensitive with any gift you might bring to a household. Reciprocal hospitality may sometimes cause a problem in certain places where there aren't many foreign boats. On occasion the port captain may request that you not have visitors aboard without first notifying his office, which will almost invariably acquiesce without comment. Traditionally, the Cuban government has looked suspiciously on foreign influences, and unfortunately this attitude may still hold in

A clown entertains children on a city street. (Photo by George Halloran)

certain areas, and there may be the suspicion that a shoreside visitor is on your boat with an ulterior motive. This concept may be hard to handle, but unfortunately it is still there to a certain extent, and until things change, it's just one of those contradictions you just have to live with. In practice it is a minor inconvenience, and your visitor is far more used to dealing with such permissions than you and accepts them as normal, ironically referring to the "control" which is everywhere.

Fishermen and other sailors, however, are usually delighted to come aboard without reference to mere officials, and they will view your boat with professional curiosity and delight. You will have to show the cabins, bring out charts, explain the various routes you have sailed, and accept advice for the next leg. Your navigation instruments will be lovingly inspected, and even your engine will be compared with theirs. Information about performance will be swapped, as between enthusiasts anywhere, except that here they are a bit more enthusiastic.

You will be invited back aboard their craft to treat it as your own too, and you'll be lucky to make that appointment you had thoughtlessly made for later on, when rum is produced and begins to flow back and forth. You will remember the first time you stagger back across from an unexpected session aboard a Cuban tugboat for the rest of your life. Your rum may help here too.

I have even been dragged all over a converted Russian corvette to comment with a proud ship's engineer on the four V-12 engines!

SILENT SLANG

One of the things you will pick up on as you become more familiar with Cuban conversation is just what is actually unsaid. Life in rigidly controlled regimes evolves like any other, and develops its own lines of casual disrespect. Even though you may find that President Fidel Castro is usually idealized and referred to as "El Commandante," later on in the same conversation, he may be referred to silently by a significant stroking of an imaginary beard. This usually signals caution on the part of the speaker at some sensitive point.

You might on another occasion be tapping gently into some stream of discontent and notice the lowered voice and conspiratorial whisper followed by theatrical glances around. Then a touching of invisible epaulettes with two fingers on the speaker's shoulder will indicate unmentioned authorities.

Never forget that this is still a police state, and those authorities can have extraordinary powers over the ordinary citizen. Always try to be prudent in both conversation and action, remembering that as happened in any former Eastern Block state, there are still informers here who can befriend you. On occasion, I have known with absolute certainty that I was being examined by parties who were not what they purported to be, and it can happen to you.

AVOID UNWISE ACTIONS

If you do get drawn in to the undeniable political undercurrent, you must know that as a prudent skipper it is incumbent on you to ensure the safety of your vessel and crew, and part of that prudence requires that you observe local laws and customs. My advice to you will be to remember this at all times.

It would be a pity to end up in serious trouble over some quixotic notion which may have been cultivated quite unconsciously in you somewhere else. I do not think, for example, that even if as a private individual you were a sympathizer of relaxed drug laws, you would wisely get your boat mixed up with traffickers off the Colombian coast. So treat Cuban politics with the same circumspection.

So now that we have touched on that subject, it leads naturally on to those authorities with whom you will come into frequent contact, and through whom most of the other official contacts will flow.

THE GUARDA FRONTERA

Literally the "Frontier Guard", this organization maintains posts at all ports and regulates the comings and goings of all marine traffic in and around the Cuban coastline. As far as concerns the boater, this is the group which authorizes any transits along the coast, and to whom you report both when entering and leaving harbor.

You will recognize their sometimes rickety installations by their frankly, military look with grey barracks, radio masts, flagpoles, patrol boats moored alongside, and green-uniformed soldiers. They may be situated at the head of a river, downstream from an inland port, perhaps even mixed up among a cluster of docks surrounded by fishing boats who also report to them. Or they might be within the main port at the entrance to a smaller harbor where the fishing fleet has its facilities.

They will normally be meticulous in their behavior to you, with an impressive courtesy and an even more impressive love of paperwork. Perhaps this is an unfortunate oversimplification, but the fact is that they have been trained to be ever vigilant for any perceived threat to the integrity of the state. Historically they have been taught to expect an invasion or some sort of infiltration, ironically along the lines of that carried out by Fidel Castro himself all those years ago.

It does not help anyone's cause that the Bay of Pigs invasion was just the sort of example that I am talking about, so we just have to live with it.

GET ACCUSTOMED TO BOARDING BY OFFICIALS

Your vessel, whether going alongside or anchoring just off the post, is likely to be boarded by one or more representatives of the Guarda Frontera who will inspect your documents, mainly your permission to leave the previous port and the indication of your destination. They will also sometimes require your passports to satisfy themselves that you are in fact those listed as crew, and then, with an apologetic look, your permission will be sought for "Un pequeño reviso," or a little search.

The endless forms which are called for may sooner or later begin to wear you down, but the Guarda is a military body, and they too have to file even more reports later, so be patient.

Many U.S. citizens might not know this, but one is subject to a similar, if less intrusive, form of control if you're a foreigner operating a boat in U.S. waters, having to inform the Coast Guard of your cruising from say Key West to Miami. I have been threatened with "astronomical fines" (their words) for not knowing this once.

The difference is that in the U.S. you are unlikely to be searched at every port, but in practice, the searches are cursory to the extreme, and usually consist of little more than a visit to each cabin and perhaps, an opening of the shower compartment. On our boat we have two compartments which have never ever been inspected, and I'm not going to divulge which!

If you are entering the country the Guarda Frontera dock will still be the first place to which you will report, and they will liaise with further inspectors such as customs and immigrations.

There will, in spite of the foregoing, be many occasions when you just dock and go about your business, while nevertheless, expecting a later visit from a perspiring soldier on a bicycle. Always show courtesy and remember that you are probably interrupting their routine as much as they are interfering with yours. Sometimes, when the same document is slowly examined and re-read by the same official who did it not three minutes before, and who now finds some other point to pause over, I find my own temper slipping too. But at these times, I can only consider that the document is the first one of its type that this official has seen. That's how it is when you're the only yacht that's entered the harbour in two years. And that has its own charm too.

ENTERING CUBA WITH YOUR OWN BOAT

Finally, you've gone and done it. And now you're crossing that invisible line beyond which you suspect anything can happen, i.e.; the 12-mile limit.

Should you stop? If not, will they send a gun-boat to blow you out of the water?

Should you call in on the VHF for permission? Will they even answer?

In my experience, the answer to all the above is... No.

If you don't stop, you won't be delayed waiting for an answer, which in all probability won't come, so just keep on going and call in as you get a bit closer.

In many of the ports which you will be using outside of Havana and perhaps Santiago on the south coast, you may find yourself communicating with officials using hand-held radios, whose range is limited by both battery power and antenna height.

Rig your Cuban courtesy flag, and below it fly the yellow quarantine flag, which denotes that you are asking permission for clearance. Continue on in towards your destination, calling at comfortable intervals in a *clear distinct voice* for official permission to enter.

If, as is most likely, you are approaching one of the major ports where a marina is located, then they will arrange inwards clearance, and you should call in to them on one of the frequencies given in the section on marinas. Only if approaching a port without a marina, will the station you are calling answer on channel 16.

There are several names which might elicit a reply, so try any of the following:

- Seguridad Marítima (Marine Security).
- Portuaria (Harbour Master's Office).
- Capitanía (Ditto).
- Morro (an old castle which guarded the entrance but now houses the port officials).

And you should always append the name of that port towards which you are headed.

Sooner or later you are likely to receive a reply requesting the name and flag of the vessel calling. At this point, you are in contact, and should follow all instructions faithfully, answering all questions to the best of your abilities. Entering some ports, especially on the south coast, you are likely to be asked if you'd like an escort in through the reef, if there is one, or just into the harbour. This is a good idea, establishing your bona fides, and moreover lessening the tension you are by now certainly feeling if it's your first visit.

Officials, such as this customs officer, are generally friendly and helpful. (Photo by George Halloran)

Note: If you're going to Havana, you don't need to be communicating with the harbour officials in the castle (call sign "Moro Havana" on 16). You need, in fact, to be calling the authorities at the Hemingway Marina who listen on a different frequency (See page 74).

When entering Cuban waters, occasionally a patrol boat may show up, and if you haven't received a reply by now, you should call them on the VHF to explain your presence. In all cases, you will be treated with courtesy, and you should respond equally correctly. Your Spanish or their English is likely to be heavily accented, so if you do have some Arkansas drawl, you should mute it into as neutral an accent as possible, and do not speak quickly. Especially emphasize your consonants and the vowels will take care of themselves.

If you are being escorted into port, let matters take their own course. Your next destination will be the Guarda Frontera post already discussed. If you haven't been escorted, then you should endeavor to find out over the radio where it is, and if you don't understand, let them know it.

Entering strange ports where there is some doubt about the location of the post, you should shout across at any sailor in the harbor as you pass his boat. If your Spanish is limited shout "Guarda Frontera, donde?" or "Gu-arda Fron-tera, don-de?", use your hands a lot, and look at his hands as he points.

Come alongside the indicated wharf carefully, having made sure your lines are all ready in advance, and do not get into discussions about documents until your boat is secure. There are likely to be a few spectators or soldiers about who will handle your lines, but you should not disembark until it is obvious that senior officers have approached to begin the formalities, at which point you should shake hands with them and invite them aboard. One thing a lot of proud skippers are somewhat picky about is having black army boots/shoes on their deck. Don't push your luck here. You'll be glad later.

At this point, if you've not done it before, it's likely to become somewhat hectic aboard. Take things as they come, and it will all sort itself out eventually.

Somewhere like Casilda on the south coast, you will probably be boarded en mass, and your cabin or cockpit might resemble a crowded subway-carriage, but in larger ports things will be done in a more structured way, so I'll explain it in logical order.

First to board will be the immigration officers from the Cuban Ministry of the Interior, who will appreciate somewhere to place their caps, and as with all officers, you should indicate a comfortable seat at a table of some sort for their papers. Someone will usually speak English, but if you can handle things in Spanish then it will be appreciated, and you might as well start learning the correct names for things.

A rare Cuban gunboat stationed offshore. (Photo by Simon Charles)

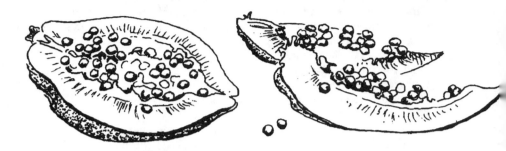

You will be asked for your "Zarpe," or clearance papers from your last port, the vessel's registration papers, and the passports for every member of the crew. If, as suggested before you have all your documents together, then you can produce them logically as they are requested, rather than letting things end up in total confusion. This is likely to be a long process, with lots of questions, and all your documents being handed around the officials, while a collection of freshly filled forms finds its way into your hands. We have found that it is handy to have already prepared a dozen copies of the crew list with passport details that is headed by the boat's name and registration number. Something similar will be required by officials all round the coast, so you might as well have it ready.

You will be asked how long you wish to stay, and no matter if you intend to leave the next week, you should ask for the maximum as: A) You will want to stay longer, and B) You will have to pay $8 for an extension or "Prorroga" when you do. The first time we entered, the immigration officer smiled at me and said, "Here, I give you maximum. You come me when you want more, eh?" I'd only really wanted 10 days that time, but stayed on, as he knew I would.

Remember that if a crewmember leaves the country later on by another means, you should have him removed from the crew-list. This signing-off process ("Desenrolo") merely entails a $15 document from the customs officer of the port rather than the immigration department.

Next aboard will be the customs officials, who will probably want the same papers all over again. More forms requiring three copies or more will be filled in, and you might as well start handing out that carbon paper you've got in your folder, and expect this process to take an equally long time.

Each of the above categories of official will have a senior officer who does most of the talking while a more junior officer handles the paperwork, and there may well be a young trainee, so your cabin is likely to be rather hot after a while. As the perspiration begins to drip, why not offer a soda from your stock? Everyone will appreciate it, and eventually your consideration will be reciprocated.

After the bulk of their paperwork is over, the vessel will be searched, but this is usually no more than an inspection of the various drawers, cupboards, compartments and so on, lasting usually no more than a few minutes. You will, however, be asked to surrender any arms which you will be carrying, and if you have any aboard this is the time to produce them along with the ammunition. Don't worry, they will be scrupulously returned to you upon departure from that particular port.

I would strongly advise against the carriage of illicit drugs.

Next comes the medical officer who will not delay you more than a minute or two, and he (or equally likely she) will be followed by the veterinary officer, or the agricultur inspector. They may take an interest in any fresh fruit to prevent infections entering, bu yours show no signs of infestation all will be well. Your fresh meats may be another ma so don't count on them getting through.

A word of warning. **All** the above may board you at the same time, so whatever happens, relax and go with the flow. Ever tried to come in at Miami airport when it's busy?

In all this confusion keep track of your documents, replacing them in their dossier when they are not in use and doing the same with the documents you will be given. You will be surely asked for them later on down the line, and at times like these the dedicated paperwork-folder shows its worth.

All in all you might end up with these documents:
- Immigration's pink slips (to be retained in your passports).
- Entrance clearance for the vessel (with space on the reverse for subsequent ports).
- Official crew-list.
- Customs receipt (approximately $35) for processing vessel.
- Customs declaration (Money, jewelry, cameras etc., brought in).
- Search party act, showing you've been searched.
- Firearms receipt.
- Ministry of Health's clearance.
- Ministry of Agriculture's clearance.

This whole process can take an hour, or even more, but is an amiable as well as formal process, and finally, you can take down your quarantine flag... You're in Cuba!

Entrance to Santiago de Cuba Bay. (Photo by Simon Charles)

ENTERING PORTS WHILE CRUISING

The main differences between the above scenario and that experienced while cruising from port to port within Cuba, is going to be not so much in the level of documentation as in the general level of officialdom with whom you deal.

As an example, you might be boarded by a single representative of the Guarda Frontera when berthing at one of the small docks which serve fishing communities. This soldier would probably restrict his interest to the boat's travel permit (the "despacho" described in the section on Leaving Port) and perhaps your passports, while in any of the international ports, you might expect all the original entry documents to be re-examined by a full complement of officials. Harking back to my emphasis on having all your documents ready and in one place, depending on your preparedness, this bureaucratic process will take anything between 5 minutes and 2 hours!

As an illustration, on our last visit to Varadero 70 miles east of Havana, we immediately presented the boarding official with the documents experience had shown us he would most likely need and no others. He departed in four minutes, saying that we were free to go about our business, but that if anything more was required someone would call round sometime. At dockside, a friendly Canadian couple who had assisted with our lines, were astounded when we promptly set off for town, claiming that the process conducted by the same official that morning had taken them nearly 4 hours involving further visits from immigration!

ADVICE ON SMALLER PORTS

In the smaller ports which line the Cuban coast, the Guarda Frontera post may not be quite so visible. It is not always necessary to actually hunt them down, as they may well come out to your boat if you anchor in the harbour, but in the event of your wishing to dock somewhere, it is as well to visit the post first. In these cases, as described before, we tend to approach as close as safety allows to whatever convenient dock has a manned fishing boat alongside. They will be only too happy to direct you further. As a description of a fairly typical procedure, see the description of the approach to say Manzanillo in chapter 7. In the majority of cases, however, you must expect a general "Reviso" or inspection of the vessel.

When wishing to merely anchor overnight in an inhabited bay which contains a port, you might see fit to anchor some distance away from the township. In this case, it is possible that sooner or later a small wooden dinghy will be rowed laboriously out to your boat with a perspiring fisherman and a Guarda Frontera. Usually, a quick glance at your papers are all that are required, especially if the remainder of the crew have gone below to rest.

Just to round off the confusion surrounding the question of establishing your presence, there will be occasions when you might find that you're merely expected to dock at a fishing-depot (or perhaps a "Base Naval" in Spanish), where a friendly Guarda Frontera is on duty. These are the best, as from then on you are more or less a full part of the brotherhood of sailors. Break out the liquor, and ready the aspirin. And clear the stove for action.

Patience in all cases of boarding is required, as the inspectors will have to submit their reports to yet another committee down the line, who in turn do the same, and it will only be a short time before you realize that your progress down the coastline has been monitored and sometimes relayed ahead.

INSPECTION IS LARGELY A FRIENDLY PROCESS

By and large it will be a friendly process, and we usually take the opportunity to offer the Guarda Frontera a chilled soda, in turn receiving useful information about the port, its services, and attractions. In a considerable departure from that which you might expect in any other country, they will usually also be only too happy to arrange these services for you or even advise about further transport if you wish to travel inland.

Patience, however, should in no way be confused with obsequiousness. As captain of your vessel you not only have duties but rights, and you may insist on being treated fairly in the most unlikely instance of a problem.

You should in all cases resist any requests for the removal of the ship's documents. If an official insists that he needs to retain your documents until the vessel leaves port, you should be equally firm that the only documents you will permit off the boat are the photocopies of the ship's papers, which you have conveniently prepared before arriving in Cuba.

Finally, if calling over the VHF for instructions, it will be a rare occurrence to receive a reply. We have received replies in perhaps once in twenty cases. Apart from the very larges ports like Santiago and Havana, we just nose on in, trusting observation and instinct to guid us correctly, and thus far we've never gone seriously wrong. Your experiences should be much different.

LEAVING PORT

Not merely a reversal of the process you went through upon arrival, the way you make your initial arrangements here may well influence all subsequent arrivals. Get it right and you will breeze through your cruise. But on the other hand, a simple mistake can cause hours of frustration and delay down the line, so the time to get it right is the very first time you do it.

The key here is to understand that to leave all ports within Cuba you need an official clearance to depart for your subsequent planned stop. The tiny, but important document you will be issued with by all harbour authorities is called a "Despacho" (or dispatch), and it will be inspected at the next stop, where it will be retained and a new one issued upon departure.

Taking Havana as our example of the correct way to arrange your documentation, you would follow roughly this format.

Firstly determine just where you are going to be cruising and for how long, then request your clearance as soon as possible.

You may, in fact, have only a general idea of your route, preferring to meander as and when you see fit, so this is the idea you must get across to the authorities.

In Cuba, as in all centrally planned and directed societies, there is a reluctance to accept that you may have no specific plan, and you will be asked for a complete itinerary with stops and schedules listed. The idea will then be to issue you with a permit to continue to the next stop, and for them to continue in the same vein. Unfortunately this will complicate matters when you encounter some spot which holds your attention for a few days, and you decide to miss out the next stop.

So, from the outset, make it clear that you are voyaging with no set plan, except that you may ultimately end up in such-and-such a place. Thus, a permit called "Permiso de Salida" can be prepared with your ultimate destination listed, along with potential intermediate stops. You may even list a circuit of the island as your purpose, and a general list of the major stops along the line.

We always request that the form notes our aim to anchor out as much as possible, using the terms "Wherever conditions are favorable," and we mention our desire to dive on scuba too. This request has never been turned down, or modified in any way by the Ministry of the Interior to whom it is submitted.

You will, as well as this document, be issued with the usual "despacho," which will list your first expected stop, but if you miss this stop, the "permiso de salida" will establish that your itinerary was vague in the first place.

Note that a different document called a "Guia de Recala" or list of ports will probably be issued along with the permiso de salida, but in any case, it has the same ultimate purpose, so don't worry overly about which you are issued with, as long as you make sure you get one or the other.

Recently, the Ministry of Transport has begun to insist on all foreign registered yachts receiving a cruising permit. This document is called a "Permiso Especial de Navegacíon" and shows that your vessel has been inspected for safety. It is valid for six months, will set you back some $50 U.S., and can be arranged upon arrival.

As recently as late 1993, it was not required, or even known about in the southern ports, but presumably it's implementation will spread to those areas soon.

It too goes into your document-folder, along with the rest.

In the case of Havana, all the above documents can be arranged by the management at the marina where you will be docked. If you are arriving at one of the smaller international ports, then I would set the process in motion by informing the immigration officers who clear you in as soon as possible as there could be a delay of a day or so.

If in fact this impressive list of documentation in your folder has daunted you, later on you'll find that in many places you will only have to present the last despacho, the list of ports received at the onset, and the passports to gain entry to harbours, so experience will begin to guide you as to which documents can be kept at the back.

These documents are initially delivered to you upon departure from your initial port of entry, when your vessel will once again be searched. It is up to you to emphasize in advance what time you plan to leave port, and that time should be of your choosing not anyone else's. It is you after all who is going to be the one affected by a subsequent late arrival at a strange port in the dark.

The actual process of leaving a major port like Havana can take up to an hour, or much more if you haven't arranged the time in advance, but subsequently you can be more relaxed about things, as along the coast there will probably be only one visitor who handles all functions. In these cases, departure can be sorted out in the time it takes to write out your fresh despacho. Say 10 minutes or less, and you're on your way.

To end off the subject of documentation, there is one thing to be borne in mind... unlike the rest of Latin America, a bribe can really get you into trouble.

A canal at Marina Hemingway. There are occasional "genuine" marinas in Cuba, however a cruising boater should not base his voyage around these destinations. Marina staff are especially helpful for necessary documentation. (Photo by George Halloran)

MARINAS

Visitors who usually like to confine their mooring to the plethora of full-service marin⸱ in the Caribbean and Florida are probably going to be disappointed here.

In spite of the emphasis on tourism, there are only a couple of genuine marinas in C⸱ and they are considerably drabber than those you will have been accustomed to.

You can find them in Havana, Santiago de Cuba, Cienfuegos, Varadero, and perhap⸱ other tourist areas, so don't base your cruise around them.

They all supply fresh-water and 110 v electrical hook-ups, with additionally a 'phone hook-up available in Havana (if only it worked). One thing to look out for here is that the standard hose or power connection which you have aboard may not work with the different fittings used in Cuba, but generally there will be an adapter available on request. You can usually purchase fuel and oil too, with access to service facilities not generally available, so try to schedule oil-changes and the like for these stops.

Some (a notable example being Havana's Marina Hemingway) may offer shops, discos, and even a sometimes usable laundry and bath-house, but in general they should be regarded as a civilized base for further cruising, rather than a mooring for your entire holiday, and you can expect to pay anything up to 45 cents per foot overnight with slightly less being the norm.

One major facility offered, however, should not be spurned and is a considerable help to novice cruisers and perhaps those with limited Spanish making their first visit, i.e. **documentation**.

The management staff of all Cuban marinas are only too delighted to arrange all aspects of your documentation, liaising between you and the various ministries more efficiently than you would be able to. So if you've had any recent problems, then take advantage of this service to rectify matters.

A point to notice here is that they usually have a different frequency for VHF work, so be prepared to use channels 72, 68 and 06, in addition to 16, if you're trying to make contact. Normally they are more conscientious about keeping a radio watch than other organizations, so you're more likely to receive a reply.

Seven miles west of Havana, the Marina Hemingway monitors channel 72, and will accept all calls for inward clearance arranging for an escort in and official reception, while 60 miles to the east, the Marina Acua in Varadero listens on channel 68, and handles the same functions. There is a Marina Chapelin at the same port, but they rarely have room for unannounced arrivals, mainly berthing local and foreign yachts engaged in charter work in the large tourist industry based there.

Along the southeast coast, the marina at Punta Gorda, inside the immense and wonderful harbour at Santiago de Cuba, can be contacted by the Morro (castle), whom you call on VHF 16 and converse with on VHF 10 when requesting inwards clearance. Once again, all formalities will take place at the marina facilities upon docking.

Along the middle of the southern cays, the best marina to contact will be at Cayo Largo, southwest of the Bay of Pigs. Call "Seguridad Maritima de Cayo Largo" on VHF 16 and "Cayo Largo Marina" on VHF 06 to spread your bets. They'll offer an escort through the reef.

ANCHORING OUT

If the lists of documentation and officials have gotten to you, or if you merely anticipate this, then note that on our first trip round from Havana to Cayo Largo (almost 400 nautical miles) we were never once asked for a single document! On that occasion we anchored out all the way through the cays in sheltered bays along the coastline, even docking alongside wharfs situated away from the mainland and offering facilities for the Cuban fishing-fleet, where friendly fishermen kept us entertained for days.

Everyone's reasons for anchoring are different, but we receive an enormous amount of pleasure from gently lowering anchor in a deserted bay at the end of an easy run. It is here, surrounded only by trees, limpid water, and gulls, that we feel most at home with nature. Our drinks are sipped in silence broken only by the splash of a fish falling back from an attempt is supper, and the shrill cry of a wild animal that has almost certainly never seen a man. You can be almost guaranteed that your anchorage will not have welcomed another vessel ight in years, and if you have arrived from more crowded parts you will be awed by ouched beauty of the cays.

It is perfectly feasible to arrive in Havana, or one of the large ports, take your fill of historic buildings, street scenes, museums, wonderful country journeys, and then leave them all behind for days or even weeks on end. You might later wish to berth in a different town many miles away, travel inland to see other sights, and thence return to the cays to repeat the process as often as you wish. Apart from certain parts of the coastline, there is neither need nor reason to hurry on to make a planned anchorage if you have the mindset for anchoring out.

In the 175 miles between Havana and the western tip of Cuba, only the first 60 miles are unsuitable for anchoring out, with the remainder containing dozens of secluded cays and inlets, where a boat might rest for however long the crew desired, taking occasional trips inland to see the undeniable glories there too.

From the eastern tip of Cuba, as far west as Havana, there are about 250 miles of coastline where anchoring would be best confined to the large regularly spaced bays, and 250 miles of countless islands and cays where shelter can be found almost anywhere.

Cliffs line the extreme southeastern coast, but travelling further west there must be hundreds of anchorages among the cays making up the next 500 miles, and encompassing aptly named areas like "Twelve League Labyrinth" and the "Gardens of the Queen".

There is nowhere between Canada and the Antarctic South Pole where you will find any equivalent cruising ground, still unspoiled, and so conveniently located.

FISHING AND DIVING

Anchoring out leads naturally into the question of fishing.

All I'll say here is that you'll have endless opportunities to fish, both statically at anchor and by trolling along your route.

Take a medium-weight spinning-rod for casting out at anchor, and if you prefer to fly-fish over the flats where the cays get shallow and the bonefish feed, then this can be done from the dinghy with a fly-rod.

En route, along the coast, you'll need to stay well outside the reef where the depth drops to thousands of feet, and where you can troll for larger fish with heavier gear. If you stray in over the wall where the depth suddenly becomes less than 100 feet you'll certainly have a barracuda on the line every few minutes. In spite of rumor, these fish are good eating as long as you don't try the very large specimens. Ask any **local** fisherman.

Inside, amongst the cays, you may trail a black and silver lure for mackerel and the like.

Lobstering is exceptional at many of the more remote cays. The crew of the good ship "Hobbes" prepares for a barbecue. (Photo by Simon Charles)

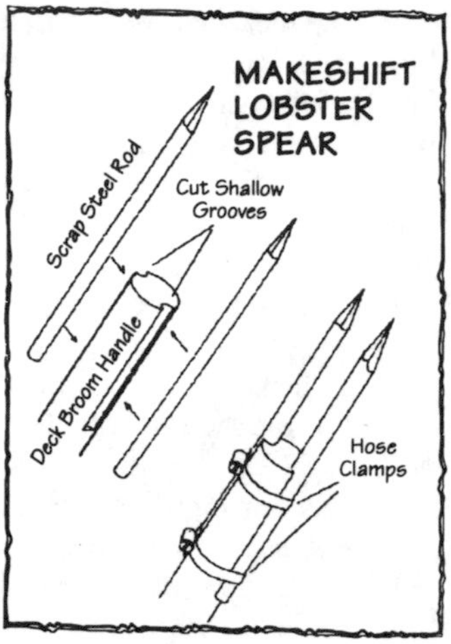

Overnight you can lower a baited hook, which more often than not will attract something of interest like a nice grouper, if you're in anything like 20 feet or more.

Apart from what you think you'll use, take plenty of hooks of all sizes, especially the large types as they make excellent gifts for fishermen who you meet along the way, and who will be endless sources of information. The same goes for line, as both these articles can be in short supply at various times.

While diving the anchor to see if it's set, you may feel it wise to occasionally take along a spear-gun and snorkel, and you'd be right. Practice going down vertically, using slow easy finning motions, and you'll be surprised how easy it gets after a while.

A word of caution here... Do not attempt to stay down beyond your limits.

MAKESHIFT LOBSTER SPEAR

Scrap Steel Rod

Cut Shallow Grooves

Deck Broom Handle

Hose Clamps

The main danger here is that of "shallow-water blackout", which is the phenomena of blacking out while actually on the way up due to the drop in partial pressure of oxygen in the lungs. You won't feel it coming on if you've overstayed your welcome at depth, and it is a real danger.

I have seen it come on quite suddenly in a couple of occasions, and only prompt rescue saved the swimmer.

A lobster spear can be made up in an emergency by using two 18" prongs hacksawed from some abandoned steel rod, and if the cut has been made at an angle, then the sharpening will be facilitated. The rods can be fastened to your unscrewed deck-broom handle by means of two hose-clips, and this set-up is the equivalent of anything a shop could sell.

Look for the antennae sticking out below ledges of coral in easy snorkeling depths, and only make your move when you are certain the lobster is at least six inches long over the back of the main shell (carapace). Aim for the center of the shell, and thrust quickly from not more than eight inches away, pinning the beast to the floor. Grasp firmly with a gloved hand, and keep him on the spear until back at the surface only removing him when certain he is "in the bag".

Marinate the butterflied lobster half an hour in a little lime juice, a little sugar, olive oil and lots of garlic. Cook only until no longer translucent (3 minutes maximum), and receive the accolades of your crew.

If you're a scuba-diver then take your own tanks. You'll be able to have them filled with air at any of a multitude of dive-shops in hotels along the coast and the diving along the southern cays is equivalent or superior to anything anywhere, as they're situated sufficiently far from the main island to be unaffected by silt washing out from rivers.

Dive the wall anywhere along a thousand miles and be assured you're the first.

AND FINALLY!

The next chapter, dealing with how to navigate safely through the cays and along the coastline, should be read thoroughly. There are hundreds of routes through thousands of cays and no book can hope to cover them all in full detail.

What we have to say about traveling safely and competently will ensure that when you deviate from any route shown here (as I know you will, endlessly), you can do so in safety, and as importantly, in confidence.

When we first traversed the coast, we had no guide and on occasion no good charts.

The thoughts contained in the next chapter are gleaned from those experiences, and used with prudence will ensure your safety as they ensured ours.

NAVIGATING AND ANCHORING
IN THE CAYS AND ALONG THE COASTS

In a sense, this chapter is going to determine your enjoyment of any cruise you make around the coasts of Cuba. Given the sheer size of the potential cruising grounds, the numerous routes one can choose between countless points, and the changes taking place in Cuba, any attempt to prescribe rigid routes will be doomed to failure. At best, the following chapters can only be an effort to show a few passages upon which you may base further cruising, and you would be unwise to think that this book could define your routes precisely. That's not how it should be.

We will attempt later on to describe in detail a number of passages, anchorages, and ports, but for maximum enjoyment you should deviate as and when you see fit. Indeed you would be shortchanging yourself and your crew if you didn't. After all, that's how knowledge is acquired, and disseminated.

Regard this chapter as our philosophy for cruising unknown waters. Use it to arrive safely into ports and harbours not covered by the passage guides in this volume. It illustrates how you may safely choose your own routes through reefs, along coastlines and into tiny anchorages. All in the knowledge that you were one of the first.

GENERAL LAYOUT OF THE COAST

In the previous chapter we touched briefly on the makeup of the Cuban coastline, and you might remember that there were a lot of cays mentioned in relation to the prospects of anchoring out.

Well, here are some figures gleaned from a variety of sources.

There are two islands (the big, long one, and the little one hanging underneath the western half).

The coastline contains over 200 bays and 289 beaches, being stretched out into an official figure of 5,746 kilometers (3,102 nautical miles). This figure is measured with all the ins and outs taken into consideration, and thus is both hugely magnified and irrelevant.

Of more interest to the yachtsman is the 10-fathom line off the coast.There are approximately 1,500 nautical miles along that 10-fathom line.

And within it, 4,010 cays and islets (although this is an inflated figure too).

Cruise Cuba and there's going to be a lot of messing about in and amongst those cays.

They stretch out along some 50 per cent of the coast, but unlike the Florida Keys where a large percentage of first-time cruisers may have acquired most of their experience, there is no well-marked Intra-Coastal Waterway to guide their steps, and apart from a few buoyed channels plied by merchant ships, the small vessel will find there are few defined routes.

The cays are more or less confined to four large areas including:
- Along the north coast between Havana and the western tip of Cuba.
- Ringing the Gulf of Batabanó on the southern side of the island opposite Havana.
- Between Trinidad midway along the southern side and eastwards to Cabo Cruz.
- A large stretch about halfway between Havana and the eastern tip of Cuba.

In addition there are two notable areas of coast which comprise steep cliffs sweeping down to the waterside, and these are contained both along the eastern portion of Cuba opposite Haiti, and along the south side of the peninsula at the western tip of the island.

Near Havana, to either side, the coasts are somewhat flatter with mountains to be seen inland, but nothing notable apart from some deep bays and beaches at the water's edge.

NO MAGNETIC DEVIATION AT WESTERN END

As a final point, it should be noted that there is no magnetic deviation to be allowed for at the western end of the island, but by the time you have reached the eastern tip you'll be adding nearly six degrees! If you have purchased an overall chart of the West Indies, such as the DMA international chart No.400, for general passage planning around the Caribbean, then along with the major current-flows it will also show the curving lines demarcating areas of magnetic variation increase or decrease.

WHY YOU'D WANT TO HANG OUT IN THE CAYS

'Cause you won't find another yacht within 50 miles.
And you won't be hassled by anyone else either.

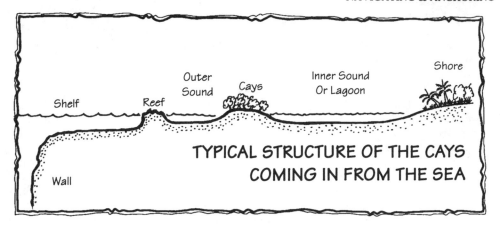

TYPICAL STRUCTURE OF THE CAYS
COMING IN FROM THE SEA

STRUCTURE OF THE CAYS

Above, you can see a fairly typical cross-section showing the undersea features you're going to come across in the cays. An awareness of what you're likely to encounter and a method of predicting what lies below will be of tremendous benefit here, and could be said to be the key to safe cruising in uncharted waters. Combining this with good charts, there's no reason to believe that a relative novice keeping his guard up should encounter any problems, if he looks for the clues.

ENCOUNTERS ON THE WALL

Taking our typical coastline above, we can see that as we come in from the indigo or dark blue waters outside, we first encounter the so-called "wall". At this point, the depth can change from perhaps 5,000 feet to 30 in the time it takes to read this, so always keep an eye out for the **color-change**, which accompanies the depth-change. It won't always be as severe as that, but by and large, it will be something along those lines.

Oh, scuba-divers just love to dive the wall.

Above the wall, the depth-change will bring a corresponding color-change to a lighter blue, and depending on the actual depth of water there may be a corresponding change in wave motion. The large swells of the deep can sometimes become shorter and choppier, occasionally making this a welcome alternative to staying outside the wall when cruising the coast. A good look-out must always, however, be exercised when utilizing this technique.

At this point, the bottom composition is nearly always coral, and will offer good holding for an anchor. Were you to experience some form of emergency while running parallel and outside the wall, it might be wise to come in over it to where the anchor could be lowered to settle properly on the floor, rather than hanging it down uselessly in the deep, and then having the jagged top edge of the wall saw through the line in minutes as you drift in. Be mindful of the fact that even if there is no fringing reef between the shoreline and the wall, as the bottom shoals the waves can begin to swell again. This can break out the anchor, so get it down near the lip.

The outer wall is not always the only change in bottom characteristics coming in, and attention should be paid to the possible existence of a "fringing reef" as mentioned above. This will show itself not only by a line of breakers or raised swells in from the wall, but once again by a color change.

This reef can be near the wall, or perhaps some way in, but recognizing this deadly hazard is one of the most vital functions of the helmsman at this point.

The color of the water will change depending on the bottom composition, and in general you will be looking out for dark patches or blotches in the water. You might see an olive color, or if for example, there was a lot of elkhorn coral reaching up, then it could show as more orangey.

Whatever, if you are approaching something odd, do not wait for confirmation but put your helm over hard and skid to a halt as it were.

For the moment, you'll want to take all the way off your boat as if it should indeed turn out to be anything like elkhorn coral, which grows vertically up from the bottom and spreads out at the top, it will hole your boat just below the waterline.

Don't worry, one of the good things about this sort of coral is that it shows up well, and it isn't that difficult to spot if you're looking out for it.

On the other side of this reef will be the "sound". This is a shallower area protected from the waves outside, and once again there will be a color change. If the bottom here is sand, then the sound will become a most beautiful light or sky blue, mottled on the floor by the light refracting through the wavelets, becoming turquoise as it shallows to unnavigable depths. The bottom can almost always be clearly seen, and any isolated coral stands will also show up well as darker patches.

If there is turtle-grass below, then the bottom will not be quite so distinct. Depth-perception may well become more difficult, but in general not so difficult as to cause any problem. Be conscious of the fact that if traversing a large area of turtle-grass, your attention may well drift, and you can ground as the terrain slopes gradually.

OUTER CAYS ALONG THE REEF

There may well be outer cays growing up out of the water here along the reef, with another sound between them and the shoreline, or there may be more cays further in against the shore. These cays will usually be relatively low-lying and thickly covered with vegetation. The edges are usually outlined with white sandy beaches or bordered by mangroves, whose roots eventually become the very land they once lined, and whose tops reach well above mast height.

Cruising the cays can be a study in contrasts. For example, along the northwest coast, the inner sound can be as narrow as a few hundred yards, making for a snug refuge anywhere, while in the southeast it can be anything up to forty miles wide and deep enough to have large waves.

And then, still further in, we come to the shoreline of the main island of Cuba, its beaches and its trees.

ENTERING THROUGH
THE REEF FOR THE FIRST TIME

The pages of children's literature have been filled throughout the ages with tales of mighty galleons ripped asunder by pounding surf. The cries of survivors sounding weakly amongst the roar of the waves.

Well, all that stuff was true. Never forget that.

Having made countless entries through or over a reef towards the refuge of a sound, and sometimes in fading light, there's still a certain tension on the bridge as we come through.

Maybe that's good, 'cause it's certainly kept us on our toes; and afloat.

IS THERE A REEF?

But, hang on, is there in fact a reef?

The charts you have aboard should certainly tell you at least that much. And if you have the before-mentioned Cuban government charts, they will even show coral heads which are far below the depths you'll be worrying about. The originals printed in color make everything obvious, but if you're using black and white copies, the reef may sometimes be lost among a mass of contour lines and figures. Be careful to check your charts closely, and be especially on the look out for the symbols for submerged rocks, which may be isolated from the main body of a reef.

If in fact there is a reef, then don't push your luck unnecessarily. There will probably be a charted entrance not far away. Very few reefs off the coast are unbroken, and the entrances which exist are usually known and surveyed, so truck on towards one of those.

If the entrance is a major one, used by cargo vessels, then it is likely to be marked by buoys, pylons, or stakes. If there is a preferred course in (to avoid some hazard), there may be range marks as well (you line them up one in front of the other and go in along that track). More often than not, if there are range marks they will be shown on the charts, but it is a different story with buoys. Storms, old age, and perhaps even collisions can take their toll, while there may also be new markers, where none were shown before.

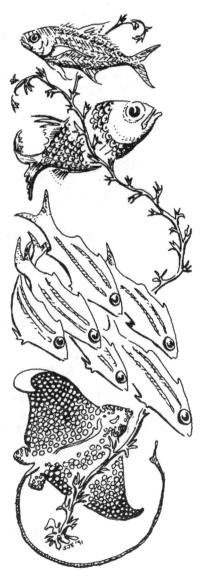

The buoys and pylons will follow conventional IALA Region B colors as used in the U.S. ("Red Right Returning"), but sometimes a single, unpainted, wooden stake may be the only marker where the vessels are smaller, and this should be treated with caution. It will not usually be obvious which side you should keep to when confronted by a stake (or even if it actually marks an entrance), so in any case you should keep a sharp eye out for signs of swells, breakers and the color change denoting coral and reef below the surface. Sometimes the stakes are not placed at the very end of the reef, and the actual entrance may be up to 50 feet away, so be circumspect.

Approaching a charted entrance and using GPS, you'll be fairly certain of your position, but if you're using your Loran receiver, then it would be wise to have corrected the readings against some known point in advance so that your own coordinates are exact. Take a reading when you are at some location whose position is charted precisely. Your instrument will probably show a slight error due to signal deviation, range and other factors, so using the instrument's manual, fill in the correcting data. This should be done every time you move far out of your normal cruising area. And especially if you've changed between transmitting beacons.

Whatever, even though you have a GPS receiver and good charts aboard, you should still be careful as the charts can often contain errors as to the lesser-used reef entrances. Go slow, and keep your eyes open.

A HEIGHTENED AWARENESS

And what if you don't have good charts; your instruments are on the blink, you don't know where you are, or you can't see any markers and you need to be inside? You'll need a heightened sense of awareness, but things will still be okay.

At this point, if you have a large motor-boat then you are at a decided advantage, as you'll need a good look around and you have the fly-bridge to steer from. If you have a sailboat and the water's not too rough, then it might be handy to have someone up the mast, but if this is impractical a crewmember should get as far forwards and take as high a vantage point as possible.

With a low sun in your face the reflections will blind you and you may have no choice but to remain at sea, but if this isn't the case then polarized sunglasses will prove their worth here, as they screen out some of the surface reflections, and allow you to see below. Amber lenses offer the best visibility under these conditions showing the coral heads better than the grey ones, but any polarized lenses will be better than even the expensive non-polarized ones, so keep a pair around, and try to keep them clean of salt and scratches.

Coming in through an unfamiliar reef, it might be as well to do it under power, as you may have to ease up close and parallel the reef looking for a break. You definitely do not want to be swept in by waves which might even broach the boat, so keep in water which is deep enough to allow adequate maneuverability in all directions, and be patient while looking for a spot which fulfills all the criteria for safe water i.e.: no breakers, sudden swells, discolored patches or distinct changes in water color.

Remember too, that the sound on the other side will have to be deep enough for your vessel, so look carefully for clues to that too. If it is very flat with hardly a ripple, then this may be a sign, so look carefully at the surface with binoculars. This also goes for navigating between cays and searching out internal channels.

When all is said and done, if there is any doubt; stay away.

Be especially cautious when swells are pushing in, and do not find yourself in a position from which you cannot escape if a hazard suddenly presents itself.

ENTERING/EXITING A FAMILIAR ENTRANCE IN HEAVY SEAS
(Or When To Remain In Shelter And How Not To Underestimate Conditions)

I used to have to do this almost daily when skippering a dive-boat which had to keep to a schedule. We knew we could find calm waters to dive on the other side of the small island we were based in, but why *you* should wish to leave a snug harbour... I do not know.

It's almost certain to be still rougher outside, and if you don't really have to go out, then why not remain in comfort-mode, and kick back with a day off? This really is one of those times when you can be seriously lazy. Break out that bottle of rum, and blame the conditions for your idle good-for-nothing attitude. If you feel energetic, then take the dinghy ashore.

Having said all that, there may be circumstances which make it imperative you leave, so let's look at the conditions, and see how best they might be coped with.

Exiting safely with seas sweeping sideways along the reef is so difficult that you may have no choice but to remain in shelter, but if the waves are headed more or less directly into the exit, and aren't curling over to break with a crash, then with care, you may make it without mishap.

The major danger in leaving into a heavy swell lies in taking heavy seas over the bow. This can smash the forward windows and swamp a motor vessel, or it could lead to the boat submarining deep under the following wave, and driving deeper, stopping it altogether. To a lesser extent, the same can happen to a yacht, so our energies will be aimed at preventing this.

Remain near the entrance, balancing the boat against the waves with the engine, and wait awhile to observe the rhythm of the swells. There will likely be a visible lull every few waves (some say every seven), and this may be your opportunity. Increase speed to full, and get the vessel as far along its way as possible before the next large swell comes at it. As the boat rises to meet the wave, let its head come up until near the top of the swell where the power can be eased right back, and then let the wave pass beneath the hull. This will prevent the craft plunging down the other side and into the following wave, instead allowing it a controlled slide downwards to lift its bow again at start of the next cycle. As the bow lifts you may again increase the power to drive upwards, then as before decrease the power at the top. Hold the vessel always head on into the swells, and with luck you can find yourself right outside without taking a drop over the bows. Of course it also depends on your not having underestimated the conditions in the first place.

As with all reef maneuvers, don't allow yourself to end up somewhere from which there is no turning back because it will not be possible to turn around safely in a narrow entrance if there is any sort of a heavy swell.

FOLLOWING SEAS ARE TRICKIER

Entering through a gap in the reef (a "cut") can be even more difficult, and boats were regularly lost doing this in the island where I worked. The first thing to be sure of is that there is enough water there in the first place. In the trough between waves, the depth may well be considerably less than normal, so allow for this, and once again do not underestimate the conditions.

Try to visualize your reactions in advance, and have the crew well braced.

Apart from "pooping" (being filled from behind by a crested wave), the main danger here is that of being broached, or swept sideways, and hit broadside by a large wave. Even if the vessel rides it out you are likely to drive straight into the side of a narrow entrance, so devote all energies and maneuverers to keeping the vessel straight.

I have found it best in familiar waters to minimize the amount of time the boat is actually stern on to the waves, and to this end, I like to run parallel to the reef as closely as I dare, which can sometimes be as little as 50 feet, if there is adequate depth. With one eye open to the possibility of being pushed sideways onto the reef and anticipating the waves as they come, I calculate my arrival to coincide with an observed lull in the swells. Here I like to make a sharp turn at the point of entry and get my speed up to outrun whatever I can, but

A small fishing boat sets out in heavy seas. Many Cuban fishing boats are extremely small for the seas that they tackle. (Photo by Simon Charles)

this procedure can be dangerous in unfamiliar waters. In this instance you won't get a feel for the waves until it is too late to abort so you may find it better to make your approach from further out. Of course it will not be possible to outrun everything and in this case you must saw the wheel to keep the vessel straight as the swells lift the stern and pass under. Sometimes as the waves pass forward under the hull leaving the boat in the trough it will veer uncontrollably off-line, requiring both a determined spin of the wheel to get it back on course, and an instant drop in power to keep the vessel from driving itself at right angles onto the reef at the entrance. Keep the power up when you can, drop it when you should, and don't think it's not going to be exciting. I always reckoned that was where we earned our corn.

As before, please remember that it is rarely the waves, but rather the coral which sinks a ship, and stay out at sea if you have to. If necessary you can usually find a broad safe entrance a little way on if you don't let impatience get to you.

THE INNER CAYS & SOUNDS

Conditions inside the sound are in total contrast to those existing outside the reef. Gone will be the swells, and instead all will be calm. There may be a chop if the sound is large and deep, but even so, there are unlikely to be any waves worthy of the name unless there is a stiff wind.

Now is the time to write-up the ship's log, perhaps putting in a sketch of the entrance and any bearings, or GPS locations of significance, buoys, ranges and other features, so do it while the details are fresh, and before the vessel is prepared for anchoring.

These notes will be invaluable later on as inevitably you will wish to return to some of your favorite discoveries, or even to merely reflect at ease one day upon your trips. A well-written log is the equivalent of all other travel-writers' books combined.

Another often overlooked point is that you may well find your notes useful if you have to leave through the same gap, and especially if you have to do it at night.

In the relative calm following entry, you may again consult your charts to compare them with what you can see, and perhaps set visual courses for promising anchorages. Remember the floor will probably now be visible, and you should begin to take note of the colors and associate them with bottom-composition and depth.

Auto pilots are useful inside the reefs too, as some of the gulfs are large enough for all land to be well out of sight, and the next marker may well be some 15 miles away. Any Cuban cruise will entail long passages on the inside, and with the auto pilot set you may go about other tasks, while always maintaining a look-out.

Hand-bearing compasses, while also useful for plotting marks and bearings on entry, will be useful if you wish to identify cays which show at a distance as you cruise past. You will find as you search for landfall among those cays that your eye-level above the water determines how soon you may expect to see them. Given the average height of the vegetation on the cays, we usually begin to pick them up from the bridge at about 8 miles off, but your different height will determine your own distance. Make a few notes in the log, and you'll soon know exactly how far off you may expect to be before picking them up for yourself.

LOOK FOR CLUES FROM FISHERMEN

As you spend time pottering about in the cays looking for anchorages, or just feeling your way amongst coral heads and islands, you will begin to notice various clues that fishermen may have left to denote entrances and passages into the heart of the cays. The charts are incapable of showing all of the entrances to lagoons, or even the myriad passages through a closely packed group of cays, but local fishermen will have almost certainly explored the area at some time. They may well have left markers in the form of "whithies" (branches haphazardly stuck into the bottom), or perhaps a buoy made from a floating bottle of bleach. At first you may be somewhat sceptical about using some branch or even a large twig as a navigation mark, but they usually mean something significant, so take note, and regard them as privately maintained channel marks. As they are used by small shallow-draft boats, sometimes powered by oars or simple sails, your trick is to determine if they show a deep enough channel for you and which side you should pass.

Often you will find that in one particular area all the marks should be passed on the left, but a little further on, the opposite convention applies. Use your observation, and feel your way if the water is shallow, always being ready to instantly back off in the event of approaching critical depth. As before, binoculars can be useful in scanning the surface further ahead for signs of absolutely flat water, mangrove tips sticking up, birds wading , or other warning signs. Depth alarms should be set on the echo-sounder, and you should observe them, rather than developing a tolerance for their squealing.

Of course, if you're inside a large gulf like Batabanó, or even Guacanayabo in the south, then the main passages are likely to be well marked with buoys and large pylons showing deep channels through and into commercial harbours. These lights and buoys are usually well maintained, but as with all man-made aids to navigation you should not rely on them absolutely.

Incidentally, the large pylon structures can have small concrete storerooms atop the legs with equipment inside for servicing their lights, and the whole affair is usually painted in a color denoting which side you pass on. In many cases, however, in spite of the best efforts of deterrent spikes, sea-birds such as cormorants will perch on the platforms to dry their wings, and their droppings can totally obscure the original color. Indeed, some may even become almost invisible in the distance due to this.

Inside the cays you are likely to have much to distract you, what with cruising past deserted beaches on paradise islands and cups of tea being handed up from below. If like us, your attention wanders frequently while you scrabble about on the cockpit floor for that

dropped biscuit, then it is as well to be prepared for the occasional grounding. The bottom can, in places, shelve so gently that the color does not noticeably differ from 10 minutes ago and besides... weren't *you* looking?

As mentioned before, we keep our depth sounder's alarm set, and amongst coral we like to give ourselves a goodly couple of feet of leeway, while keeping a rigid no-mistake look-out, and steering clear of coral heads which could well puncture a hull. However, cruising above the turtle-grass or sand of the inner sound, and feeling out an unfamiliar entrance to some lagoon with the alarm on the bare limit, we have occasionally come to a lurching stop. The key here to getting off is to get the power down as soon as possible, letting fly the sheets, or dropping the revs and putting the engine into neutral at once. If your speed was low in the first place, then it may be a simple task of backing off, but if this does not work then sterner measures may have to be taken.

A couple of strong crewmembers in the water may well provide enough force when pushing from the bows to assist the engine, while on occasion a rocking movement from side to side has also proved successful in dislodging our boat. Extreme care must be taken here, and good communications between the helmsman and those in the water is essential, while needless to say, only a responsible adult should be in control of the motor to prevent what is only a minor event from becoming a life-threatening disaster. It is as well to note that there isn't much in the way of tide inside the cays, so your vessel will not be left keeled over on its side, and unless the incident took place at dead high tide, there may still be enough to lift it off later. You may often find it best to just wait.

If none of these methods prove successful, then stop the engine to prevent it sucking in silt through the intakes and apply the kedging-off technique, which essentially means that an anchor is taken out away from the boat by foot or in a dinghy and lowered to provide a point from which force may be applied, perhaps via one of the boat's winches.

Yachts may be heeled well over sideways, either by crewmembers hanging onto the boom swung far outboard, or by a rope attached at one end to the tip of the mast and at the other to a block on an anchor securely embedded in the bottom. Don't worry, the mast can take it. This may decrease the draft enough to allow the engine, or another anchor astern to drag the vessel off.

If these still fail, there is always the likelihood of decreasing the weight at the point where the vessel is most firmly grounded. A substantial amount of weight can always be found at one end of the boat or the other, and in relays this can be moved aft quite quickly and easily. Scuba tanks, anchors, rolls of spare line, bags of diving equipment, spare fuel, tools and other items can easily add up to a couple of hundred pounds, and not only will you have removed the weight from the affected area, but in transferring it to the other end you will still further lift the lightened area.

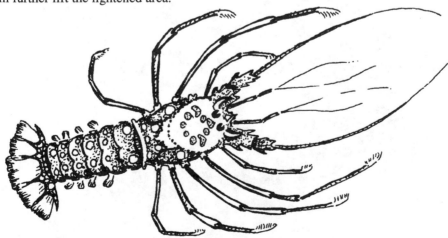

Having made sure you have already placed your anchor off the stern, that line should be under tension to prevent further grounding, and a crewmember should pull it in quickly as the engine powers the boat backwards, and so prevent it from wrapping round the propeller shaft.

BEWARE OF FLOATING NETS

While on the subject of wrapping things about the shaft, we have come across a multitude of nets with floats strung along just below the surface. These seem to have no common denominator, being made from easily-seen white polystyrene, or difficult to see cork bundles in equal quantities. There are fleets of fishing vessels which operate nets in the Gulf of Batabanó, or other similar large protected bodies of water, and the vessels used range in size from large ferrocement or steel boats of over 60 feet down to smaller wooden craft around the 35-foot range, all with a couple of dinghies as tenders.

The mother-vessels play out their nets, while the dinghies arrange it neatly in the water and attend to lobster pots some distance away.

It must only be our imaginations, but it seems that they only begin their maneuvering to lay out the nets as we approach, causing much swerving and swearing under our breaths, so be aware of this little foible. It's worth noting that sometimes the nets are floating some 4 or 5 feet below the surface, and we have safely passed over them on occasion, but I'm sure it's only a matter of time....

Then there are the lobster-pots, which in some areas are as thickly laid as in the Florida Keys. Not only will you see the floats bobbing on the surface, but there will be passages on which you may see what appear 4-foot square objects on the bed below as you pass. A quick drop over the side with a snorkel will show them to be full of lobster awaiting collection. Under no circumstances should anyone ever molest fishermen's gear. If you do, you deserve all you get, and additionally may bad karma be upon you... God will see.

CRUISING THE SOUTHERN GULFS

While cruising those same gulfs in the south, like us, you may be forced to dodge what appear to be large translucent lobster-pot floats just below the surface. Finally, losing patience after 20 or 30 occasions, you will slow down to discover that they're in fact jelly-fish rhythmically pulsing along their way and were it not for having thoroughly irritated you already, they might appear quite beautiful.

And then there are those silver-grey torpedoes, which burst out of crystal waters to leap and skim across the wavelets, while dancing on their tails and turning sharply. They're the houndfish and their smaller cousins, the needlefish. Sometimes these aptly named needle-nosed beauties will put on their display twisting and turning for a hundred yards or more, while you look on fascinated, and wonder what would happen if they ran into your inflatable.

At rest over the sand in the cays, you may find an inquisitive stingray taking his pleasure below your vessel, much in the same way that the friendly barracuda takes his in the deeper waters over the wall, but outside the reef. Please don't be frightened as you'd have to be startlingly unlucky to ever be molested by either of these much maligned creatures.

Oh, try feeding the seagulls from your hand as they sail in low overhead, cocking their heads sideways to check on you. With patience it can be done.

An interesting behavior can sometimes be observed outside the reef where occasionally a pair of gulls will take up station 50 feet or more above the bows. They're waiting for flying fish to be flushed out of the water into flight, and as they do this, the gulls swoop like fighter-planes twisting and dodging in pursuit between the waves. Sometimes they win, and sometimes they merely splash down to rearrange their feathers with an embarrassed look.

ANCHORING & ANCHORAGES

As noted elsewhere, shelter may be usefully sought near the reef if you don't wish to venture far inside to seek out a temporary anchorage. If there are breakers on the reef outside, it's fair to assume that the force of the waves will be dissipated before crossing it, and we have found that overnight anchorages here can be surprisingly comfortable, while in addition you may be assured that there will be no mosquitos. Lobster may well be found in the lee of the reef under coral ledges, so while diving the anchor why not go take a look?

One advantage of this anchorage is that speedy exits are possible if you need to make a long outside passage the next day, but in this case, good bearings and an easy exit channel are required if you're going to be leaving in the dark. If you have just come in, it may well be prudent in any case to take a bearing on the exit while it is fresh in your mind, as the next day uncertainty may have crept in, and you could waste time searching it out again.

Of course, you might prefer to anchor near any of a few thousand cays. Determine from the charts whether there is a handy lee in which to moor, or even whether there is a small inlet which might afford protection from all sides. Often a closer look can show useful nooks where the charts are vague on the subject, so it pays to start browsing in advance. You don't want to be caught in fading light, and faced with a mutinous crew snarling back from the anchor while you say, "Hmmm, not here either. Maybe over there?".

Taking advantage of the lack of significant tides, we like to anchor with only a foot or two under the keel, and while bringing us into range of the local mosquitos, it does allow us to get in close to the cays for both shelter and a certain peaceful communing with nature. But whatever, we always endeavor to be at rest before the light begins to go.

There have been occasions when due to our own greed, we pushed the day's journey to the limits and were faced with a low sun off the water, and into our eyes. At this point, no sunglasses will suffice and trusting to luck, while occasionally successful, cannot but result sooner or later in disaster. In fact, we have twice run aground in a perfectly familiar channel, due to a blindingly low sun in our eyes.

If you are into taking the dinghy ashore then you might as well be tucked in close so that later on a tired, and perhaps well-wined crew, do not have to do battle with anything more than their condition can handle. But be aware of potential wind-shifts which can easily mean nightly 180-degree changes due to the kabatic effect. I well remember a memorable barbecue one night on Cayo Blanco, where we each consumed two lobsters and three-quarters of a bottle of rum, then promptly fell asleep on the sand next to the smouldering embers. The four of us grudgingly awoke later to bury the ashes and mount a clammy dinghy out to the boat in ill-natured silence. Two hours later, I was forced awake by the banging of the rudder against its stops, as the wind-shift swung the stern all the way round onto a bank near the shoreline! We were not happy-campers that time; no, not at all.

TRADES ARE PREDICTABLE

By and large, the trades will make for a fairly predictable breeze (and on the northeast coast will be hardly affected by the kabatic effect). In general, you can look to the western shores of a cay for shelter, but winds may rise sufficiently to negate your shelter, so be careful of bottom composition, which may have a bearing on the available holding.

We have touched upon the anchors you may be carrying, but no amount of fancy anchors are going to make up for poor anchoring itself, so it's well to establish early on a good routine for this. Remember that an anchor which doesn't hold with the engine in reverse probably won't hold in a blow. Now it's obviously impractical to apply full revs if you're one of the over-powered brigade, but you must put enough force on it to know if it'll take strain, and to this end, we run our engine up to half speed, and if there is any doubt then take the engine a bit higher to see if there's movement. At the end of this exercise you should be able to get the rode tight enough to "thrum" under the strain.

DIVE YOUR ANCHOR

The subject of diving the anchor has been brought up before, but if you're going to be having a swim at even tide, then why not do it early enough to see where the anchor is, and how well it is dug in.

With a snorkel you can observe the anchor's behavior under stress, and if it repeatedly pulls out of turtle-grass before your very eyes, then there's always the option of swimming down to it and either forcing it in by hand, or placing it right side up in a depression or a gully into whose sides it can dig. The anchor will weigh a lot less below water, so this is certainly not as difficult as it sounds.

You really want the flukes of your anchor to get right down below the surface, so as to pull the anchor further in. Anchors seem to dig in a lot better where the bottom is not covered with a mat of grass, so this process is probably going to be easier in sand or heavy mud, but there's not going to be a lot of mud on this trip.

In regards to coral, your anchor will get a good grip on something here, but you must be extremely careful about the rode being sawn through on something else if there isn't enough chain to keep the rope off the bottom, so be careful. At these times you're grateful for the extra chain you've fitted to the anchor rope, or that all-chain rode, but to be honest there will be few occasions when you need to anchor overnight on coral, in fact, you should try to avoid anchoring in coral as it causes irreparable damage to live coral, so the extra weight of an all-chain rode may be an all-round disadvantage. A combination chain/rope anchor rode would seem to be best, unless you have a good winch.

We'll want the angle of pull to be nearly horizontal on the anchor, so be sure to play out enough so that the curve of the rode under tension lies as flat as possible along the bottom (weight is one of the functions of the chain at the business end). For normal purposes, you should have about seven times the distance from anchor-roller to the bottom. E.G.: If anchoring in 6 feet, with an additional 4 feet from the waterline to the roller, use around 70 feet of line. While in dodgy bottoms, or cases of high winds and waves, then you should let out 10 or 12 times the distance so that the rise and fall of the bows will not wriggle the anchor loose.

Of course, if the wind is getting up you may need two anchors out, so here's where your spare comes in handy. Most serious cruising yachts keep twin rollers with two anchors in the bows, but if yours is not so equipped, then you should have at least 200 feet of rope/chain permanently bent (attached) to your spare, and the whole lot close at hand for emergency deployment. It will not do to have it in some inaccessible spot, so keep it clear of junk and the like. You deploy this one by lowering your primary anchor, and then under power moving some distance at right angles to the wind, to lower the second on. Allow the boat to drift back, and make fast when you have played out as much rode as possible, and

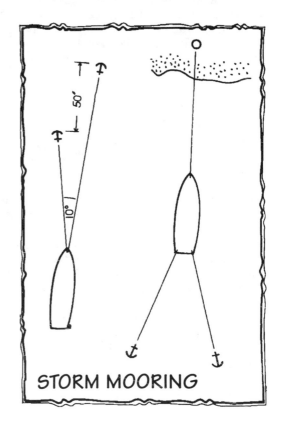

STORM MOORING

hope for an angle of about 10-20 degrees between the two.

This is a good time to record GPS readings, or a series of bearings with a hand-compass to compare later on at night when a worried looking guest comes to shake you awake, and a note of the depth will also go a long way to reassure him. Of course, allowance should be made for the swing of the boat too.

All these precautions may seem excessive at first, but you will probably have need to remember them later on if you neglect your duties here.

One summer we anchored near the northeast corner of Isla de Juventud (or "Pines" if you prefer) in a rising wind. We brought our boat to within about 150 feet of a nice, broad screen of unbroken cays with vegetation reaching at least 40 feet high for protection, then dropped anchor (a Bruce), set it somewhat casually and retired below to supper, a cup of tea, and the first three tapes of "The Hitchhiker's Guide to the Galaxy".

Two hours later as the wind now sang in the in the darkness, I casually glanced at the depth-sounder. It read 18 feet! And we'd recorded 7 feet earlier on!

Still there was no thought of panic, until the restarted GPS showed a difference of over half-a-mile!

We battled back as close in as before, and hung out two anchors this time, with an extra 50 feet, but we still slid out again.

The second anchor (a Danforth) had seemed to be holding well by the look of the line, until I merely grasped the rope and pulled by hand. It came in so easily that I gasped ,"The damn thing's come loose from the shackle at the end!", and looked about for someone else to blame.

It was still there, however, firmly attached to the chain at the end, but planing and sailing smoothly over the thick mat of turtle-grass below.

It took us a few tries, but we finally set the main anchor properly, and its rode hummed all night, but this time didn't drag.

That night in the dark we hadn't been able to see any shoreline, so we couldn't tell where we were apart from our earlier records, and we were lucky to have picked up the drift before it became serious, and luckier still that the wind hadn't swung round.

AT ANCHOR

A good routine should be established here so you won't forget anything, and while the boat is being put to bed, so to speak, the log should be written up.

I know this point has been harped on, but it's such a simple thing to do, only taking a minute while the details are still fresh in your mind, and hey, someone else is doing all the real work!

We record all the positional data like depth, latitude, longitude, bottom composition, and in addition note the recorded engine hours, so we can always update fuel figures periodically.

The boat having been settled, the crew can drop over the side for a swim (water temperature off the coast of Cuba will be around 82° Fahrenheit in the cays), and if there was any doubt about the anchor, it can be inspected by snorkel. It's unlikely you'll be in water much over 10 feet at anchor, so you'll have a good view, and if it's not well dug-in you can have someone aboard run up the motor to rearrange it while you're in the water screaming instructions no-one understands.

Turtle-grass is host to a surprising amount of life if you take the time to hover motionless above and drift lazily. You'll probably notice conches--good to eat raw in salads or stewed (ask a fisherman to show you how to get the meat out), anemones, sea-urchins lurching slowly amongst the vegetation (a good reason not to jump in so deep that your feet get punctured), equally slow moving starfish and multi-colored fishes who get friendlier with familiarity. There's a lot more too as you get in close to the shoreline into about two feet of water.

Look for the depressions and gullies, duck-dive down, and look under the ledges. As a coral-reef diver, I was stunned by the life in an area I'd previously thought practically uninhabited.

If you're anchored in deeper water or over sand and coral, you'll find a practical use for the early evening swim if you keep a spear-gun aboard. Your spear is, after all, the only piece of scuba equipment you'll ever buy which actually pays its way!

Take only what you need, and remember fish are magnified 25 per cent by the water, so don't bring back something which is undersized.

There are plastic fish-identifying cards and waterproof books which you may even take with you to consult under water, and these will add immensely to your pleasure as you'll remember a lot more if you can actually put a name to the fishes. We do keep aboard a couple of books to consult in greater detail later, and they're the most popular references at anchor.

A TIME TO RELAX

Back on board, you can dry off with a towel solely dedicated to sea-water use, or take a quick shower if you've got the water to spare, and then relax with a drink.

If you're into mixers, then actually keeping the sodas in the 'fridge will necessitate less ice, so keep it stocked up during the day when perhaps the engine's alternator is putting out lots and lots of volts, which can be usefully used for cooling. And of course, it will cause lots of aggravation if whoever used all the beers didn't replace them. However, don't do that now. At this time the 'fridge should only be opened for taking stuff out, and it should be closed immediately.

Don't stay below, even if the day has been hot and sunny, this is when it cools down, and the time spent on deck in the twilight hours with a cool drink in hand will be the abiding memory of your trip, long after you've forgotten that cobbled street with the old cathedral at the end.

If you feel like it this is a good time too for fishing as the fish begin to feed, and with skill and luck you might find you've got a self-sustaining boat.

Of course, speaking of fishes and fishing, there are always the occasional visits from friendly fishermen who may be in the area. Their boats stay out away from harbour for days on end, and like anyone else after a while they get bored. You can pass hours on end, if your command of Spanish is anything more than basic, and if you have a genuine liking for gossip.

The advice, information and just plain fun that can be had alongside a salt stained wooden fishing boat can't be re-created anywhere else, and as a further benefit you'll find almost unlimited opportunities for bargaining for seafood.

LISTEN TO WEATHER FORECAST

As darkness descends we still have the weather forecast on short-wave to attend to, and maybe you should try to fit it in while supper is being cooked. Remember, there's an

91

irritating gap in the shortwave broadcasts between 8 p.m. and midnight, so don't get caught out if intending an early night and an early morning departure. More conveniently, on the northwest coast, you'll be able to pick up the Key West transmissions on VHF (Wx) at any time.

On the shortwave, it's always best to listen to the forecast areas nearby, and to blend them into one if you're near the border between two sea areas. If listening to the VHF forecast, then you may have no choice but to extrapolate somewhat for the weather in your area.

Finally, as you prepare to shut down for the night, you can help with conserving both water and electric power by turning off the master switch to the water pump (leaking joints) then restocking the 'fridge with soft drinks and filling the ice-trays. These will then have a chance to freeze overnight as the 'fridge won't be opened again.

GOING ASHORE

Well, you've been lugging the dinghy all over the place, so why not get your money's worth?

Getting the inflatable into the water is the easy part, but the engine can be a bit more difficult, and many are the men who have dropped it in by mistake. If you took my advice about power to the extreme, you may well have an outboard at the limits of not just your stretch, but your strength!

It takes but a moment to fasten a line to the transom-brackets, and this way if you do drop it in (you will one day), you can get it out a moment later. Don't worry, take the plug out to clear inside the cylinder, and sooner or later it'll run again, even though you may have

ominos is a popular Cuban and Caribbean game. (Photo by George Halloran)

to drain the carburetor floatbowl if it's in for any length of time. Pour bowls of fresh water over the motor and spray it down thoroughly with one of those magic water-dispersing sprays they sell.

Everyone has their own method of mounting the outboard, but in all cases you should tie the dinghy in close so it won't drift away as you handle the motor, and make sure you have a good footing before beginning the process.

Before going ashore for a picnic, you might rather fancy a couple of nice fat lobsters, and if everyone partakes in the hunt, then the whole crew will have even more fun later on.

You're going to be looking for areas of coral which have overhangs under which lobster like to shelter, so trickle the dinghy in a search pattern, looking down at intervals for the patches which seem to have potential. Someone can drop over the side with a mask, or just lie over the sides and look down. When you're in a really good area you'll maybe see their antennae waving out from below the ledges, but in any case, if there are likely overhangs, then drop a mushroom anchor, and someone should go down for a look. See the last chapter for descriptions of how to catch them, and the kids can stay aboard the dinghy to mind the goody-bags if they aren't going to be involved.

Ashore you'll always be able to find some driftwood to build a fire, but don't go overboard and build a hazard to the environment. Make a low wall of rocks around the fire, leaving a gap through which air can enter to support combustion, and you can bury foil-wrapped fish or lobster in the hot embers for a few minutes to enjoy food cooked in its own juices. You may, of course, prefer to just impale your prepared catch and cook it above the flames, being careful not to scorch it.

These affairs are inevitably marked by someone or the other stepping on a hot ember in bare feet, so if a glowing coal spits out of the fire, don't just shove it into the sand with a stick and cover it with a sprinkling. Bash its life out with a big rock if you can't get it back into the fire, and bury it deeply.

Please remember you are a visitor in someone else's country, and as such, are also responsible for the image of your own, so make sure you don't leave litter or do anything that might be construed as vandalism. Make sure the embers are all well covered with sand, and clean the area of any signs of your presence. Even if it doesn't affect you, your behavior will certainly affect those who come behind you.

On a more somber note, most boating accidents take place when not actually aboard your vessel, so always be careful in dinghies, and especially if you're somewhat judgement-impaired after a good evening ashore.

Whether or not you take the dinghy aboard will be your own call based on your condition at the time, but remember that it can be a hindrance later on in the water.

MORNING PREPARATIONS

If you're leaving your present anchorage (or mooring), there are a few tasks that need to be attended to. You might like to pick up the shortwave forecasts while breakfast is being prepared so you can discuss the weather later on like any civilized couple ashore, except that here it's more than just a polite interest. You'll need it to plan the day's sail.

Afterwards, with the table cleared, the charts can come out and the passage looked at in detail. Remember that while plotting your courses, it will be a good idea to make jottings in a passage notebook showing bearings, cays, anchorages along the way.

Even if the day's passage is not expected to be rough, the vessel should still be made as shipshape as if it were putting out to sea. Clear the decks of all those drying towels, or if they just have to be left out, then at least make sure they're fastened to the lines.

We make exactly the same checks every day on the engine, and this can be done by one person while the other sets about the other aspects of departure preparation.

The engine's oil and water must always be checked, as must the water-pump/alternator belt, and any topping up or tightening should be done as soon as needed. It's a good idea to make exactly the same log-entry detailing oil, water, fuel, and belt checks at the beginning of each passage so there is no danger of forgetting them. If the belt shows signs of wear, then it should be replaced before it breaks and subsequently causes a rise in engine temperature.

While this is going on, the cockpit can be arranged by someone else. The plotting instruments can be laid out, navigation instruments turned on, pencils sharpened, and binoculars, cushions, caps, sunglasses and other gear all need setting out as well.

Raising anchor can be a strain on the elderly or the just plain bad-backed, so if you don't have a winch, then go ahead slowly, and do pay attention to the bowman's directions. This can be an ill-tempered job, so try to look sympathetic too. It will help to allow the person up front to occasionally make a few turns around the post with the line, and rest for a minute or two before you slowly go ahead again.

When the chain hangs down vertically, you may sometimes need to power the boat right over it to break the anchor free, but if it still won't come loose, then you might just have to take a look with a mask on. If you habitually anchor in coral, then you should have a buoyed anchor trip-line fastened to the other end of the anchor. You can haul on it to reverse the angle of pull, and draw the anchor out backwards. If you have to abandon the anchor temporarily, the buoy will mark the spot too.

Don't allow the more discolored splashes of water brought up on the anchor rode to remain for long on the deck, as mixed with a little organic matter they can be the very devil to remove later. Brush it into the scuppers with your deck-broom dipped over the side.

In the relative calm that follows raising the anchor, and while the engine is still coming up to temperature, a final glance round the decks is in order to see that all has been put away. The anchor should be pinned and the ropes coiled, while if a boathook or a broom is lying about on deck, it will go overboard as soon as the first wave hits.

FINALLY

In addition to the last couple of chapters, there will be further advice scattered throughout this book, sometimes not in any logical order, and information given in one chapter is also probably applicable to another where similar circumstances exist. Read all the chapters through, even if you only plan to cruise one particular area.

The following chapters will describe passages around the coastline and through the cays, but they will not give every route possible. For better enjoyment of your particular cruise you should use them as a guide only, deviating as and when the fancy takes you.

Please, in the instance of discovering new (hopefully better) passages and anchorages update the author, while if you also discover errors or glaring omissions, I would be grateful for prompt corrections, which may benefit future editions.

Many of the drawings shown later are subjective and made clandestinely or from memory, as there have been occasions when I have not thought it wise to sit in full view of the Guarda Frontera making sketches of what might possibly be considered sensitive locations. Forgive the cruder aspects, they have all been done with the best of intentions, if not always under the best of circumstances.

Cuba is changing daily. New vistas are opening up as you read this, not only in the world of cruising, but more importantly in the social aspects of day to day and political life. All these have a bearing on the future of not only Cubans, but visitors as well. Shoreside information is scarce too, with whole towns still largely unknown as to the services or attractions available. The next chapters will likely be rendered obsolete, or in need of revision within a year or two as these changes begin to take effect. Please bear this in mind as you cruise, and take delight in the fact that you are indeed part of that change.

PLANNING YOUR ROUTE

On our first visit to Cuba a couple of years ago we didn't know a thing about the country. We just turned up, cruised the island, and took our chances. We didn't know what we would find, but what the heck, we had time to spare.

You on the other hand, having been graciously allowed two weeks paid vacation, might still be counting on returning to your job. Perhaps it would be best if you managed your time better than us. If it is just a stop-off along a greater route, all well and good, but if your journey is a holiday cruise, then what you want from it will determine where you go on it.

So, just what are you expecting from your trip?

WHERE YOU WANT TO GO

Your own particular route is going to be determined by two major factors which we will discuss later; wind and current. But within those parameters...

A HOLIDAY CRUISE ON THE NORTH COAST

For a holiday cruise with lots of snow-white beaches for the kids, hotels, entertainment, a marina berth and assorted tourist facilities, your best bets are along the north coast. This would start in Varadero, and looking east, along the cays where the majority of the newer self-contained, hotel-resorts are being constructed. Varadero, in fact, has a convenient airport from which you can fly to any part of Cuba, as well as offering regular flights to Nassau, Bahamas. This is very convenient if you need to get to the U.S. quickly and from Nassau there are countless daily flights to Ft. Lauderdale.

From Varadero you may visit Havana by road.

Further west after the cays, the coast is deeply indented with huge "pocket bays" evenly spaced about a day's sail apart.

HEADING WEST FROM HAVANA

Going the other way, west from Havana where the cays stretch out along the north coast of Pinar del Rio province, your vacation takes on a different aspect. The few resort areas that do exist here are smaller. Any cruise in this area might require more self-sufficiency, but the cays are far more accessible and the waters more easily navigable. This would be the best bet for a short trip over from the U.S. if you wish to combine cruising the cays with a few days spent in Havana.

THE SOUTHEAST CLIFFS

At the other end of the island in the extreme southeast, the coast is unlike anywhere else in Cuba. Sheer cliffs, rocky walls undercut by the pounding surf, and enormous boulder-

TABLE OF WINDS

Compare place names with charts on pages 100 and 101.

Cabo San Antonio	Jan	Feb	Mar	Apr	May	Jun	Jul	Aug	Sep	Oct	Nov	Dec
wind direction	E	NE	NE	NE	SE	SE	ENE	ENE	NE	NE	ENE	NE
speed	10	15	16	15	16	14	9	9	5	10	13	11
turbulent days	3	2	3	4	8	16	19	23	18	8	4	2

Caibarien	Jan	Feb	Mar	Apr	May	Jun	Jul	Aug	Sep	Oct	Nov	Dec
wind direction	E	NE	ENE	E	ENE	ENE	ENE	ENE	E	NE	NE	E
speed	13	14	15	15	12	11	14	13	11	12	13	12
turbulent days	5	2	1	3	11	12	10	10	13	8	2	1

Punta Maisí	Jan	Feb	Mar	Apr	May	Jun	Jul	Aug	Sep	Oct	Nov	Dec
wind direction	ENE	ENE	ENE	ENE	ENE	E	E	E	E	E	ENE	E
speed	17	16	18	23	20	16	23	20	18	16	22	23
turbulent days	1	1	2	2	6	6	5	4	5	4	1	2

Jucaro	Jan	Feb	Mar	Apr	May	Jun	Jul	Aug	Sep	Oct	Nov	Dec
wind direction	NE	NE	N	NE	S	NE	E	E	NE	NE	NE	NE
speed	24	22	19	21	21	12	16	14	14	17	23	24
turbulent days	0	1	1	3	12	16	20	20	21	12	3	1

Nueva Gerona	Jan	Feb	Mar	Apr	May	Jun	Jul	Aug	Sep	Oct	Nov	Dec
wind direction	E	E	E	E	E	E	E	E	E	E	E	E
speed	14	14	14	14	14	14	14	14	14	14	14	14
turbulent days	0	1	0	0	4	9	10	10	5	2	2	0

strewn mountains sweeping right down to the sea. There is also the historic city of Santiago (the "Heroic City" in modern Cuban mythology), from where a rental car provides easy access inland to the prehistoric parklands and valleys. This coastline is without a doubt the most spectacular in the whole of Cuba, and has harbours evenly spaced out along it.

THE INNER CURVE OF THE SOUTH COAST

The inner curve of the south coast is ringed with cays to both sides of the Island of Juventud (itself easily as large as most of the British West Indian islands). Along the coastline, far inside the two major gulfs, the terrain is flatter with the historic city of Trinidad and other notable ports offering communication by road and rail to Havana and the rest of Cuba. Cayo Largo is the only tourist resort out among the deserted keys, and communication to the mainland from some of these can require a journey of a day or more.

Being so vast and due to its location, this area will require the most commitment from a cruiser but is also the most rewarding.

THEN THERE IS HAVANA

Havana itself is worth a separate visit even if you've just got a long weekend.

WHAT DETERMINES YOUR ROUTE

Winds

As you can see from the adjoining table, the predominant winds around the coasts are from the east, with swings to the east northeast (especially during periods of low pressure). The winds are regular and can be counted on about 70-80 percent of the time, and the days on which you might expect turbulence are concentrated in the summer months. There are five locations shown from which you can calculate what you might reasonably expect in any of the main cruising areas.

Note the wind directions shown are **median monthly directions**, and not shown in the tables are the frequent swings to the southeast and northeast under the influence of low barometric pressure. Neither are the high winds from the north and northwest, when the cold fronts come sweeping through in winter.

There are also short local disturbances in May and November which affect the north and south coasts. The Gulf of Batabano is especially affected by a west or southwest wind called "La Virazon" by local fishermen. This wind can be accompanied by storms and small cyclones. It is considered a harbinger of further periods of bad weather. However, heavy storms (while not rare) are unusual. You should not be overly preoccupied if you miss a forecast or two, as long as you do not make it a habit.

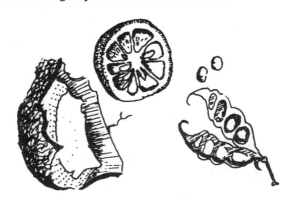

ON THE TOPIC OF HURRICANES

One cannot discuss the weather in the Caribbean without mentioning hurricanes, so we had better get it over with. Apart from advising a certain caution over the question of travelling down to the West Indies in the season, there's not a lot that one can advise here.

The hurricane season begins in June and lasts until the end of November. In the unlikely event of a hurricane coming in, its normal path would be along a northwestern track. The main shelters available are along the north coast, where there are several deep pocket bays with high steep walls.

You probably would not be heading down to the West Indies during that season, but it is comforting to know of the existence at these refuges.

Along the southeast coast there are a couple of really good refuges like Chivirico and Santiago, but as mentioned before there is not much that one can do in the event of a direct hit. Instead, apply all your energies to getting out of the way.

A youth relaxes on the fender of a vintage American car on a Havana street. Older cars, still operable, are common sights in Cuba. (Photo by George Halloran)

Currents

A major influence while passaging along the coast is the current found on both coastlines.

As a general rule, the Bahamas Current comes in from the east and sweeps up alongside the northeastern coast. There it gets necked down and speeded up by the venturi between the Bahamas and Cuba.

A small quantity of this current is earlier diverted west along the southeastern coast, seeking to join the current which flows up along the southern side of the island chain. However, here it meets a different current closer into the coastline. This small counter-current, flowing eastwards along the Cuban coastline, diverts it down to the southwest before finally hitting Mexico. There it becomes the Yucatan Current and squirts northeast as the beginning of the Gulf Stream.

It is as well at this point to look at the drawings of the currents on the following pages as this will make it clearer.

CONCLUSIONS

Circumnavigation

This guide is formatted to allow a logical progression with one cruising area leading naturally into an adjacent area. That way the reader may guess relatively easily where the information he seeks is located. Thus, the guide will be approached as though the reader were actually conducting a circumnavigation of the island.

Taking the anticlockwise (or counter clockwise) route, we note that the south coast is largely made up of cays. Through these easily navigable waters the average yacht might wish to meander. Courses would therefore be off the wind for much of the time. The prevailing easterlies would be much modified by the shelter of the island. The current, which might otherwise sweep northwest, is negated and even pushed back by the counter-current described above. Coming around the eastern corner to turn west along the north coast, the sailor will find an exhilarating run with the current and winds favorable all the way.

The clockwise route would leave the sailor with the task of beating into stiff headwinds and currents east of Havana. At a glance the cays along the way might offer protection, but in fact the water inside those cays on the north coast is shallower than first appears and much of the inside route is not navigable by yacht. Along the south coast, journeying west, the winds would to some extent be favorable, but the current would not assist as much as might be hoped.

I would go anticlockwise; so that is how the rest of the book will be structured.

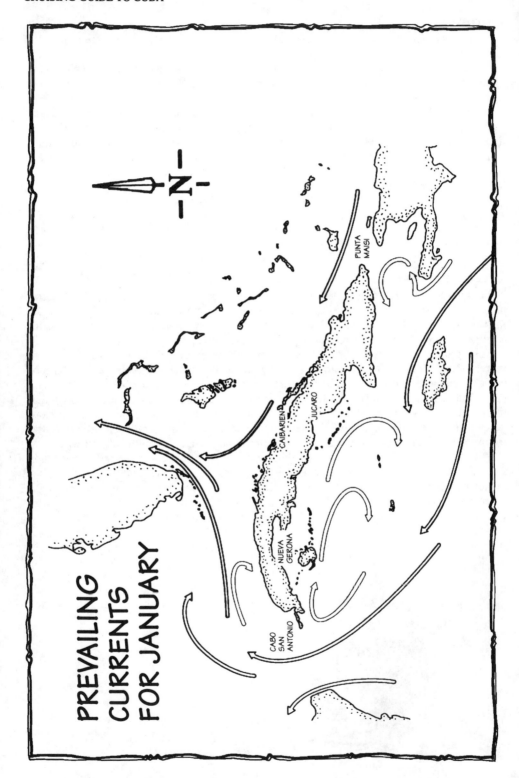

PREVAILING CURRENTS FOR JANUARY

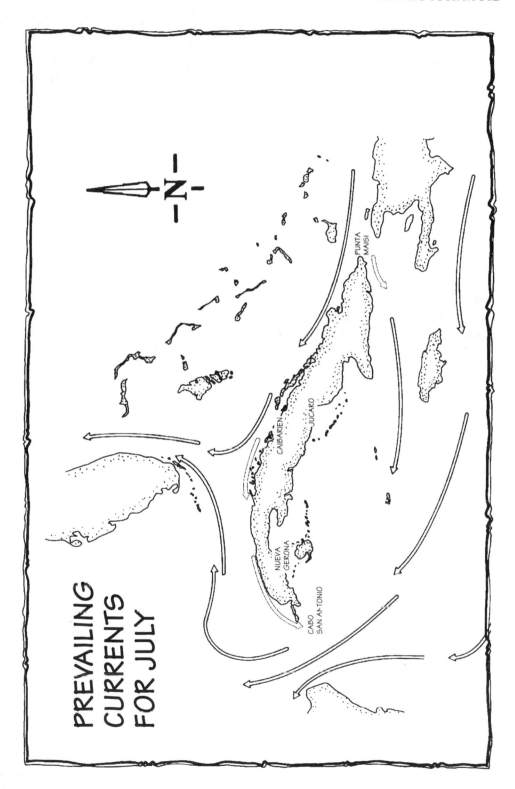

PREVAILING CURRENTS FOR JULY

CRUISING SECTIONS

Havana Westwards to Cabo San Antonio

This route will take the reader to the Marina Hemingway in Havana, then on to the cays along the northwest. On the way, we shall stop overnight in Bahía Honda, as the cays are too far to allow a daylight run to the first of them. Along the cays, we dock at two small islands where there are wharfs and hotel complexes, allowing an easy introduction to Cuban cruising. Following that, we will cruise westwards through more cays, where you may wish to anchor overnight, or visit ashore at a couple of the towns along the way.

Finally, at the western extreme of the island there is the option of returning to Havana, leaving Cuba, or continuing on to the next section.

Cabo San Antonio Eastwards Along the Southern Shoreline and Cays to Cayo Largo

Rounding the cape we cruise along the cliffs east to the bay of Corrientes and the dive resort of Maria La Gorda (Fat Mary). From here, it's an easy run towards a couple of towns on the mainland inside the Gulf of Batabano. Then we divert over to the Isla de Juventud where you might wish to rest for a day or two. Later we visit the stretch of cays ringing the gulf to end up in Cayo Largo, from which you may leave for the Cayman Islands or continue on.

Cayo Largo to Cabo Cruz

Leaving Cayo Largo, we visit the harbour of Casilda, serving the beautiful city of Trinidad. This is one of the two Cuban cities UNESCO has placed on its world heritage list (Old Havana is the other). From here, we cruise the spectacular, deserted cays heading east, until we come to the mainland city of Manzanillo, finally stopping at Cabo Cruz.

Cabo Cruz to Punta Maisí

The next stretch is the most impressive in the whole journey, with sheer cliffs and mountains lining the coast. Halts can be made at secluded ports along the way, stopping for a much longer time at Santiago. Then we continue on past the U.S. naval base at Guantánamo (you may even wish to enter the bay) until we round the cape at Punta Maisí on the southeastern tip of Cuba.

Punta Maisí to Havana

Our last leg will be the fast northwest run up along the coast, past huge deepwater bays with narrow entrances (some with cargo facilities further in). There are holiday resorts and complexes dotting the cays further along with more being built. This is Cuba's premier vacation area, and we shall stop awhile in Varadero before the easy run up to Havana to complete our tour.

An ornate balcony provides an excellent viewing spot for a Cuban woman watching the activities on the street below. (Photo by George Halloran)

From eggs to rum, what you need is U.S. dollars. Cold, hard cash is the easiest form of payment. Here, a street vendor peddles fresh eggs. (Photo by George Halloran)

A cigar maker prepares his hand-rolled cigars for sale. Cuba is still known worldwide for fine cigars. (Photo by George Halloran)

Classic architecture in a grand style provides interesting sights in Cuba. The main square in Old Havana is pictured above. (Photo by Simon Charles)

Colorful buildings frame a uniformed school girl on a Havana street. (Photo by George Halloran)

The Cubans are hospitable and friendly, and they love to invite you to their homes. Here two school children prepare to share a stalk of sugar cane. (Photo by George Halloran)

A youth plays baseball as others look on, oblivious to the propoganda graffiti on the wall to her left. Baseball is the favorite Cuban sport. (Photo by George Halloran)

Verdant rolling hills reflect a pastoral scene in a Cuban rural area. The countryside provides spectacular beauty. (Photo by George Halloran)

Marina Hemingway consists of a series of canals with modern yachting amenities and a helpful marina staff. (Photo by George Halloran)

The more picturesque harbour at Jaimanitas nearby is utilized by Cuban fishermen. (Photo by Simon Charles)

Ingenuity at its finest. A Cuban bicycle rider "hitches a ride" by grabbing the tail of a cow being transported aboard a trailer. (Photo by George Halloran)

Horses play an important role in the agriculturally centered society found outside the major metropolitan centers. (Photo by George Halloran)

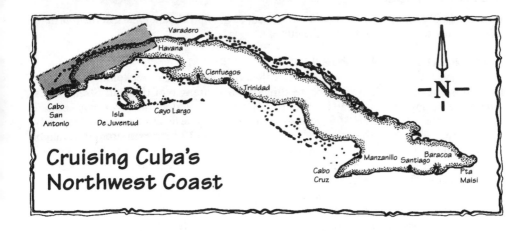

Cruising Cuba's
Northwest Coast

HAVANA TO CABO SAN ANTONIO

PASSAGING FROM MIAMI

We've all got to get to Havana from somewhere else. And I suspect that, with the greatest respect to those who arrive from the rest of the West Indies, the majority of visitors to Cuba will pass through Miami, or at least its sister port Ft. Lauderdale. It is after all, one of the last stops on the North American continent where you can get every aspect of your boat seen to professionally. With regard to my earlier chapter on boat preparation, that's not such a bad thing.

But an Irishman once responded to a stranger's request for directions to a nearby village by saying, "Well sor, if I were going there, I wouldn't be going from here!". Nor should you.

A direct journey from Miami would needlessly expose you to endless slogging into the teeth of the Gulf Stream.

Leaving the port of Miami sinking under the Biscayne Bay horizon, you should head for the Florida Keys to make your crossing from Key West. You might as well take the inside route along the Intra-Coastal Waterway, stopping as you see fit in Marathon's Boot Harbour, Plantation Key, Big Pine, or any of a dozen snug anchorages along the way. This way you'll get a chance to right any wrongs your friendly mechanic may have done you on the last service, before it becomes critical. You might call it a shake-down cruise within a cruise.

The weather forecast is easily obtained from the NOAA transmitters on VHF, and they also give the position and strength of the Gulf Stream which you need for dead-reckoning. In addition, you can go upstairs at the airport in Key West where the cooperative staff will give you not only the latest weather, but a pretty good passage prognosis.

You don't want to be caught with a rising wind in opposition to the stiff current which already exists. It will only get rougher, so delay your journey if it is your first such crossing, and wait for relatively settled conditions.

The first time we went to Cuba, we thought the marina was at Havana, so that was our first mistake. In fact all foreign yachts are cleared in approximately 9 miles west of the entrance to Havana's harbour at the **Marina Hemingway**. The direct course (91 miles) from the final channel marker outside Key West to the first channel mark at the marina is 208°M, plus something added for the current.

MAKING ALLOWANCE FOR THE GULF STREAM

I don't wish to tell anyone how to navigate their boat, but for dead-reckoning you'll need to make some sort of allowance for the direction and strength of the Gulf Stream. Just where it is on any particular day is open to conjecture as you don't always come across it at the same place, but the VHF forecasts gives its approximate location several times daily. The current will probably have a course of anything around 70 degrees, a strength of maybe 2 knots, and could be positioned anywhere up to 40 miles off the Florida coast, but this should be checked before making your allowance. At best, it'll be a guess where you actually begin to be affected, so if you don't have an electronic navigation aid aboard, then you should allow the current to take you east towards Havana. This way, when you hit the coast you can just turn right. If you've never done dead-reckoning in current before, read up on it, and remember that what you allow for the current should take into consideration your anticipated boat speed (haven't you been making notes on this in the various logs?). Don't be surprised if the actual allowance is well over 10 degrees. But plot it all out in advance, even if you do have a GPS set aboard, and enter it in your passage-notes.

Your final day in Key West will be best spent at dockside making your final checks on the boat, so if you haven't filled those extra canisters of fuel I talked about, then you can do it here at any of the marinas. Don't leave, as we once did, the fitting of a larger bilge-pump to the last minute, but get everything sorted out in advance. Leaving is going to be stressful enough as it is.

OUTWARD CLEARANCE NECESSARY

You'll need outwards clearance from U.S. Customs, whose offices are conveniently situated in the middle of Key West. It's a simple process: you presenting them your vessel's papers and money (U.S. $9), them presenting you a Certificate of Clearance to a Foreign Port. This can be done in a few minutes, so you might easily schedule some final shopping around it, or even that visit to the airport weather offices.

A point to note well is that from here on you have no passengers, and everyone aboard must be listed as crew on these and all further documents.

Neglecting this will involve you in countless bureaucratic hassles, so short circuit the whole process by taking the easy way out.

If your boat is not a speedster, set your departure for afternoon so that you leave all channel marks behind in good light, and allocate watches throughout the night, allowing you to arrive in the middle of the day. You'll be crossing the Florida Straits, one of the most heavily traversed stretches of water in this part of the world, but with due care there shouldn't be any problem. Any lights however should be closely monitored so as to ascertain the course and speed of the other vessel. But do not, like us once, mistake the rising moon for imminent collision!

KEEP AN UPDATE OF YOUR POSITION

We like to update our position every hour, plotting the position on the chart, and especially on long night passages this can make for a welcome break in the monotony. If this is your first long night passage, you might find it wisest if all watches were double-manned, until at least the early hours of daylight, when if you're satisfied that all is well with the world, the crew can go below to nap in turns.

Building columnades frame a visitor to Old Havana (Photo by Simon Charles)

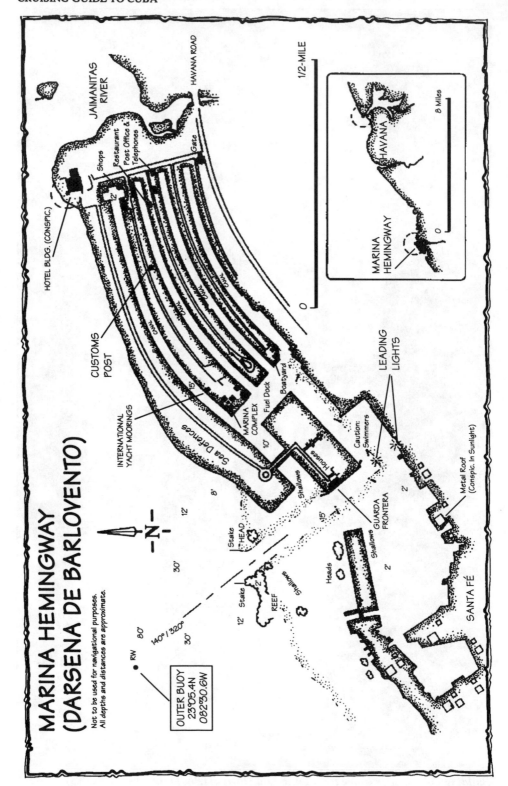

MARINA HEMINGWAY
(DARSENA DE BARLOVENTO)

Not to be used for navigational purposes.
All depths and distances are approximate.

OUTER BUOY
23°05.4N
082°30.6W

RW

80'

30'

140° / 320°

30'

12' Stake

REEF

Shallows

12' Stake

HEAD

Heads

Shallows

Stake

2'

2'

8'

12'

10'

15'

GUARDA FRONTERA

Caution:
Swimmers

LEADING
LIGHTS

2'

2'

Metal Roof
(Conspic. In Sunlight)

SANTA FÉ

Houses

Fuel Dock

Boatyard

MARINA
COMPLEX

Sea Defences

INTERNATIONAL
YACHT MOORINGS

CUSTOMS
POST

15'

12'

HOTEL BLDG. (CONSPIC.)

Shops

Restaurant

Post Office &
Telephones

Gate

JAIMANITAS
RIVER

HAVANA ROAD

1/2-MILE

8 Miles

HAVANA

MARINA
HEMINGWAY

0

0

Having crossed what you believe to be the 12-mile limit, you may begin to call in on the VHF for clearance. Do not be surprised to receive no reply at first, but continue onwards towards the marina, while calling at regular intervals on **channel 72** to the **Marina Hemingway**, where someone will usually have a rudimentary grasp of English.

You will hear countless calls early in the morning on channel 16 to the Morro (Castle) in Havana from various larger vessels awaiting instructions and the like. Their desperation should convince you that it's best to call the marina, so persevere with them, only calling Havana as a last resort.

The marina office should reply sooner or later, asking you a series of questions about your vessel and your visit, then they will contact the various immigration functionaries so that all will be ready upon your arrival. See chapter two: Entering the Country.

RECOGNIZING MARINA HEMINGWAY

Marina Hemingway is situated a mile or so to the west of the Dársena (harbour) of Barlovento, at the mouth of the river Jaimanitas, and just east of the town of Santa Fe. It can be recognized at a distance by the sun reflecting off a low curved metal roof just to the right inside the entrance, and there is also a large squat grey-white hotel block (which has been under repair forever) three-quarters of a mile east.

The entrance to the marina is guarded by a reef not a quarter-mile offshore. Look for the large red and white marker-bouy (Fl.10s) at 23°05.4N/082°30.6W in about 120 feet of water. Pass it close on your port then come in along a course of 140°M, lining up the range-markers inside the harbour, a leading diamond (R) and a trailing post (R/W spiral). This will take you a couple of hundred yards on between two red and green markers marking the gap through the reef, and along a narrow passage dredged to about 18-20 feet. The channel is only about 50 yards wide, so do not stray off line until you are into the harbour proper at the Guarda Frontera post.

An additional hazard which you will face here are snorkellers who spear-fish around the entrance. Be on the look out for them.

ENTERING THE MARINA, CUSTOMS & IMMIGRATION
CHART NO. ICH 1124 (CUBAN)

The Guarda Frontera post is immediately inside on the left, and just past it is a stretch of concrete dock alongside which you can moor using handily placed cleats. The wall here reaches some 5 feet above water-level, and you might wish to mount your fenders high as there is a protruding top lip. If there is a swell entering, then station a crewman there to fend off.

You will understandably be a bit nervous, but don't worry, it's all been seen before, and if you've earlier been in contact with the marina, they will have notified the immigration officials who should already be on their way from Havana. Wait on board for their arrival rather than walking over to the nearby swimming pool and demanding a beer.

You'll probably be tired, and even if you've already read the section on entering the country, might not be prepared for the invasion of officials, but don't be alarmed. Handle things with aplomb by having all your documents ready, and exhibit a gracious manner.

The whole affair should only take an hour or so if there is no problem, and even if there is, you will find that the officials will try to sort things out as best they can.

Once clearance has been given you may take down the yellow Q-flag and proceed to the marina itself, so call them again on VHF 72 to say you'll be there in three minutes and depart the dock.

From the Guarda Frontera post you proceed slowly, about 50 yards further on, and turn sharply to port between the green shoreside mark on the corner and the large red marker-boxes in the water. Remember to keep a sharp eye out for the hordes of young swimmers who climb those very marker-boxes to dive in from the top.

Turn port (northwest) again 200 yards further down the line, and off your starboard bow will be the fuel docks and the marina offices.

MARINA HEMINGWAY

Most foreign yachts dock along the last of four concrete-lined canals on the right (the closest to the sea), and heading there you should be especially cautious. There are always curious swimmers and small pleasure craft in the basin, which is only about 70 yards wide anyway.

The canal itself is even narrower (only about 60 feet), so enter carefully to starboard, and dock either where indicated by waiting marina personel or at the first available space.

A hint here, if you do moor close to the entrance you will also be close to the marina's restaurant/disco whose noise will keep you up all night, so move along at least 100 yards or more.

Don't fret, the canal is about half a mile long and has a turning basin at the far end if you don't feel like turning round in the channel.

Finally, the prevailing winds are from the east so if your cabin is aft, then turn the boat round so the breezes can enter more easily for cooling. I once carried a max/min thermometer in our aft cabin, and it showed daytime temperatures of 104°F and 80°F at night in mid-September.

Make up some skipper-like excuse to the rest of the crew in front who will not be aware of what you're doing, and tie up to the impressive cast-iron cleats.

Something to look out for: The cleats are set back about a foot and a half from the edge of the wall, so if there's a low tide with a bit of movement, you can find your ropes being frayed where they run over the lip and down to your boat. Chafe-guards are called for.

American tourists jog past the Marina Hemingway landside entrance. (Photo by George Halloran)

MEETING THE MARINA STAFF

The first contact you will usually have with the marina staff in person will probably be Lazaro, a lovely wizened gentleman. It is he who usually indicates your dock-space, takes your lines, sorts out all the power/water connections at dockside and handles all gossip. Your standard connections will probably be at variance with those used in Cuba, so he will provide adaptors at no cost. Provided he has not been replaced (there was a dismaying rumour once), he will be the one who notifies you when the water is actually on too.

The marina staff will sometimes provide a dockside welcoming committee of sorts, whose job it is to give you as much information as possible about the services offered. They are almost overpoweringly friendly, but take everything they say with a grain of salt, as they tend to make light of obvious supply problems and within each other's earshot spout the official party line.

It is also not unusual to receive a further visit from the local customs officials who are stationed in the marina. They too are a friendly bunch, passing many a happy hour in idle chat with yachtsmen, and they just love Madonna's recordings!

ON THE TOPIC OF MARINA CHARGES

Marina charges in late 1993 were 45 cents per foot per day all found, and there is fuel available at around 65 cents per litre for diesel, 90 cents per litre for gasoline, and oil was $1.75 a litre.

There were telephone hook-ups available too, if only you could get one that worked!

You will, if cruising further afield, be expected to purchase a Cruising Permit/Safety Certificate here for $50, and the marina officers will handle all your future requirements as regards documentation. Let the current take you lazily along and don't fight it.

Arrival of your documents will take about 2 days, so start the process at once if planning to cruise the cays.

A DESCRIPTION OF THE MARINA OPERATIONS

This is the first stop for the majority of visitors, so at the risk of burdening the reader who may want to get on with it, I'll give a somewhat expansive description to things in and around the marina. Later on down the line, the stops will get lesser versions as the reader becomes more familiar with things and how they work in Cuba.

There are usually some six or seven foreign-flagged and occupied yachts moored along the canals, along with a couple of Cuban yachts which moor there in between day charters.

The marina's office is open until 9:30 p.m., and is situated between the outermost canals.

Here, all aspects of your stay may be dealt with, including the documentation required for further travels. The amiable staff will order taxis for you and can advise on further travel inland, if you so desire. We once had to leave our boat here for a month, and they were happy to hold our keys to enable the boat's bilges and systems to be periodically checked. In fact, you will be surprised to find how many boats are left there unattended for extremely long periods of time, with mechanics carrying out routine maintenance for absent owners.

Inside the northeast corner office upstairs, you will find a full weather forecast and a chart of the Caribbean areas with all isobars and fronts drawn in daily.

There is a medical post with a rotating staff of doctors where all manner of minor ailments can be attended to, and if anything serious crops up, they will accompany you to a local hospital.

Over the last two years, a splendid bath/laundry-room building has been constructed (we felt privileged to witness the awesome sloth with which it was constructed, and amazed to see it eventually finished) at the west end of the docks, near two tennis courts. Laundry charges were complicated, so it's best to hand over a full black plastic-bag which will all get washed, dried, and folded overnight by the attendant at the desk in the bath-house for about $4. La Fiona says that's still a lot, so don't be shy!

There's a scuba depot halfway along the main avenue leading out of the marina, and I've been able to get air-fills there. You rarely see overt signs of much activity, but I know they offer dive-trips out along the reef. It's marked by a large red and white scuba flag painted on the wall and an illuminated sign.

The 110V electrical hook-ups are via supply-boxes at dockside, much like anywhere else, except that your connection won't fit. Lazaro, the man who gets all things done, will sort you out with an adaptor.

He has fittings for the strange pipe-spigots too, so be prepared to remove your old connection from your hose, and fit one of his with a cheap clip from the boat's stock.

Actually getting water is another matter, however. Despite all assurances to the contrary, it has always been difficult for marina residents to get showers daily, and then only from around 6 p.m. onwards.

They usually say, "the pipe's broken," but then again it's always broken; every day until after five p.m.

The water doesn't in fact come by pipe, ever. It's brought in late by truck, and pumped up into the overhead tank, just in time for groups of outside visitors to hog it all.

PERSISTANCE IS A KEY TO WATER

If you're persistent enough, refusing to accept obvious excuses, the bored attendant will nod her head wearily and say to somebody around there, "Go and turn the pump on." So you get your shower, even if she's only just told you to come back at ten o'clock when the pipe will have been repaired! As I said before, you just have to be firm about so many things in Cuba. Perhaps the service has been perfected since, but probably not.

A YACHT SUPPORT SERVICE?

As this was being written, a new yacht-support operation opened for business in the marina. I obviously have not dealt with it, but it seems to duplicate some of the existing services supplied by the present management as well as providing others. Run by "Yacht Support Services Ltd" out of England (tel. 44-424 774888 from abroad) and seemingly aimed at the larger "super yachts", they aim to provide general agency services, and worldwide sourcing of parts from abroad. Time will tell if they succeed or not, but on the subject of super-yachts, I should mention that I have occasionally seen absolutely enormous craft moored in the marina's canals. With permanent crew, and owners who arrive infrequently, some of these could be considered more or less permanently berthed in Cuba.

A SMALL MARINA SHOPPING COMPLEX

At the end of the avenue leading out is a small shopping complex containing some five or six shops, which accept foreign currency for provisions and rather tacky items of clothing. Further along, there is a telephone-office, and if you turn right at the office you come across two restaurants.

The only place you'll get any service worthy of the name is along the middle canal at the "Fiesta," some 200 yards down on the right. Their food, unusual for Cuba, seems to have been inspected both before and after cooking, and is actually served warm.

Don't bother to visit the one closest to the entrance unless you're a masochist.

There are discotheques, both at the shopping complex and at the marina proper. If this is your first experience of Cuban dancing it will knock you out! The one at the far end of the avenue is only for serious party-people. Incidentally, the girls from the marina disco will tap lightly on the side of your yacht at night. You make the call, but don't be foolish.

There is a dry-dock area between the first two canals closest to the main road. Boats are attended to on the concrete apron where they can haul anything up to 6.35 tons on the marriage of a Japanese telescopic boom and Russian controls, with a 20-ton crane available on call. When I visited the mechanics, they assured me they could handle almost anything, from keel repairs and engine overhauls to fiberglass work. I was also told the stainless welder on duty was particularly good.

In the middle of 1993, a new service was introduced, whereby a van came around taking orders for groceries, vegetables and other supplies at wholesale prices. We received a quantity of *Pig's Eye* (a startlingly named, but perfectly drinkable American beer) at 60 cents, compared with $1.20 in the diplotiendas (see chapter two: Food & Water). The rest of what we ordered never arrived, although we were several times told that it was already in the back of the van and ready to be delivered, tomorrow.

At the entrance to the marina is the main Havana road. Turn left and take your bike if you want a work-out. It's about six or seven miles into the center of the city, but just half-a-mile along as you come to the first bridge; stop and look out towards the north. It will be your first view of a small local Cuban harbour. Just a tiny pool, but full of the most fascinating boats.

ENJOY A RIDE DOWN SHADED AVENUES

Continuing on your work-out, turn off diagonally to the right another half-a-mile along, where the sign directs you towards the New Latin-American Cinema. Here, you'll enjoy a most wonderful ride down dim avenues perfectly shaded in the middle of the day by huge overhanging banyan or bearded fig trees, and lined by amazing old houses. Dark and cool, even in the scorching heat of a midday sun, the area is called Residencial Siboney. Try Calle 190.

A taxi, called for you by the staff at the marina, will set you back about $12 U.S. to get into Havana, so make sure you plan your day properly. You will never forgive yourself if you miss spending an afternoon in Old Havana (Habana Vieja), one of the two Cuban cities placed on UNESCO's World Heritage list. It's worth every minute you spend there. And check out the surrounding streets, there are nuggets among the decaying structures.

TIENDA DE NAVIGANTES

Conveniently, the Tienda de Navigantes (where you can buy local charts) is in Old Havana, so you might wish to drop in there at the end of the day to obtain what you need.

It is beyond the intended scope of this book to function as a shoreside travel guide, but be prepared for a certain amount of culture-shock. If you've never before visited a Latin American city, your conception of noise and crowd etiquette may be at variance with normal practice, so get a good guide-book in Havana, or order one or two up in advance of your visit.

You may, for one reason or the other, need to leave the country by air. As mentioned before, you can leave the keys to your boat at the marina, whose staff will need to know of your plans, and if you wish you can make an arrangement to bring in any needed spares for your boat in your luggage. Ask the customs officers at the marina. They will only be too happy to give you a letter stating that you have a vessel docked there, and this will help with over-enthusiastic airport customs officials when you return. If you're doing this, why not ask around at the office to see if they need any bits and pieces which you could bring in for them?

Normally, you have to show a return ticket when entering Cuba by air, but if the original ticket has been bought in Havana, they won't put up a fight over this. If going to the U.S., there are direct flights weekly (unpublicized) to Miami, but you may prefer to fly to the Bahamas and then cross over to Ft. Lauderdale. Tickets are available through Havanaturs at around $145 return, and the trip from Nassau is around $60. No one knows it, but you can get an entry-visa for Cuba at the airport in Nassau at the airline desk.

Remember your passport will not be stamped upon entry or departure.

Flights are also available to Mexico, Jamaica, Ireland, Spain and other countries, and the airport ride will cost you around $18 by taxi.

The Russian Embassy building in Havana, imposing behind a barbed wire fence. (Photo by George Halloran)

LEAVING HAVANA
CHART NO. ICH 1124 (CUBAN)

It is important to have arranged all aspects of this procedure as far in advance as possible, so you should have already notified the marina staff in the office (señor Sanchez is the chief, along with señors Villorio, Gorki, Aramis, and whoever else is new) about your plans. In addition to being very friendly, they are always extremely helpful and efficient.

Presuming you are cruising the cays, then you should have already researched your probable route. Following the guidelines given before (chapter two: Leaving Port), ask for documentation allowing a certain flexibility, and do it at least two days in advance.

To ensure that all is right, you should make sure you've been issued with the Cruising Permit and Permiso de Salida (the Departure Permit with your route,) at least the night before leaving.

Once you have it, speak with the local customs officials at their post, halfway along the avenue in the marina, and assure them that you wish to leave early next morning. Seven o'clock will probably be a good time, and you should emphasize that your plans are not at all flexible in this regard.

If you need to top up your tanks, then inform the staff, and take your vessel round to the docks opposite the offices where the splendidly color-coded supply lines deliver clean fuel. Do not delay this operation until departure, as the immigration officers quite rightly won't wait long at the Guarda Frontera post.

On that subject, be firm when requesting their presence at 7 a.m. at the post as they've got to come 8 miles to clear you out, and you don't want them only just leaving Havana at the very time you should be clearing out. Failure to emphasize your departure day and time, can result in a three or four-hour delay, as I have witnessed several times.

MAKE YOUR DEPARTURE CERTAIN

Mind, you need to be sure that you're actually leaving, and not just sticking your head out to see what the conditions are like outside. A couple of years ago we tried three times to leave the harbour, each time arranging visits from all and sundry, only to abort in the face of the stiff northeast wind that had cooped us up for a week, as it drove heavy swells over the sea defenses. They'd come down to the boat, and we'd be so embarrassed.

We actually did manage to leave once, but were driven back in two hours, as the boat was on its beam-ends all the time. Returning, we had to go through the whole check-in procedure all over again, but this time accompanied by jeers!

You'll have to pay your bill at the offices, so get a receipt in case anyone asks about it in the morning and the office is closed.

Having crawled out of bed at 5 a.m. to prep the boat, you will be understandably disgruntled when 7 a.m. passes without a visit from the customs officer, but never mind, you can walk over to the post halfway along the main avenue and rouse him out of bed. He'll then show up grumbling and muttering, but otherwise in a cooperative enough frame of mind.

His part can be sorted out dockside, but sometimes if he's bored he'll choose to accompany your boat for the ride round to the Guarda Frontera post at the mouth of the harbour. If so, bring him aboard, slip your lines and depart in the early mist.

At the mouth of the harbour you will again have to stop for the usual formalities at the Guarda Frontera post. Here you will be visited by immigration, your vessel will receive a quick search, and they'll clear you outwards. The Guarda Frontera too will have their say in the matter before you get the all-important despacho, but if as before you've put all your relevant documents in their folder there won't be much trouble. Don't expect much change out of three-quarters of an hour though.

Exiting the channel is straightforward, 320°M with attention being paid to the width and the existence of snorkelers who will be in evidence as far as the outer channel marker, but as soon as you've cleared it you'll be in deeper water and can set course for Bahiá Honda.

PASSAGE TO BAHIA HONDA
CHART NO. ICH 1124 (CUBAN)

If you leave in a north or northeast wind of any strength you're likely to be in for a rough passage as the seas will be on the beam. Hopefully, you've scheduled things for an east wind, and even if it's blowing a bit outside the seas will be calm in the land's wind-shadow with only a gentle swell pushing you down the coast.

If you have decided to make an overnight run along the coast to arrive in the cays without a stop, then you can set a course of 268°M for about 40 miles while staying 2-3 miles offshore. This may be fine on a moonlit night, but be careful as there are likely to be few house or street lights ashore later on at night, and you will have to rely on navigational aids if there is no moon. The wall here is steep and close inshore without much warning of shoal-waters so let caution rule.

ROUTE TO BAHIA HONDA

At around longitude 083°15.00W, you'll be coming up on the cays and can begin to veer further round to the south. If by now it's still dark, then you may steer 250°M for the next 10 miles, whereupon it should be light and you should be ready to pick your way through the reef into Cayo Paraíso.

If, however, you're doing your first run in daylight, then an early departure should get you into Bahiá Honda in good time as it's only some 36 miles away. Position yourself a mile or so offshore, and you can make a visual passage all the way along a coast largely free of dangers.

Close inshore there won't be much in the way of current to slow you down, and you'll even get a little lift from a slight counter-current heading west southwest down the coast.

Along here the terrain is generally flat with lots of houses around Playa Baraco which gives way to green open spaces further along and a large flat topped hill, the Mesa de Mariel some 5 miles inland.

Your first notable landmarks will be the cement plant's chimneys smoking away some 15 miles further along the coast at Mariel, the port made famous by its boatlift to the U.S. some years ago. We won't be stopping here, but if you did wish to do so, it's a busy port (400 boats annually) inside a deep protected bay with a dredged entrance suitable for the deepest keel, and an entrance well marked and wide enough for all tastes.

FORBIDDEN AREAS

Within the bay it is strictly forbidden to approach to Angosta Peninsula with its airstrip or the Laza harbour (both southwest from the entrance), but you may proceed to the other large docks for instructions. The port is notable only for the boatlift, and there's not a lot of reason presently to visit unless you are fascinated by cement works and the dust they

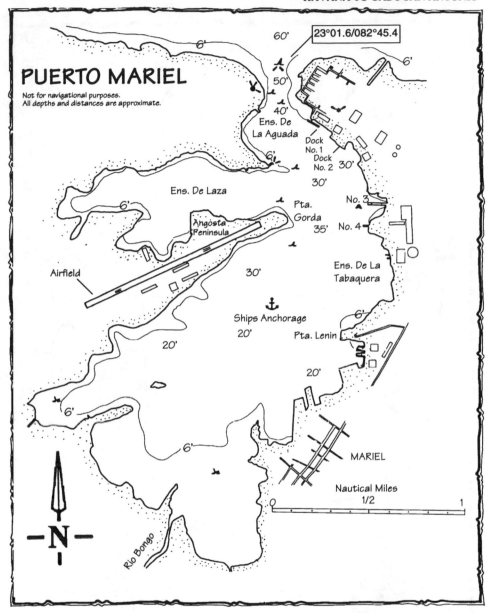

PUERTO MARIEL

Not for navigational purposes.
All depths and distances are approximate.

23°01.6/082°45.4

60'
6'
6'
50'
40'
Ens. De
La Aguada
Dock
No. 1
Dock
No. 2   30'
30'
Ens. De Laza
Pta.
Gorda
No. 3
35'   No. 4
Angosta
Peninsula
Airfield
30'
Ens. De La
Tabaquera
Ships Anchorage
20'
Pta. Lenin
20'
6'
6'
20'
6'
6'
MARIEL
Nautical Miles
1/2
0   1
Rio Bongo
–N–

spread, but it does appear to be a good shelter from a storm even if it meant abandoning Marina Hemingway.

Further down the coast you come to the Bay of Cabañas, a naval base off-limits to commercial traffic and cruisers. It is prohibited to anchor along the coast between longitudes 082° 57'W and 083°00'W. Ashore you'll see evidence of military training with the occasional beach defended by anti-landing craft devices, so I'd pass by unless I were interested in a really long-term stay. Around here you may encounter your first patrol boats too.

The terrain is still low-lying with slight escarpments on the western side of this extremely large bay, but right inland we begin to see the first glimpses of the Sierras de Rosario which may be strange for a North American visitor.

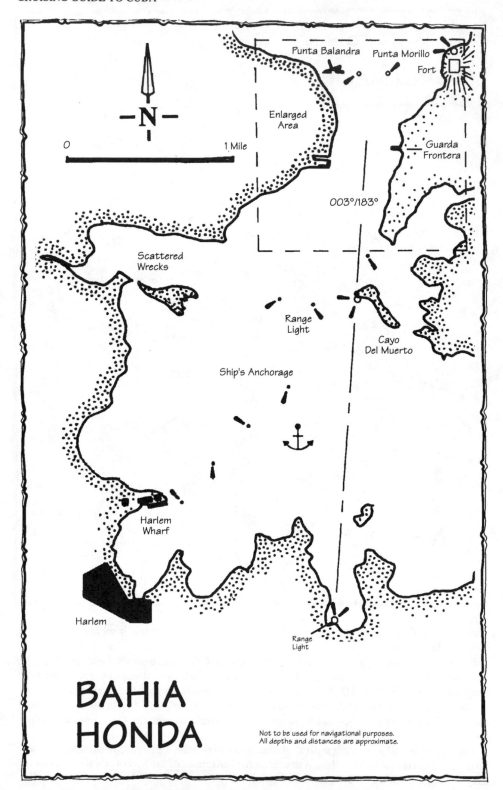

Punta Balandra

Punta Morillo

Fort

Enlarged
Area

Guarda
Frontera

003°/183°

Scattered
Wrecks

Range
Light

Cayo
Del Muerto

Ship's Anchorage

Harlem
Wharf

Harlem

Range
Light

BAHIA
HONDA

Not to be used for navigational purposes.
All depths and distances are approximate.

0

1 Mile

–N–

BAHIA HONDA

Among other things, a one-time graveyard for boats, this is where old or damaged commercial vessels were brought to be decommissioned and stripped for salvage. A point not lost on the cruiser, in light of the amount of wreckage he will see along the coasts.

Approaching the Bahiá Honda from Havana, you first see a large crane on the western side in from the entrance where there is a prominent lighthouse and a large rusting wreck run hard aground in the shallows. The eastern side has a small hill with conspicuous trees completely overgrowing the old fort of San Fernando, and in front of this is a short silver pylon-lighthouse partly concealed by vegetation.

Waves break inshore on the shallow fringing reefs, so you should remain a mile or so off (just along the wall), and aim towards the wreck outside the entrance at Punta Balandro. When you come into line with the range-marks and buoys in the channel, turn south heading 183°M, past more wreckage inside the point.

If you were coming in along the wall from the west, then your course should be a heading towards the hill with the invisible fort and the barely visible light, keeping slightly outside the wreck, then turn with the markers in line.

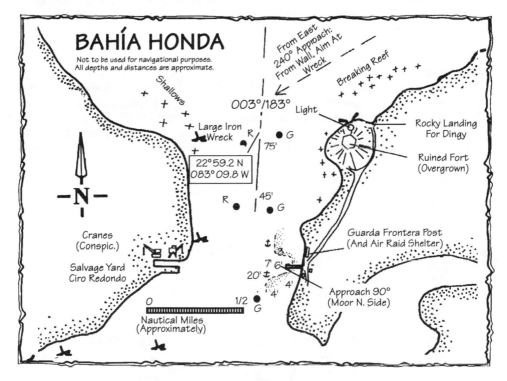

To port, just a few hundred yards past the fort's elevation, you will see a small dock with a shed on the end and fishing boats moored all round. A patrol boat stationed there gives the clue, so this is the Guarda Frontera post we need to contact.

Alongside the spindly little wharf, there is a small beach and a couple of scattered buildings painted drab grey, near the pink Guarda Frontera hut with its antenna and flag.

Trickle in at 90°M towards the rickety dock, carefully, because the depth is extremely shallow anywhere off line, and pull alongside the left of the low wharf, ensuring your fenders are properly positioned equally low-down in advance. The passage from the main ship's channel is quite narrow, perhaps no more than 20 feet wide and 6 or 7 feet deep, all the way over soft mud, but can be accomplished without drama.

There will be masses of spectators slack-jawed at your approach; old fishermen, girls scratching their bellies, naked children and hurrying Guarda Frontera. We once found them openly butchering a cow on the dock as we docked there, throwing the offal into the water off the end!

Your papers will be inspected, as though this were the first time it's happened, and further conversation will indeed confirm this. They don't get a lot of visitors here.

As always, it is important to inform the Guarda Frontera that you are going to be using your dinghy later on, and once your papers have been attended to, you should pull away carefully towards deeper water.

If you wish to be near the fort, you can anchor northeast of the large green buoy to the south of the dock in about 20-40 feet, or wherever the press of fishing boats allow.

On the other side, opposite your dock, there is a concrete harbour facility (the Dársena Ciro Redondo) with cranes and other equipment for stripping vessels. It has the appearance of disuse, and as confirmed by local fishermen, most of the six or seven wrecks around here were sunk before they could be attended to! In fact, given the relative newness of some, I doubt that they all actually arrived with this intention in mind.

At the bottom end of the bay you will see the port of Harlem with its square housing blocks (eastern block architecture prevailing over good taste), watched over by the Sierra del Rosario.

The wharfs there are used for hazardous cargos.

APPROACHING THE FORT

The fort can be approached by road from the dock, but you may find it easier to use the dinghy, going round the point to a protected, if shallow, landing area northeast of the hill. The fort is seriously overgrown, and the mosquitos are going to thank you for your visit, but this is what you've come to Cuba for. Entering, you'll have to scale the walls, using vines, if you can't find the breach in the northeast corner.

After this you can take the dinghy further in towards the south of the bay and cruise around the cays inside. There are beaches on the Cayo del Muerto (Hmm...), near the first range-mark at Punta Difuntos, and if you prefer this environment, you can ask the Guarda Frontera if you may moor there instead of near the dock. They shouldn't give you any trouble about this.

If you wish to leave your tender in the water overnight, attach it carefully with regard to security, and in the morning when you're ready to resume your cruise, take it in to the dock to collect your despacho rather than maneuver alongside. It's always quicker this way.

When leaving, follow the line of the range-marks (003°M) at least 200 yards past the outer mark. If you turn along the coast too soon you'll be in shallow water in no time at all. Make your turn along the coast when abreast of the light or the low wooded headland, and follow the wall a half-mile off the breakers on the reef. If you do stray in over the wall, you'll still find 50-70 feet of water, which is good enough for me, and as with all coastal navigation around here, if you can't see anything below you're "off the wall."

COURSE TO CAYO PARAÍSO
CHART NO. ICH 1124 (CUBAN)

It's only a 15-mile run further down the coast to the first of our stops along the cays, but it's best to leave early in the morning so the sun will be high for your first reef entrance. When you're at the cay, you'll also have time for some exploring, or maybe a sunlit wreck-dive in shallow water.

By now the coastline has begun to curve gradually towards the west southwest, bringing it into the lee of the prevailing easterly, and the waters should exhibit only a gentle swell as you can fishtail along with the genoa boomed right out.

Remain in over the wall in whatever depth keeps you happy, and you'll gain at least a knot by staying out of the northeast current. For the first couple of miles the bottom will become dark green at around 30-40 feet from the turtle grass which grows in such depths.

After you pass the small harbour of Morillo (8 miles along, around 083°19'), you'll begin to see the cays and the Colorados Reef, which will now extend all the way along the coast as far as the western tip of Cuba and the first of those cays is Cayo Paraíso. Remain a bit further off any breakers along the reef now (about 500 yards) in 30-40 feet of water, as closer to Cayo Paraíso there are scattered heads of elkhorn coral in 15-20 feet, and these reach up to within a foot or two of the surface. The waves this far in from the wall may not be strong enough to cause breakers, so look out for the other clues, such as swells or color change (orange/olive tinge).

CAYO PARÁISO (PARADISE CAY)

Cayo Paraíso is a small cay shaped much like an inverted crescent, and is currently undergoing a rather half-hearted refurbishment with a view to installing facilities for tourists and yachts. Nevertheless, the work is progressing in such a desultory fashion that I wouldn't hold out too many hopes that it will be completed when you get there. When we were last there, the two inhabitants had only reached the stage of collecting palm-fronds for roofing the hut frames, but Cuba is still full of occasional surprises.

Be aware that you are not the first to visit this delightful little spot. Ernest Hemingway beat you to it some 50 years ago, making it his cruising base for quite some time, even to the extent of conducting naval operations from there during the second world war!

The entrance does require some care, so study the two drawings, which give very subjective impressions of both the entrance and the layout. As you cruise west parallel to the reef, make your turn 180° south some 300 yards east of the cay at about 083°25.50'W (roughly as shown). There are elkhorn coral patches below the water approximately

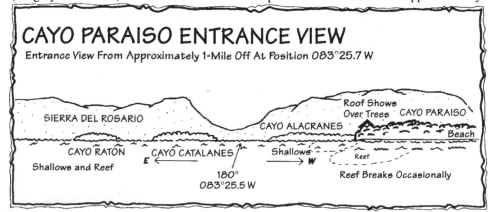

CAYO PARAISO ENTRANCE VIEW
Entrance View From Approximately 1-Mile Off At Position 083°25.7 W

SIERRA DEL ROSARIO

CAYO ALACRANES

Roof Shows Over Trees   CAYO PARAISO

Beach

CAYO RATON   CAYO CATALANES   Shallows   Reef

Shallows and Reef

E ←   → W

180°
083°25.5 W

Reef Breaks Occasionally

1/4-mile east of this longitude, so be on the lookout, and if you've come within 200 yards of the island, you've come too far west also.

Enter along your course, being aware of the shoals close to the island on your right, and aim to the left of a turquoise patch of sand ahead where the water is too shallow for safety. At this stage, paralleling the eastern side of the island, the depth will be 10-12 feet, and continuing on you can begin to make a gradual right turn through two sandbanks off the southeast tip. One of the sandpits extends some 300-feet out from the island, but both are are quite obvious through the water and are also marked by stakes or whithies between which you pass (25°55.2'N / 083°25.9'W).

Once into the underbelly of the island in 10-feet of water you can anchor or ease up to any of the narrow docks extending from the left side near a collection of thatch huts, and go about your business unmolested by any form of officialdom or Guarda Frontera.

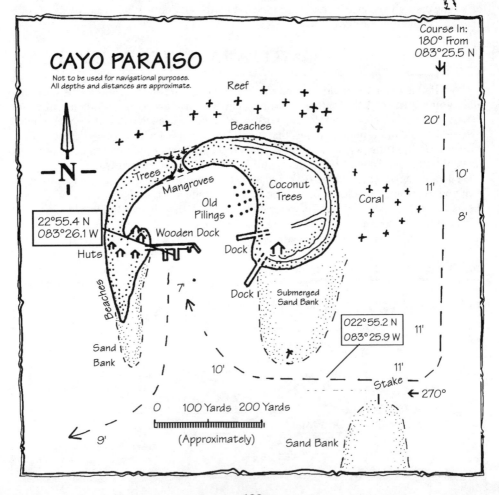

CAYO PARAISO

Not to be used for navigational purposes.
All depths and distances are approximate.

Course In: 180° From 083°25.5 N

Reef

Beaches

20'

10'

Trees

Mangroves

Coconut Trees

Coral

11'

8'

22°55.4 N 083°26.1 W

Old Pilings

Wooden Dock

Dock

Huts

Dock

7'

Dock

Submerged Sand Bank

022°55.2 N 083°25.9 W

11'

Beaches

Sand Bank

10'

11'

Stake ←270°

0   100 Yards 200 Yards

9'

(Approximately)

Sand Bank

> *"From the beginning of the 1940's this place was the refuge of the great North American author Ernest Hemingway who visited it assiduously, sometimes remaining on the cay for up to 20 days at a time. Here he wrote, rested, roamed the beach, swam, and loved it so much he used it as a base for anti-submarine operations from his yacht "El Pilar" during the Second World War. In his memory, on the 90th anniversary of his birth."* **Provincial Commission of Monuments. Piñar del Rio, 21 July, 1989**

As evidence of the veneration in which Ernest Hemingway is held by literate Cuba, there is a small monument placed close to the dock on the southwest end of the island. It is translated roughly into English in the box to the left.

There is a small diesel generator behind the huts, so perhaps by the time you get there the island will have electricity, but in any case you will find this an ideal spot for a short stay in peaceful surroundings. You may walk around the island in 20 minutes using the beaches and an internal track through the trees, but if you prefer not to deal with the low lying area between the two halves, then take the dinghy across to the eastern side.

If you feel like a swim, dinghy out towards the reef to hunt lobster (lots around here), or northeast of the island where there are the flattened remains of an old iron vessel wrecked in about 15 or 20 feet of water. Anyone on the island can tell you where it is, but if you have a hand-held GPS the coordinates are: 22°56.3N / 083°25.2W. In any case, the wreckage is spread about over an area the size of two tennis courts, and it can be clearly seen from the surface. So if you wish you can prospect for it from the dinghy and snorkel down over the wreck.

In early evening, the already considerable insect noise will rise somewhat, and you'd better be ready with the repellant. This will probably be your first real onslaught.

CAYO LEVISA

This is a larger (but still relatively small) cay not more than five or six miles to the west of Paraíso and visible from your overnight mooring. It's a straightforward inside run across the calm sound, and if you leave in the morning taking either of two routes, you can find yourself enjoying a wide variety of cocktails by midday.

Using the inside route, leave Cayo Paraíso past the sandbank, which extends out from the southwest tip, and take up a visual course (240°M) towards the northern outside edge of Cayo Levisa where you may faintly make out buildings and huts. Along this inside route the water is largely free of danger and never less than 8 feet, but over by the reef, you will see bright turquoise patches denoting shallow sand.

Coming up on the protruding end of Cayo Alcranes to your left, the water will shelve to seven feet for a second if you go too close, so hold your course looking back frequently to see that you are still in line with the southwest tip of Paraíso and continue towards the northern edge of Levisa.

Begin to veer left about half-a-mile off Levisa (at 083°30.0'W), taking a course of 212° M towards the northeastern tip of Cayo Dios, which sticks out from the mainland over to the southwest, and this will take you past a sandbank on the east of the island and round underneath it.

When you are clear of the sandbank, you may once again go west between the two cays towards the derelict barge and the wharf now showing halfway along the bottom edge of Levisa.

AN ALTERNATE ROUTE

If you don't feel confident about such shallow water navigation, then you will find a deep and wide marked channel, the Pasa San Carlos, about 2.5 miles west of the cay at longitude 083°35.0'W, and you could quite easily take the outside route there and back round. Enter the marked channel and make your turn east, when Cayo Levisa shows well clear of the mainland cays at Punta Purgatorio.

A STRAIGHTFORWARD APPROACH

Cayo Levisa has a sturdy dock on the south, just east of a couple of irregular mangrove protrusions out from the shoreline. The approach is straightforwards apart from a shallow patch southwest of the wharf, and you can come in from almost head on. The depth is anything up to 20 feet, but the various boats which bring in fresh water and supplies to the island use the outer end, so you take the western edge where it is a bit shallower. A couple of curious sailors might assist with your lines, but apart from this there won't be any official reception, and you can just wander in and about the island at your leisure.

The dock is about 8 feet wide and 100 feet long, with quaint lamps along its length and a green light at the outer end (which will shine in your windows). Following the elevated wooden walkway 200-300 yards through the mangroves will bring you to the hotel com-

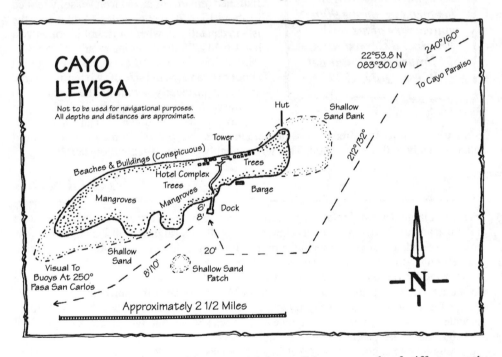

plex over on the north coast, where you might as well have a couple of stiff ones at the outside bar while getting the lay of the land.

The hotel complex is Spanish owned (Euroeste), but entirely Cuban operated and has a bar (naturally), restaurant, bakery, scuba shop, and some 20 cabanas. Visitors are ferried in from the mainland to the dock, and if you're there when anyone arrives in the off-season, you might see the congregated staff singing songs of welcome with guitars twanging, maracas shaking, much shouting, back slapping, and bags held high overhead as they're carried along the duckboards.

Emotional yes, but what a way to arrive. And no, it does not seem some propaganda-show staged by the government. The hotel also has a VHF base station, "Cayo

Levisa" on 19, if you fancy a similar welcome.

Tours are offered to the mainland, which might be one way of taking in as much of the rugged hinterland as possible, without having to rent cars. You can visit tobacco factories and rum distilleries, all-inclusive for about $35. There are boat-tours offering submerged rivers in the caverns near Piñar del Rio in the mountains or out to the cays, where you can cook your own fresh-caught lobster.

Tourism is mainly concentrated in July and August when a lot of Spanish visitors arrive, but off-season the place is likely to be quite deserted, and you will have the 3.5 km of white sandy beaches to yourself. You can play with the hotel's Hobie-Cats and catch up on really quick responsive boats, like the ones you used to sail.

When we were last here (late September), there were only four guests, and we did some diving along the coast as guests of Alberto, the Harley-Davidson owning hotel dive-guide. He's been exploring some new sites (among the forests of black-coral along the walls at Pasa San Carlos), which were quite spectacular, especially when compared with the Florida Keys not 90 miles away to the north!

It's well worth taking supper at the resort, both for the break, and also to give something back to the local economy. Dining is buffet style, and considerably better (for less too) than anything offered in the cities like Havana. A local idiosyncrasy here is the custom of weaving your name into the various songs you'll be serenaded with during supper.

Various members of the staff also eat in the communal dining room, serving themselves along with the guests, and this brings up another point with which the visitor may not be as yet familiar.

Perhaps in part due to your being a bit weird (all cruisers are...), and perhaps in part due to Cuban egalitarianism, a staff member with whom you have been earlier chatting (we always chatter away with everyone), may well catch your eye and bring his plate over to accompany you at your table during your meal. As long as you're not deliberately looking for solitude that evening, it's a great way to dine.

We always end up eating with delightful people, and loving it.

Leaving Cayo Levisa for the west is merely a matter of watching out for the shallow patch off to the southwest of the dock, and heading towards the inner buoy at the Pasa San Carlos along a course of roughly 250°M once past the island. From there you can head on towards Cayo Jutías along the outer route, or if you'd prefer to be slightly more adventurous you can take the inner passage most of the way.

If you're really adventurous you can take the inside *all* the way, but this is very tricky. You'll need a draft of 4-foot or less, a high vantage point (e.g., a flybridge), and probably a long keel to minimize the consequences of occasional grounding, but if you can do this one, you can go anywhere!

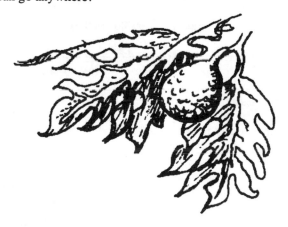

A bicycle provides the means for transporting two large water containers. (Photo by George Halloran)

ROUTES TO CAYO JUTIAS, ESPERANZA OR SANTA LUCIA
CHART NO.ICH 1123 (CUBAN)

There is no substitute for the correct charts here if you wish peace of mind along the inside, so if you do not have the Cuban charts, then it will be best to take the outer route only entering along marked channels. The older large-scale U.S. charts don't have the required detail for much more.

Outer Route:

You should head out through the main channel at Pasa San Carlos (083° 35.0'W) 4 miles west of Levisa, and parallel the wall outside the reef, following your usual method of coasting until coming to the marked entrances.

Quebrado San Cayetano for La Esperanza (enter 083°43.0'W and go southeast after entering).

Pasa Honda for Santa Lucía (wide and clearly marked at 083°59.0'W).

Quebrado la Galera west of Cayo Jutías, cutting back into a well-sheltered nook called Nombre de Dios.

These entrances are sometimes a bit vague on the charts, but on approach they become quite obvious and combined with any sort of vigilance, you will have no trouble at all nipping in and out through the reef. In fact the charts, even the most up to date revisions, do not show the recent buoyage into the above channels.

No matter which route you do in fact take, there will nevertheless be a marvellous view of the Sierra Organos running the length of the mainland here. This steep-sided range of velvet mountains makes a beautiful inland backdrop, with a slanting sun shadowing valleys into the deepest green, rather like the mountains of Macchu Picchu or Rio de Janeiro. They are not enormously high, but perfectly amazing, especially if you're coming in from somewhere low-lying like the Gulf or East Coast of the U.S.

Inner Route:

I've been assured by local fishermen that there are no coral heads along the edge of Cayo Levisa, but the depth does oscillate between 8-18 feet over turtle-grass until you leave the cay behind.

Go west towards the inner range-marker at San Carlos pass, then approximately 245°M to pass between two small cays (Arenas and Berracos) some 4.5 miles across the bay at 22°51.0'N / 083°35.1'W, whereupon you aim outside of the outermost cays another 7 miles west, looking out for depth changes and steering round the shallower spots.

There are two routes further on, both requiring care. One goes outside of those cays ahead, and the other, more interesting, takes you through a narrow channel in the southwest corner of the bay of **Playuelas** close to the town of La Esperanza (there's a slipway there if you needed one).

The first route requires no explanation, but for the second, you should turn towards La Esperanza when it lies due south, and then closely parallel the coast until you're almost sure you're going to run into the cays.

PLAYUELAS ANCHORAGE

The entrance will suddenly open up right in the corner at 22°46.3'N/083°45.3'W presenting a short (100 yards) channel which is marked by stakes. It is 30 yards wide and has good deep water once inside, especially if you keep to the southern bank.

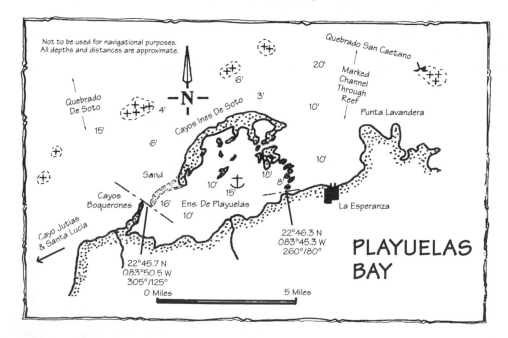

Not to be used for navigational purposes.
All depths and distances are approximate.

Quebrado San Caetano

Quebrado De Soto

Cayos Ines De Soto

20'

Marked Channel Through Reef

Punta Lavandera

15'

10'

3'

10'

6'

6'

4'

10'

Sand

10'

15'

10'

8'

La Esperanza

Cayos Boquerones

16'

Ens. De Playuelas

10'

Cayo Jutias & Santa Lucia

22°45.7 N
083°50.5 W
305°/125°

22°46.3 N
083°45.3 W
260°/180°

PLAYUELAS BAY

0 Miles   5 Miles

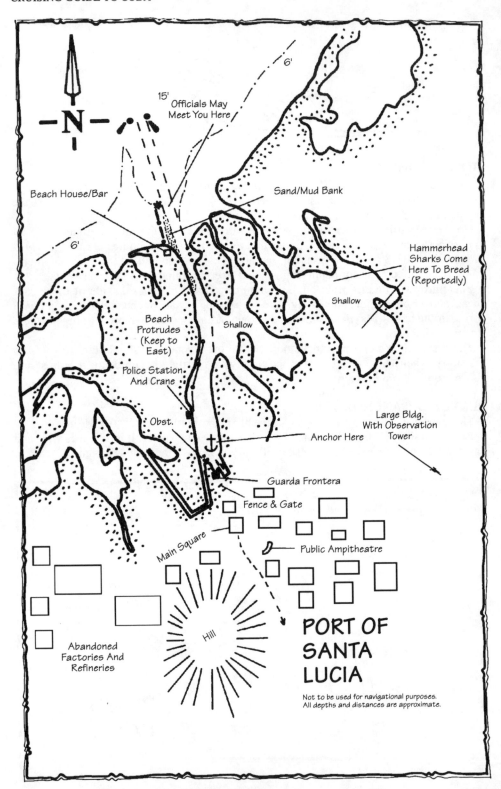

-N-

6'

15'
Officials May
Meet You Here

Beach House/Bar

Sand/Mud Bank

Hammerhead
Sharks Come
Here To Breed
(Reportedly)

6'

Shallow

Beach
Protrudes
(Keep to
East)

Shallow

Police Station
And Crane

Obst.

Large Bldg.
With Observation
Tower

Anchor Here

Guarda Frontera

Fence & Gate

Main Square

Public Ampitheatre

Abandoned
Factories And
Refineries

Hill

PORT OF
SANTA
LUCIA

Not to be used for navigational purposes.
All depths and distances are approximate.

Having passed through, you will find yourself in a secure, enclosed bay some 2 miles wide with cays curving round to the north. The other exit is 4 miles over to the other side, right at the tip of the cays reaching out from the land on a course of 260°M. A sheltered anchorage indeed.

The exit is narrower than shown on the charts due to a spit of sand extending down southwest from the end of the northern cays at Punta Hicacal. It is not clearly marked on charts, but again the bank is quite obvious, and once there you can take up a course of 305°M out through a short staked channel 50 yards wide at 22°45.7'N/083°50.5'W.

Once back into the main sound inside the Colorados reef, Cayo Jutías will be visible 10 miles away, where it sticks out from the land just past Santa Lucía. So you have time to make your decision about your destination over the next hour or two.

SANTA LUCIA

Santa Lucía is a smaller port catering to the shipment of sulfuric acid and copper ore, offering repair and towing facilities for vessels in difficulties. It actually is a sub-port of Mariel and comes under the administration of the port of La Coloma over on the other side of the peninsula. There's not a lot here, and the facilities are presently a bit run down, but you may wish to visit if this sort of thing appeals to you.

The port itself is set back inside a buoyed channel through the mangroves, as per the adjacent drawing, and if you do wish to enter, you will likely be met by a Guarda Frontera boat at the entrance and escorted to the Guarda Frontera post inside. Suggestions may be made about anchoring away from the actual docks themselves, but if you do this, you'd best look-out for swim-aboard thievery as friends of ours experienced.

They were moored inside the harbour, working on a burned-out alternator below with a couple of officials actually on board, when someone attempted to climb in quietly.

A PROTECTED ANCHORAGE

If you wish to anchor out, then you may seek shelter over to the cays a mile or two northwest of the port, on one side or the other of Cayo Jutías.

This is a long cay along the line of the coast, and joined to it by a loose series of smaller cays with a rock causeway (pedraplén), currently under construction for road access. Unless you wish to search for space amongst the creeks at the northern end, the best shelter is available on the other side to the west.

You can exit the reef at the well-marked channel north of Santa Lucía through the Pasa Honda, 2.5 miles east of the light on the cay, then continue on until the entrance, just past the reefs west of Jutías at Quebrada La Galera. Apply normal precautions when re-entering.

Although there is a beautifully sheltered bay inside Jutías at the anchorage Nombre de Dios, it is important to note that there is a soft shallow bar some 6 feet deep extending from the tip of Jutías towards the small protruding landside cay. If you prefer not to have to deal with this, then progress on to the shelter at Rio del Medio 5 miles southwest of the entrance instead.

AN EXCITING, TRICKY ROUTE

If the pedraplén (the causeway) one mile west of Santa Lucía has not progressed much further than 22°42.0'N, there is an exciting and tricky way through the cays joining Jutías to the mainland, but this should only be attempted with a shallow draft vessel and an adventurous spirit. Behind the unfinished causeway, there is an area of shallow water into which you may gently pick your way looking for the break, but speeds will have to be low, a look out must be posted and be prepared to back off.

If the following appears a bit imaginative, we nevertheless did it with no instructions or guidance, using our 34-foot trawler, a vague rumor and nothing else.

An example of Cuban art is this portrait in a museum. (Photo by George Halloran)

Rounding the tip of the causeway at 084°00.5W, you turn back to the south into sometimes not much more than 4-5 feet, (over turtle-grass) while looking for a couple of whithies marking the channel through. Remain in the exact center between the causeway and the cays, while trickling along until at 22°41.48'N, and suddenly in 7 feet of water, you can turn west towards the two small whithies, marking an extremely narrow (no more than 35-40 feet) channel, with no obvious exit.

The channel at first narrows after the entrance (at 22°41.47'N / 084°00.71'W), and you'll be so close to the banks that overhanging trees will sometimes brush your rigging, leaving small branches and twigs all over the decks. I won't track all the twists of this amazing labyrinth of tributaries surrounded by the cry of birds, leaping needle-fish, and tightly closed in on all sides (including above), but make progress generally westwards, and look for the current at the forks where there is no obvious indication of the correct channel.

Note the current inside the first few yards and remember the direction. It will likely be flowing through from one side of the cays to the other, so if the tide is moving the reeds below in the correct direction, then you are likely on the right track. Slack water in one tributary compared with another, can be an indication of no exit that way.

So, press on (okay, if you have to use directions then take the first fork right, and the next is a left) for half-a-mile, and after the most amazing passage, you'll burst out into the full light of day again. Stakes mark the western end at 22°40.93'N / 084°01.05'W, and you can now head for a welcome anchorage in the snug shelter of Nombre de Dios bay.

If you can't manage the shallows near the causeway, but can still get round into Nombre de Dios, then a dinghy ride into the maze here will be a welcome diversion. I still remember every minute of my time here.

ANCHOR ANYWHERE IN THE BAY

Anchor anywhere you want in Nombre de Dios Bay. Around here, you sometimes see the most marvelous jellyfish pulsing along their way just below the surface, and flights of herons or cranes gliding above with extended necks and inquisitive beaks. The mosquitos here can be fierce in the evening and morning during summer, so you may prefer to remain further away from the cays. Remember this exposes you more so check the anchor's holding.

In the bay here, I remember the mosquitos were relatively invisible during the day, later descending in an avalanche of lust at some secret signal in the early evening and dawn. Your screens had better be tight-fitting, as in the morning you might just see 30-40 of them gazing in hungrily at you.

ROUTES TO LA FE AND CABO SAN ANTONIO
CHART NO. ICH 1122 & 1123 (CUBAN)

This route will take you along the Clorados reef, past the end of the Sierras de Los Organos and into the Gulf of Guanahacabibes (you'll need to practice this one), where continuing as far as the tip of the peninsula at Cabo San Antonio the land becomes progressively more uninhabited. The Peninsula de Guanahacabibes is lined with mangrove along the northern shoreline, but for the rest largely covered with scrub. It is more or less a nature reserve now, with a few buildings at the extreme west where there are facilities for tending the lighthouse and pilot services.

LEAVING THE BAY OF NOMBRE DE DIOS

Leaving the bay of Nombre de Dios, pay attention to the bar which exists at the western end, then steer about 238°M to clear the tip of the little cay Alonso Rojas, 6 miles away. There are a couple of buoys (uncharted) just off the cay, so continue on outside them towards Punta Tabaco, the next cay, another 5 miles across the bay. These buoys also mark a convenient pass through the reef to the outside.

Caution: About 2 miles north of **Punta Tabaco**, and east of the large white-girdered lighthouse, there is a charted reef which seems to have grown considerably since survey. It now has trees growing there and extends eastwards with scattered obstructions below the surface to 22°36.0N / 084°12.1W (just where the chart shows 8-9 feet of water).

The lights erected on the reef grow more numerous along this stretch, but judging by the scattered wrecks near any of a dozen lights around the coast, I'd not be attracted to them at night like a moth, but rather use them as warnings to stay away. Passing about three-quarters-of-a-mile below the light at Punta Tabaco, you can see the breakers along the reef, and even though it may be mirror-calm inside, you'll be surprised to see the amount of waves over on the horizon outside the sound.

By now there should be a collection of cays (Rapados Grande and Chico) coming up ahead of you, and first steering close to the light at Cabezo Seco, you can approach them from the north. Here you will come across the first of the wharfs, which are a feature of Cuban fishing practice.

These freestanding wharfs are not necessarily connected to any body of land, but rather built onto piling in water deep enough to enable fishing craft to moor alongside. Here, the catch may be landed temporarily, stores taken on, and the crews may rest a few days. For a description of these "acopios," see my later remarks in the section dealing with Cayos de La Leña towards the end of the chapter.

If you wish to anchor overnight around here, you may find the best shelter is available in the lee of these cays, or even a mile or two on at Cayo Buenavista. We've used them all, dodging from one to the other depending on wind-shifts.

A WARNING OF AN UPCOMING BLOW

A couple of years ago (having arrived dog-tired after an overnight run from Havana), we moored in the shallow bay on the north coast of Buenavista and fell asleep early in the afternoon. Some time later a fishing boat with uniforms aboard drew close alongside, roused us naked from our bunk and promptly shouted across that they didn't want to see any documents. They had only come to tell us they expected the northeast wind to rise later, and why didn't we move around to better water on the other side, or over towards Rapado Chico.

On that occasion, we showed our papers only *once* after Havana, and that was when clearing out from Cayo Largo halfway down the south coast near the Bay of Pigs!

ROUND OUTSIDE THE CAY

Going round to the south of Buenavista can best be done outside the cay, between it and the reef.

If passing through the shallow inside passage, keep in the center of the Santa Maria channel, and beware an even shallower patch protruding slightly west southwest of that shown on the charts at Punta Las Orillas. The water around there is crystal clear, and this at least makes for good vision to the bottom. My records, in fact, say that we could see, "Every blade of turtle-grass, every starfish, every urchin...," and we still ran aground adding our propellor tracks to those already scarring the bottom off the point.

If going to Los Arroyos behind Buenavista, the best approach would be made from the northwest head on in 10-feet of water.

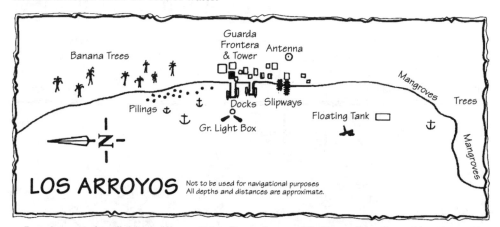

Los Arroyos is a fishing village with a fleet of some 50-60 small craft working the gulfs of Mexico and Guanahacabibes. The boats anchor off the port, having discharged their catches alongside the two small docks, so exercise caution when approaching. There is a watchtower, a green light guiding you in, and two small slipways here too, which you could use in an emergency. It's surrounded by banana trees and connected by road to the nearby town of Mantua, but you're still going to be a long way off from any good highways elsewhere.

THE GULF BEGINS TO WIDEN

The Gulf of Guanahacabibes now begins to widen considerably, with depths dropping gradually down to 60 feet, and criss-crossed with deep stands of coral separated by sand. A scuba diver or snorkeler can spend a lot of time there, and along the reef with the outer wall only a few yards further off. The waters are crystal clear, and the abundance of marine life is a tribute to benign neglect.

Your Loran too will still be giving excellent information, so it can be relied on where there are no landmarks or buoyed channels.

On the other hand, if you prefer to remain close in to land, you may set a visual course all along the coastline from now on, remaining a few hundred yards off in whatever depth you choose.

Continuing on from Arroyos, the coastline veers south, and the inland terrain becomes flatter with slight hillocks and open areas dotted by isolated trees.

Along here, you may see smoke quietly rising from the sugar-cane fields as they burn off the leaves and scatter the snakes prior to harvesting, and you might occasionally also hear loud explosions too, with its own distinct type of smoke. We thought it was from quarrying, but one of the local officials informed me it was from army maneuvers.

The **Ensenada de Guardiana** is a deep bay east of the widest point of the gulf, itself containing a smaller bay further in the extreme eastern corner. This is the bay of Juan Lopez, with the town of La Fé nestled inside at the entrance to the river Guardiana.

The first part of the river is navigable by shallow draft boats and is used as a refuge in times of really bad weather, but in any case the whole bay at Juan Lopez is enclosed on most sides.

LA FE & JUAN LOPEZ BAY

The entrance is marked by a large red/white buoy (22°01.24N / 084°19.93W), which is in fact, now only white with accumulated bird-droppings. The outer mark shown on the charts is no longer there, but this is a perfectly straightforward entrance which needs no aids to navigation at all.

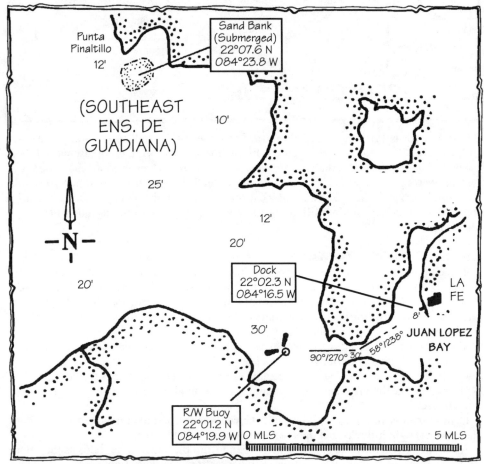

Enter via the center of the channel, and you can head directly across the bay on a general course of 60°M to La Fé, which will be visible 2 miles away against a lovely backdrop of hills.

It's a tiny picturesque little place with red-roofed white buildings, a red and white antenna and a watchtower looking suspiciously over the bay, in case the enemy ever does arrive. The better buildings tend to be along the northern end of the town, with more humble affairs closer to the only wharf on the south side.

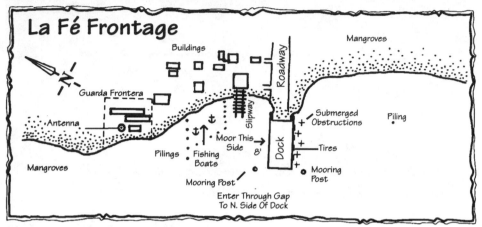

La Fé Frontage

Approach the sturdy Russian-built concrete wharf only on its left (north). Although there are tire fenders strung along the right side, the bottom there is fouled by debris jettisoned over the edge. Slip between the mooring post off the end and the wharf itself (the gap is about 20 feet), and moor alongside.

There is a slipway right next to the dock with a couple of yards depth outside, and in spite of its rather dilapidated appearance we have been told it could handle our boat if necessary.

The Guarda Frontera barracks is a grey building 100 yards to the north, and they'll come out to the wharf as soon as you approach, but do not allow them to remove your documents. They do not get much in the line of visitors here, and may even request that you don't take the dirt roads far inland, but the local inhabitants are friendly in the extreme. Your vessel will be the center of attention, and what appears to be a goodly proportion of them will find themselves out to the end of the dock, where they'll sit with their legs dangling and stare curiously inside your cabin.

PLANNER'S THEORY HAS BROKEN DOWN

You may notice along the coasts out here that the centralized distribution and grandiose theories of the planners has somewhat broken down. The townships along here are more obviously deprived, compared to what might pass for basics in the more privileged (yes, privilege does exist in Cuba) areas of Havana, but the people who actually have to live with it are still remarkably friendly, in spite of it all.

In the morning you may be roused by large black vultures coughing and flapping their wings as they strut the wharf outside. So, having collected your despacho (remember that one?) and departed the southeast corner of the Gulf of Guanahacabibes, you are left with an easy run along the low coastline to the west. Navigation along here is purely visual along an unremarkable shore for the next 30 miles, whereupon **Los Cayos de la Leña** (firewood cays) stand out from the peninsula and offer an enclosed shelter.

A Cuban fisherman sets out in a small boat. (Photo by Simon Charles)

CABO SAN ANTONIO
CHART NO. ICH 1122 (CUBAN)

This is the final destination on the northwest coast of Cuba. It is the place to rest up for an early morning trip round the cape and on towards the southeast, or from which you start your return journey back up the coast.

FISHERMAN'S DOCK AT CAYOS DE LA LENA

As you can see from the chart showing Cabo San Antonio in the following chapter, these cays offer excellent shelter within the bight, while still remaining close to the cape. A little distance off the western side there is a small dock offering facilities for local fishing vessels, and it may be approached along a direct line from the tip of Punta Cajón over to the west. We have been invited (always request permission before docking) to remain a day or two, waiting on suitable weather for rounding the cape, and have enjoyed tremendous hospitality from the simplest of people here.

A wire netting cage in the water can, rather unfortunately, sometimes contain empty turtle-shells being naturally cleaned of bloody shreds by fish. Sad, but that's how it goes.

The dock, at a position of 21°53.9N/084°50.7W, is constructed of wooden pilings and situated well away from land to allow access by various types of small fishing vessels. There is a small shed at one end with a diesel generator supplying power to the main building, and there are living quarters for the four or five workers who call it home. When we were there last we saw a litter of piglets suckling noisily away in the back room!

At the front in the main room, which doubles as an office, there were the most fascinating posters depicting a smartly dressed group of middle class citizens, complete with shirts, ties, and creased trousers, calmly leading frocked children to safety while a mushroom-cloud rose behind in the background. Meanwhile, Che Guevarra smiled benignly down from the walls, with a cigarette dangling negligently between his fingers.

If you dock at the southern end, you'll be well out of the way, well placed to observe a life which few people are even aware of, and if you're at all sociable your boat will be the scene of much friendly coming and going.

There is casual tarpon fishing right off the dock, and I have actually witnessed an epic battle between one of those fighting monsters and an elderly Cuban with a *hand line*! You should have seen the state of his hands by the time the heroic fish broke free.

A portion of the catch brought in is salted here too, so you may want to bargain for some which can be prepared in a variety of delicious ways particular to the Caribbean. Try it in fish-cakes, or even in a coconut and tomato sauce (a Bahiána, Brazilian style).

Finally, ice is kept there in an insulated storeroom off the main building, and if your boat is running a bit low it's a good time to stock up.

If you choose instead to anchor a mile or two closer to the cape, in the wide-open bay of Cajon, then be careful about the holding near the shore. The bottom there can be smooth rock in some places, offering little or no grip, and northeasterlies can set up swells which are capable of dislodging an anchor only half-set on a single fluke. Better to moor a little further out where the grip is better.

Interestingly, the water close inside this area of the coast is extremely dark, obscuring the flat, shallow bottom in a few feet, whereas off the desolate tip of Cajon the waters again become as clear as a fine vodka, and half a mile or so northeast of the point the bottom is scored with ravines.

Along the coastline where it swings northwards at Los Morros, there are a couple of small landing areas, and there's even a tiny concrete step at the waterside where you can moor a dinghy if you wish to trek into the peninsula.

Mostly, however, the area is pretty much deserted following a rehousing program which transplanted the population some time ago. We've met loyal Cubans who just love to tell you how the original inhabitants have wonderful housing now, in big concrete apartment blocks with televisions, occasional electricity and water. Ha!

If you are going on, then this is the place to prepare for rounding Cabo San Antonio to visit the southern coastlines and the much larger cays along that side. But if you are going to be returning to Havana, then this is the end of the line.

By now you will have quite enough experience to take up your own route back.

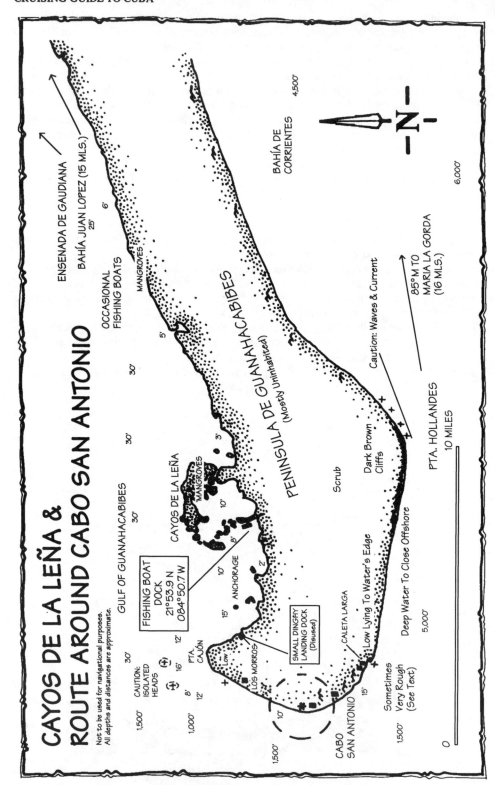

CAYOS DE LA LEÑA & ROUTE AROUND CABO SAN ANTONIO

Not to be used for navigational purposes.
All depths and distances are approximate.

ENSENADA DE GAUDIANA

BAHÍA JUAN LOPEZ (15 MLS.)

OCCASIONAL FISHING BOATS

MANGROVES

GULF OF GUANAHACABIBES

CAUTION: ISOLATED HEADS

FISHING BOAT DOCK
21°53.9 N
084°50.7 W

PTA. CAJÓN

CAYOS DE LA LEÑA

MANGROVES

ANCHORAGE

LOS MORROS

SMALL DINGHY LANDING DOCK
(Disused)

CALETA LARGA

CABO SAN ANTONIO

Sometimes Very Rough
(See Text)

Low Lying To Water's Edge

PENINSULA DE GUANAHACABIBES
(Mostly Uninhabited)

Scrub

Dark Brown Cliffs

Caution: Waves & Current

85°M TO MARIA LA GORDA
(16 MLS.)

BAHÍA DE CORRIENTES

Deep Water To Close Offshore

PTA. HOLLANDES

10 MILES

N

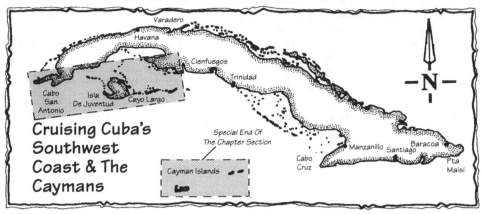

CABO SAN ANTONIO TO CAYO LARGO

GENERAL

This is a fairly straightforward cruise, along the mainland at the western end of Cuba then through the cays as far as Cayo Largo 200 miles to the east on the outer reef.

The land along the northern (top) edge of the gulf is low-lying, but within the gulf, depths are more than adequate to allow most transits. There is a ring of cays along the southern edge forming a protective barrier against the seas, and additionally there is a large island more or less half way along, giving even more shelter and opportunity for landside exploring. Finally, the cays are broken by several passes which make for easy entrances and exits across the barrier.

CHARTS

Once again the best charts to use are the most recent updates of the official Cuban ICH series.

If they are not available to you then any of the best DMA or Admiralty charts will have to do, but as these are produced from different sources and to a different scale, be more cautious in your interpretation of the data.

If you do have the opportunity to purchase ICH charts in advance of your trip (Bluewater Charts in Ft. Lauderdale is best for copies, or Havana itself for originals) then the numbers you need for the gulf are as follows: ICH 1147, 1146, 1145, 1144, 1143. Plus of course, ICH 1122 (which deals with Cabo San Antonio).

ROUNDING CABO SAN ANTONIO
CHART NO. ICH 1122 (CUBAN)

A doddle if it's done right, or a bummer if you get it wrong.

If you are using a larger scale U.S. chart you might wonder about the nifty little waves which are drawn on it. They're there for a reason.

And if you've got the Cuban charts, well, the annotation "Perpetua Rpte" on the point means "Always Rough!"

This, the narrowest point between the island and the Yucatan peninsula in Mexico, is where all that water coming up from the Caribbean Basin gets squeezed down. It then

137

meets all those minor counter-currents which confuse it into a state of nervous agitation, and it only needs one little thing to set it off... a southeast wind.

Squalls too, whip themselves up out of nowhere, and we have been calmly cruising round the point under fair skies when suddenly huge waves have appeared on the horizon and borne straight down on us. We once made this trip in an unfavorable southeast wind, and it was a miserable time, mostly spent clinging on as the boat rolled onto its beam-ends or submarined into vertical walls of water.

But on the other hand if you wait for a northeast wind, then protected by the mainland, you're subject to little more than a gentle rolling motion. This then, is the secret.

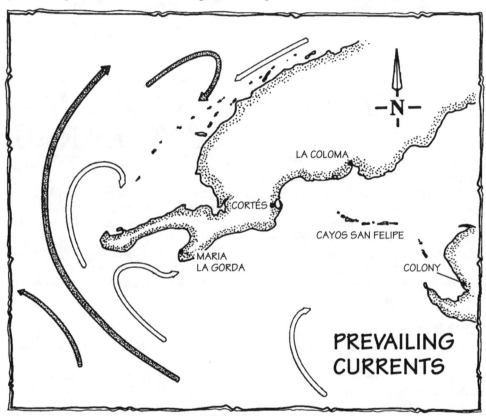

PREVAILING CURRENTS

Prepare the vessel overnight by bringing down and furling the Bimini, wedging all loose objects with cushions, and in general readying the boat for an early departure. If all notes, charts, instruments, engine-checks, etc., are sorted out the night before, then you can be on your way by sunup, when the winds are likely to be at their lowest. The forecast should be listened to, but you should have a pretty good feel for it by now, and if you've been anchored near the tip, then you'll pretty much know what the wind is up to overnight, and all you want is three or four hours of any wind out of the northern quarter.

SHALLOWS AND A WRECK

There are a couple of shallower spots, with a submerged wreck a bit north of Punta Cajon, so you can go round at 22°57.0 N to avoid these. But you might equally choose to pass between them and the mainland at around 22°55.5N, heading east from your anchorage, then turning south whenever you feel comfortable with the depth. A half-mile or so offshore should have you in about 10 feet, and you'll be out of any unfavorable swells.

Passing the well-built light and radar station at Cabo San Antonio, swing outside the shallows at Los Cayuelas and the wreck at Caleta Larga (21°49.9N / 084°56.0W), then once the coast has curved east you can come in close again.Provided you've been lucky with the weather, you'll have been rewarded with a gentle run in the morning sunlight, but in the event that your schedule has not allowed you to pick and choose your time, then stay a bit further offshore to give yourself some sea-room. In unfavorable conditions there can be some dangerous onshore currents, so be careful to note your position and heading. It's not a long run, but it can be a bit uncomfortable.

The deserted coastline continues east to the cliffs at Pta. Hollandés, dead into a blindingly low sun which is also reflected into your face by the water. Your darkest glasses will help, but they will reflect even more light back onto your long suffering nose, so remember to slather on the strongest sunscreen you have, or the next few days are not going to be too pleasant.

Low black cliffs mark the approach to Punta Hollandés, and the base of the point is surrounded by a shallow bank extending out a mile, so give it a bit of room as you come out of the protection of the land and into the Bay of Corrientes.

MARIA LA GORDA (FAT MARIA)

A dive resort, situated on the eastern shoreline of the Bahia de Corrientes, this lovely spot is surrounded by deserted wilderness and coconut strewn beaches. The waters within the bay are of unparalleled clarity, and host to an amazing variety of fish. I will even go out on a limb to say that I have never dived in a more beautiful environment below the surface.

AN EXTRAORDINARY BAY

From Punta Hollandés, set a course of 85°M across the bay towards the resort of Maria La Gorda (16 miles), and revel in the deepest blue waters which now extend on all sides. Within this extraordinary bay, frigate-birds will soar, and the sea-gulls take up station overhead looking out for any flying fish that panic at your approach. You might even see hunting packs of tuna or dolphin rounding up other smaller fish and herding them into small compact schools before the feeding frenzy whips the water on the surface. The bay is also host to the occasional whale-shark too so look out for the disturbances as its huge spotted body slowly passes close to the surface.

At about half distance across the bay, you'll begin to see a small promontory ahead of you on the other side, so adjust your course to the left of this where a small group of red roofed buildings will soon become visible.

The white-painted concrete dock (21°49.2N / 084°29.8W) is about 150 feet long and 10 feet wide, and you should moor on the southern side to leave the local dive-boat its usual berth across the way. Use the bollards, even if they are on the other side, and do not attach your lines to the light-posts on the end. When last seen they were only sitting on concrete blocks and could be easily dragged over and onto your deck.

A dock extends from the beach at the resort on Maria La Gorda. The resort is largely dedicated to scuba diving with more than 20 superb dive sites. (Photo by Simon Charles)

Checking in with the Guarda Frontera here is an informal process and should only take five minutes if he's around. If not, you may have to wait until he get's in from fishing with the rest of the guys.

Having cleared-in then you will probably be expected to moor some 50 yards off to the northwest of the dock in about 30-40 feet where there are a couple of small buoys. Later you can bring your dinghy to the dock at any point along its length.

The hotel has about 48 beds in a collection of neat concrete cabins fronted by tended perriwinkle flower-beds, and the restaurant serves a great variety of well-cooked food at around $15 per plate. Just ask Juanito in the kitchen for Lo que hay ("Whatever there is"), and you'll be glad you got out of Havana.

The resort is largely dedicated to scuba-diving, but does arrange tours into the hinterland of Guanacabibes if you wish. Rental cars are available, but they need to be booked the day before as they have to be delivered some distance to the hotel. Look at the map to see just how isolated this place is.

There are more than 20 superb dive-sites along the wall just in front of the hotel and within 2-3 miles of the dock, with tunnels, caves, vertical drop-offs, and fronds of wisteria-like ferns hanging down into the depths from the coral towers. Those dives I have done here, in company with Nelson (the extremely pleasant dive-master/instructor), will remain with me forever. If you're going to dive with them remove at least four or five pounds from your normal weightbelt to compensate for the heavy steel cylinders they issue to divers. Well over 100 cubic feet capacity, compared to the U.S. norm of 80 cubic feet.

Departure is a simple affair, visual past the Tetas de Maria (no, I shall not translate), two protuberances out from the cliffs at Punta Caiman 2 miles south of the dock, and on to Cabo Corrientes in water of cut-glass transparency. Just keep the pale-blue stuff to your left, the dark-blue stuff to your right, and cruise along the wall 200 yards offshore.

HEADING FOR ISLA DE JUVENTUD

If you wish to go straight across to the Isla de Juventud, then head 80°M to Cayo Real 23 miles away, and follow the keys all the way. For a new experience, take a dive along the wall just south of the westernmost point of the San Felipe Keys to confirm the existence of undersea freshwater springs.

Be very careful, however, of the Canal de Los Indios just after those keys when you're coming in through to the inside near Juventud. There is a substantial bar across the entrance, as you may find it better to continue down as far as the SW corner of the island, and come in through the major channel there.

If you wish to remain awhile closer to the mainland, then go to Cortés or Coloma.

ROUTE TO CORTÉS
(45 MILES) CHART NOS. ICH 1122 & 1147

This is a straightforward run along desolate scrub-lined escarpments with rocky under-cut cliffs. There are no offshore reefs and you may tack freely along the first section, but there is a shallow shelf extending well out from the buildings and the light at Punta Frances (084°02.0W). This can get you into trouble as it's quite abrupt and there's no real warning, so go wide round the point there and remain at least a mile offshore for the last run NNE to the bay of Cortés.

LAGUNA DE CORTÉS

Note: Do not attempt this entrance if you have a deep-keeled yacht (6 feet), but rather anchor in the bight of the Ensenda de Cortés a few miles further on.

A large enclosed lagoon with a tricky entrance, this offers shelter from all sides and is a placid overnight stop especially if any winds are expected later.

By now the sun will be setting,so exercise caution as you approach, shade your eyes and be ready to back up in the event of any unexpected obstruction ahead.

There are two entrances to the lagoon as shown on the charts, but on no account should you try the wider,more northerly of these. It is barred by a shallow bank and you will ground.

Follow the sketch for the entry route, approaching from a mile out to avoid the shallows close inshore along the coastline and do not aim straight at the channel from outside.

Rather, come in from slightly below (say 22°02.6N) and head west towards a point about 200- 300 yards south of the entrance.

When 80-100 yards offshore turn approx. 300°M and continue slowly towards the mouth and through the confusion of small markers.

Having come round the point it is shallower in the center, and there is another obstruction just after clearing the entrance, so remain close to the left bank (50-80 yards) all the way through and continue slightly southwest as you come into the bay itself until you clear all keys. Now you can steer a gradual arc towards the town of Cortés some 2 miles away on the western edge of the lagoon.

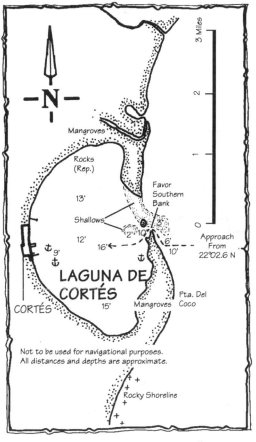

The town's a picturesque little spot with 20-30 medium-sized fishing vessels, a working drydock and lots of roofs nestling amongst a multitude of trees.

The Guarda Frontera post seems to double as the ice-house on the central wharf where the fishing boats cluster, and you should approach this on the left side. If there are any patrol-boats there then draw up a few feet off and shout over for instructions. If the wharf is too crowded they will doubtless wish you to anchor in front of the dock so find a clear spot and anchor there. There is little wave-action within the bay and the holding is good so let out just enough rode for security but not so much that you swing into the other boats, and await the small boat which will bring out the official. They rarely (if ever) get foreign boats here but documentation will only take a couple of minutes if your technique and your papers are right, which they should be by now.

If you're coming in from Mexico, this is not an international port so don't even think about it. Instead, go on to the Isla de Juventud.

Early in the morning you'll see the crews being rowed out to the fishing boats which then

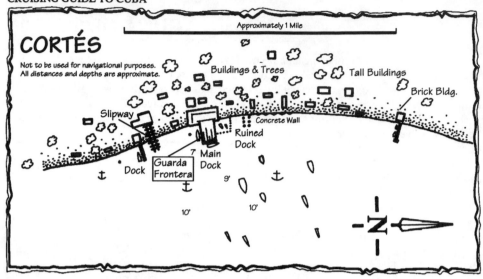

CORTÉS

Not to be used for navigational purposes.
All distances and depths are approximate.

Approximately 1 Mile

Buildings & Trees

Tall Buildings

Brick Bldg.

Slipway

Concrete Wall

Ruined Dock

7 Main Dock

Guarda Frontera

Dock

Dock

9'

10'

10'

-N-

go alongside the wharf to collect their despachos and other necessities before streaming out of the bay. As luck will have it, the morning sun will be in your eyes now, so note the direction the fishing-boats take and hunt down the dark glasses again for your departure.

Remember the dangers coming up to the mouth and keep close to the right bank when going through, then having made your exit along the coast go east towards deeper water.

ROUTE TO LA COLOMA
(26 MILES) CHART NO. ICH 1147 (CUBAN)

A short easy run to a larger town along the northern coastline of the gulf, this passage can be made directly across from Cortés or if you prefer, along the low coastline. When going directly over, the most convenient starting waypoint is the large marker 4 miles east southeast of the exit at Cortés.

From here a course of 70°M will put you off Punta Santo Domingo and further on between the marks leading into the harbor at La Coloma (see La Coloma Waypoint sketch). A jolting ride sometimes, reminding you that the gulf is quite large enough to have waves of its own.

Along the way you are likely to see a variety of the grey rust-stained ferrocement fishing boats typical of the southern side of Cuba. Steered from a position on the stern, they contain a large hold up front and favour carrying their cargo of empty lobster traps on the roof of the main cabin. A friendly lot these fishermen, we have even been halted by one vessel which despatched a crewmember in a skiff to present us with a bucket of crabs!

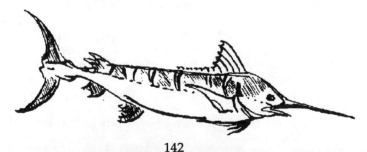

Situated at the mouth of the river Coloma, the town's principal commerce is fishing and other associated industries. It can be seen clearly on any sunny day by the white reflections from the warehouses, the tall ice-making plant, apartment buildings, and the large mushroom-shaped water-tower behind the docks.

The town also serves as a transport hub for passengers and freight travelling by water to the Isla de Juventud, and overland to the city of Pínar del Rio in the mountains to the north.

In the case of a major storm the river is navigable for some distance if you need to seek refuge.

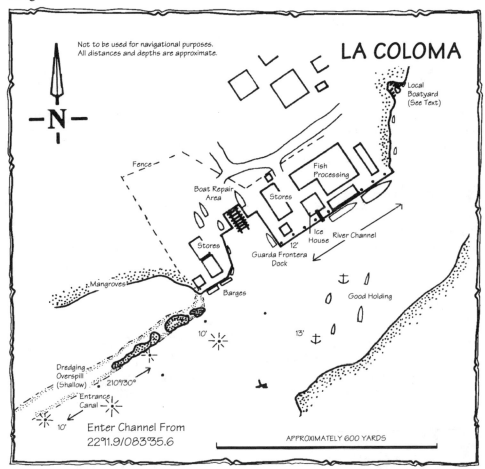

From points south, the outer Santo Domingo light is at position 22°09.5N / 083°36.5W, and then you head 20°M for 2.5 miles to the dredged channel into port.

Enter the canal itself along a course of 30°M at position 22°11.9N / 083°35.6W slightly south of the beaches at Las Canas, themselves visible from well off with their cabanas, white sand, and other buildings. (See following sketch.)

The 2.5 miles long channel is 40 yards wide and 10 feet deep but keep to the center as it is shallower at the sides. It is marked by large sentry-box type lights on alternate sides so look back frequently to see that you are still in line between the markers, and on no account stray too far left as the dredged overspill has been deposited there.

Once inside, the easily-recognized Guarda Frontera post is on the far outer corner of the first basin which also houses wharfs and shipyards. The dock is a well-built affair which contains the ice-plant and a number of buildings comprising the fishing fleet's base and warehouses.

Moor alongside the guardhouse at the base of the flagpole and present your papers. The last time we were here, checking-in took not more than five minutes and we were given permission to depart in the morning without having to return to the dock, so request this facility.

We've been offered all kinds of assistance by the authorities here, and our logbook once noted that they were the most helpful officials we'd met.

You will probably be asked to moor a little way out from the dock and amongst the other fishing boats at anchor. The holding is excellent anywhere in the harbor so just make sure you're out of the main channel, and dinghy back ashore to have a look around.

Leave the dinghy at the dock, walk between the warehouses near the Guarda Frontera post to the main gate and let the gateman know you're leaving. Strange sights await you following the road round to the right.

Grim Eastern-Block concrete apartment-buildings, miserable huts, nicer streets with neat dwellings, a baseball stadium, and squealing pigs contrasting with children playing happily at the side of the road.

The walls of the more primitive huts amongst the mangroves are made of roots bound into wall-sections and they are peopled by charcoal-burners using only the most rudimentary of techniques (they don't exclude the oxygen). There's even a tiny rural boatyard where you'll see boats being carvel-planked at the side of the road.

A fleet of fishing boats crowded into a protected harborage at La Coloma. (Photo by Simon Charles)

ROUTE TO DÁRSENA DE SIGUANEA (ISLA DE JUVENTUD)
CHART NOS. ICH 1147 & 1145 (CUBAN)

It is important to note here that you cannot travel in a straight line the 48 miles southeast from Coloma to Siguanea, the small harbor near the Hotel Colony in Juventud. The shallows of the San Felipe and Los Indios cays intrude slightly on the course making it necessary to take a gentle eastern arc on the journey.

If you don't wish to skirt those keys visually, you can go east along the mainland for some 12 miles after the outer light and steer a direct compass course from there. Avoid the shallows just southeast of Coloma by going out to the outer Santo Domingo light and then going east, following the 15-foot contour. When the prominent Punta Fisga headland bears 280°M and you can just see the village of Playa Guanal through the mouth of its bay (say 8°M), then a direct course of 145°M should take you to the Punta Buenavista marker off the west coast of Juventud. You can now go SSE, paralleling to the coast for about 10 miles to the harbor.

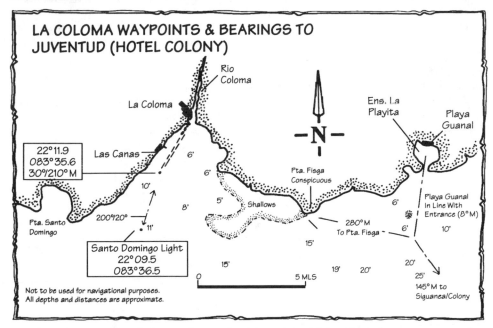

LA COLOMA WAYPOINTS & BEARINGS TO JUVENTUD (HOTEL COLONY)

Otherwise, just use whatever electronic aid you have aboard in order to get to a point 21°37.0N / 082°59.2W where the Siguanea entry channel begins.

On the latter stages of this run you are likely to come across a haphazard multitude of lobster-pots. It would be a bit of a pity for you to blot your copybook and be towed ignominiously into some village harbor in your shiny white motorboat, so keep an eye out for them. The assorted dinghies attached to the major fishing-boats tend the pots, but only God knows just how they find all these scattered cages below the surface. We've looked down with snorkel and masks and found the cages absolutely packed with lobster... Do Not Molest.

Be especially aware if you see dinghies fussing about close to the mother-boat as they may be laying out nets. They seem totally unconcerned by your presence and will gaily watch your approach until the last minute and then begin to lay their lines directly across your path.

Meanwhile just to let you know it's not personal, they're waving happily all the time.

Oddly enough, the fishermen on the northeastern side of Cuba are not as demonstrative and perhaps this is a natural outcome of the officially encouraged paranoia over there.

But there is also a lot more evidence of needle-fish, leaping hound-fish, playful dolphins and the like on this side too... Are the two features connected?

ISLA DE JUVENTUD

This island (population 100,000) has had other names since it was discovered by Columbus on his second journey to the New World in 1494. He called it La Evangelista then, but it has also been called the Isle of Pines, by which name it is still known in some places.

Previous to his arrival however, it was home to other groups of Cuban indigenous peoples like the Ciboney Indians who left their marks on the walls of caves in the south and at various other sites inland.

The island was colonized by the Spanish between 1494 and 1898 and after the Spanish-American war the North Americans had bought up half of the total land area, excluding most Cubans from the territories by 1925!

During 1870 the Cuban patriot José Martí (whose name is still invoked by both sides of the political debate) was deported here, and in the early 1950's Fidel Castro too was imprisoned near the capital Nuevo Gerona.

In 1978 the name was changed to the "Isle of Youth" after the agricultural facilities dedicated to training young people from all over the socialist world.

Although the island is relatively flat (the highest point is 950 feet) the mountains which do exist are close and easily seen from the coast, making the place look most impressive from some angles.

DÁRSENA DE SIGUANEA
CHART NO. ICH 1145 (CUBAN)

Merely a notch in the coast immediately above the bay of San Pedro, this small but sheltered harbor serves the Hotel Colony, originally built for the exclusive use of the North Americans who controlled the island before the revolution. In addition, it is near the site of one of Columbus' original landings in 1894.

Perhaps conveniently for some, this tiny harbor can handle international arrivals even though you may have to wait some time for the officials to arrive from the main port of Nueva Gerona 30 miles away by road.

On your approach to the harbor you will see the hotel a mile or so north. The hotel (itself a mile or two south of a couple of iron wrecks), is easily recognized being a large white flat-roofed two-story building with a long narrow walkway leading out to a pavillion/dance-floor 100 yards from shore.

Do not be tempted to approach the pier as the water there is just barely enough for shallow-draft boats. We found less than 4-foot on the approach and even the hotel dive-boats collect their divers from the harbor down the road.

The hotel itself caters mainly to scuba-divers from Germany and France, but the harbor is also a convenient cruising base from which transport and other inland tours can be readily arranged.

ENTERING THE CHANNEL

Enter the marked channel from pos. 21°37.0 N / 082°59.2 W steering 075°M towards the large white "screw" on the inside. You'll know it when you see it.

Keep to the right of the channel until inside the staves holding back the banks and dock at the Guarda Frontera wharf immediately on the left where the large patrol-boat usually moors.

You will have noticed the relative speed of the formalities along the coast here and this is no exception. Ten minutes after arrival you should be mooring amongst the dive-boats lining the concrete docksides a bit further in.

The marina supervisor's office is in the building alongside the eastern edge of the dock and also serves as a storeroom for marine supplies and the dive-shop. Marina charges are about .30 cents/foot and electricity is available by twisting the bare ends of a supply line onto your plug, with water from the dockside tap by your boat.

Most of the diving takes place off the western tip of the island (the tail of the comma) but the area is also a submarine preservation site, so in a scandalous effort to extort money from you a guide is required to accompany you from the dock. It seems to cost much the same if you take one of the organized dives, but the $56 fee (2 tanks, with a beach-lunch) might be a bit over-the-top for a cruiser with all his own boat, gear, and hundreds of miles of unaccompanied diving immediately behind or before him.

HOTEL CROWED WITH DIVERS

Nevertheless the hotel is crowded with regimented German divers (upwards of 150 when we were last there) who arrive on package holidays. Weirdly (to this more relaxed Caribbean diver), they are allocated cards which are subsequently clipped every time they dive to ensure they don't do more than the package allows.

In the mornings you will be woken by trucks bringing the divers to the docks where they board the boats. Check out the compressor system near the gate. It's the most sophisticated I've ever seen in daily use anywhere in the West Indies.

The hotel is a mile away down a straight road. You know you need the walk, but rub on lots and lots of repellant. Tours to the decorated caves at Punta del Este, rental cars and

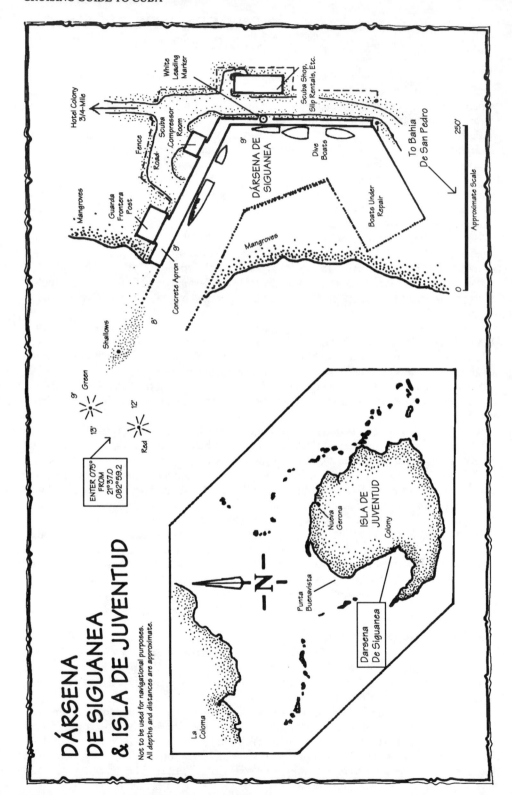

DÁRSENA
DE SIGUANEA
& ISLA DE JUVENTUD

Not to be used for navigational purposes.
All depths and distances are approximate.

ENTER 075°
FROM
21°37.0
082°59.2

13'

9'
Green

12'
Red

La
Coloma

—N—

Punta
Buenavista

Nueva
Gerona

ISLA DE
JUVENTUD

Colony

Dársena
De Siguanea

Mangroves

Guarda
Frontera
Post

Fence

Road

Scuba
Compressor
Room

Hotel Colony
3/4-Mile

White
Leading
Marker

Scuba Shop,
Slip Rentals, Etc.

Concrete Apron

9'

8'

Shallows

DÁRSENA DE
SIGUANEA

9'

Dive
Boats

Mangroves

Boats Under
Repair

To Bahia
De San Pedro

250'

Approximate Scale

0

other island transport can be arranged there.

The restaurant is particularly good and there is a games room for the bored children aboard.

You can have quite a good night here, and if you are at all sociable you will have already been befriended by the dive-boat sailors and the dive-guides at the dock, some of whom may have been temporarily seconded from Havana and might already know you. The sailors will doubtless encounter you somewhere near the bar/game room of the hotel and when that environment palls the party will move to the pavillion at the end of the pier. Purchase your booze by the bottle in the hotel store early so as not to have to drink expensive shots at the bar later on. You can keep it at your table.

This is one of the places where you realize that as a member of the fraternity of sailors a yachtsman can have a much better time than a normal tourist, and in any case you'll need to be a bit merry to survive the mosquitos on the walk back.

There is also the sound of the watchman patrolling on the concrete outside your window all night. As is the norm in Cuba, he peers in unashamedly at every opportunity until he gets bored and slips away to sleep.

DELAY CLEARANCE UNTIL DIVERS DEPART

Clearance out is best delayed until the divers have left at 9:15 a.m., but you should be able to leave immediately afterwards.

There are two potential routes east from here. One will take you over the top of the island via the port of Nueva Gerona, and the other allows you to take the outer route along the south coast of Juventud and along the keys.

SOUTHERN OUTER ROUTE EAST
CHART NO. ICH 1145 (CUBAN)

If you're going outside, then head for the point 13 miles away due west and come round along the bottom edge of the island. The 44 miles of southern coastline is rocky and sloped, but sometimes, due to the trees, it can appear to be an escarpment.

There are few natural harbors along here but if you don't draw more than 5-6 feet you might be able to use Caleta Grande at 21°31.0N/083°07.0W. There is a small dock inside serving the tiny villages of Cocodrillo and Jacksonville, originally settled by Cayman Islanders in the early part of this century. English is still occasionally spoken here as a result, and family ties loosely bind the two regions.

The eastern half of the coastline is mainly beach protected by an offshore reef, but once past that you can come into the large sheltered sound on the southeast corner of the island.

Enter around a position of 21°32.6N/082°30.5W and anchor inside, anywhere you see fit.

A billboard welcomes visitors to Nueva Gerona. (Photo by Simon Charles)

NORTHERN ROUTE TO NUEVA GERONA
CHART NO. ICH 1145 (CUBAN)

This 35-mile passage is a visual run north along the coast, round the northwest corner, then east to the mouth of the Las Casas river where the port is situated a mile or two in.

Prior to that however there is a convenient shelter inside the keys just off the tip at the Ensenada de Los Barcos where you could stop overnight if you weren't headed for Nueva Gerona but merely travelling east along the inside of the keys.

The mouth of the Las Casas river lies 1-mile west of Punta Coloma, a narrow point made up of steep mountains which sweep right down to the sea. The point can be identified by a tiny island just in front of it, and large commercial vessels use the bay formed there to anchor while awaiting attention within the harbor.

Note: If you're coming east from the Pasa de Quitasol then the river lies after the second (larger) of the two promontories you'll meet, and in the morning sunlight it can be an especially impressive sight.

NUEVA GERONA

Just inside the mouth of the river Las Casas and specializing mainly in the export of grapefruit and other citrus products, this commercial port has all Customs and Immigration facilities for international entry or departure.

From outside at 21°55.7N / 082°47.5W markers lead in along a course of 218°M through a channel dredged to about 20 feet. Do not venture to the west of the channel as the dredged soil has been deposited into a bank there.

As you come in, be ready to avoid the large hydrofoils which speed in and out of the river delivering passengers to the other side of the gulf of Batabano. These amazing Russian-built craft (Cometas), looking rather like something out of "The War of the Worlds," rise up on thin foils as they accelerate through the channel until they are some ten feet out of the water and travelling at a ferocious speed. Snorkelers in the channel (another thing to be aware of) take one startled look and dive, dive, dive; abandoning their rubber-tire rafts in a serious hurry to preserve life and limb.

There is a Guarda Frontera post at the end of the markers in a collection of low white buildings dead ahead and on the right-hand bank. There isn't anywhere to moor, so draw up as close as you can and shout across for permission to enter.

You will be directed to the main post some way in so continue slowly about one-mile along the narrow river just off the large concrete wharfs, marine repair facilities, and the roadway.

A MOST BEAUTIFUL SURPRISE

Passing here in 1993 we received a most beautiful surprise when we encountered a group of about fifteen tiny schoolchildren casually walking the road alongside the river bank beautifully neat in clean white shirts, red neckerchiefs, skirts and shorts. They immediately formed up a hurriedly-measured arms-length from each other, and in front of a beaming teacher they sang to us as we passed slowly in our boat!

Sometimes, just sometimes, life is so sweet.

THE PORT CAPTAIN'S OFFICE

The first major building after the open areas which follow the commercial wharfs is the Capitanía (the port captain's office), so pull up on the right at a filthy, rundown wooden dock at position 21°53.4N / 082°42.0W and explain your presence here.

Despite that other sweeter welcome, the officials here can be a bit brusque, wondering just why you've chosen to interrupt their routine. Don't be fobbed off with excuses (no space/security), but present your despacho showing your route. Indicate you'll be responsible for your own boat if something runs into it and you should be permitted to continue on to somewhere past the hydrofoil terminal on the right, a few hundred yards ahead of the bridge.

In this instance, the officials are probably correct, there really isn't much space. But what's a little crowding amongst friends?

Raft alongside the tugboats pressing together and settle in for your stay. Doubtless another official will show up to check on your final berth, but he will also be able to advise on the city so don't despair. They get very few private boats here, and you're probably the only entertainment they've had in a while.

The river here is rather dirty, with small carcasses and empty grapefruit skins drifting idly downstream, but your neighbors will make you welcome, and as usual you will likely be taken onboard various other vessels to visit. One rather unfortunate feature of the port is the incessant broadcasting of local radio stations over crackly speakers mounted on one of the larger boats nearby. You will not be happy after having to listen to the sugar-cane harvest statistics for each province, random speeches by/to the local women's group, soap-operas, and dissertations on Congolese folk art.

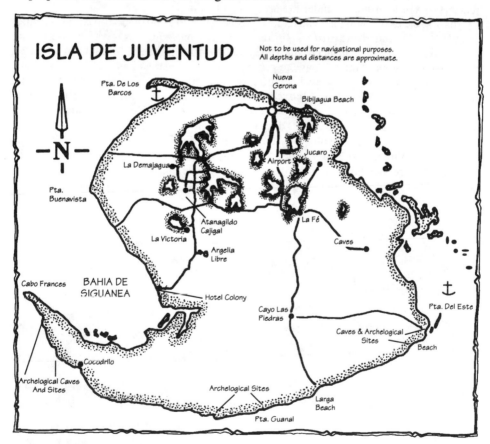

ISLA DE JUVENTUD

Not to be used for navigational purposes.
All depths and distances are approximate.

Immediately ashore you will find the large ancient ferry-boat *El Pinero* used to transport Fidel Castro to prison on the island. Now up on blocks and scheduled someday (as much as anything ever is in Cuba) to be opened to the public, it makes a strange backdrop to a crowded mooring, especially contrasted with the rather "Flash Gordon" hydrofoils just downstream.

Incidentally, you can take a ride over to the Cuban mainland on one of these: Purchase a ticket at the terminal 300 yards north of the bridge. They leave at three-hour intervals and the trip takes a bit more than two hours.

The busiest part of town runs from Calle 32 at the bridge, north to Calle 18, between the riverside and the Calle 41. Note: The odd-numbers run parallel to the river.

There are a couple of restaurants close to the center of town, but current economic difficulties make it almost impossible to give a recommendation so make inquiries locally. There should in any case be a couple near your mooring site.

Despite its rather flyblown aspect, the city is a friendly enough place, perhaps due to the influx of foreign students who made it their home in the boom years of Communism and the multitude of "International Youth Brigades" it spawned. Spend a day wandering aimlessly and you are bound to be kidnapped by someone or the other who invites you back (sometimes to a different town altogether) for tea.

Transport around town can best be done by flagging down and sharing any of the horse-drawn carriages which ply the streets. They're also available for hire around the Parque Central at the junction of Calles 28/39, which is the best place to hang out in any case.

If you wish to rent a car to tour the island then you can obtain one at the hotel some three quarters of a mile upstream under the bridge (go by dinghy).

Crossing the bridge will take you to the old prison (the Presidio Modelo) some 2-3 miles east of town. Modelled on a prison in Illinois and now a museum, this is where Fidel Castro was imprisoned after the unsuccessful 1953 assault on the Moncado Barracks in Santiago.

When clearing out, you will have to proceed 1/4-mile upstream again to the Capitanía for your despacho. The officials here are more accustomed to commercial vessels with more rigid schedules and their relative inexperience in matters concerning private boats will show. Stress that you cannot guarantee your exact schedule further down the line (you'll be anchoring out in the cays) and they'll finally get the picture.

There is a provedor establishment at the next major wharf along your route, so stop there on your way to the entrance if you need supplies for the next leg. It's the wharf with the big crane, where they haul-out the hydrofoils for maintenance.

The ferry-boat "El Pinero," used to transport Fidel Castro to prison on Isla de Juventud. (Photo by Simon Charles)

A boy amuses himself with a simple homemade toy, consisting of a wagon wheel rim and a stick. (Photo by George Halloran)

ROUTE TO CAYO LARGO
CHART NOS. ICH 1145 & 1143

Delay your departure until the afternoon and you will be able to find a sheltered anchorage dead east of North Gerona near the Pasa de Quitasol by early evening. The following leg is somewhat longer than desirable and an early start through the canal can enable you to make the passage without an intermediate stop.

CAYOS DE LOS INGLESITOS (KEYS OF THE LITTLE ENGLISHMEN)
Close to the dredged canal going through to the other side of the keys, this offers shelter from the east and northeast even if the holding is somewhat poor.

Anchor as near to the edge of the keys as your keel allows, but do check your mooring carefully as the bottom is a thick mat of turtle-grass. If there is any chance of the wind rising you should double-check by diving and force it in manually if necessary (see earlier chapter).

In spite of the windbreak provided by Cayo Inglés we once carelessly allowed ourselves to drag over half a mile in the space of two hours when the wind got up to 25 knots, but luckily for us we blew westwards into the bay instead of going ashore.

PLANS BEFORE SUNUP
Prior to sunup you can make your way round to the western end of the canal at **Quitasol** and by the time the light is good you will be poised to go through from a position of 21°55.8N / 082°39.4W.

The canal runs 80°/260°M with a depth of 16 feet along its 1.5-mile length, and we have experienced strong through-currents on occasion. There is a free-standing wharf halfway along and some 400 yards north of the canal but otherwise the water is shallow on both sides.

From the eastern end of the canal (21°56.1N / 082°37.6W) the Gulf of Batabano opens wider still and you are over 30 miles away from the moderating influence of the mainland so choose your route further on with regard to the forecast and wind direction.

You may wish to make your way directly across to the major exit through the outer keys at Cayo Rosario and whilst we have made this 45-mile run in perfect weather, this open run can also be subject to high winds. Our depth-sounder once drew pictures showing 8-10 feet waves over what was nominally only 16 feet of water.

There are few closer exits and little real shelter before Rosario, but you can hide just west of the pass itself near the cays which extend northwards from Cayo Cantilles to Tabalones.

A "Flash Gordon" styled hydrofoil speeds across the Gulf of Batabano from Nueva Gerona. (Photo by Simon Charles)

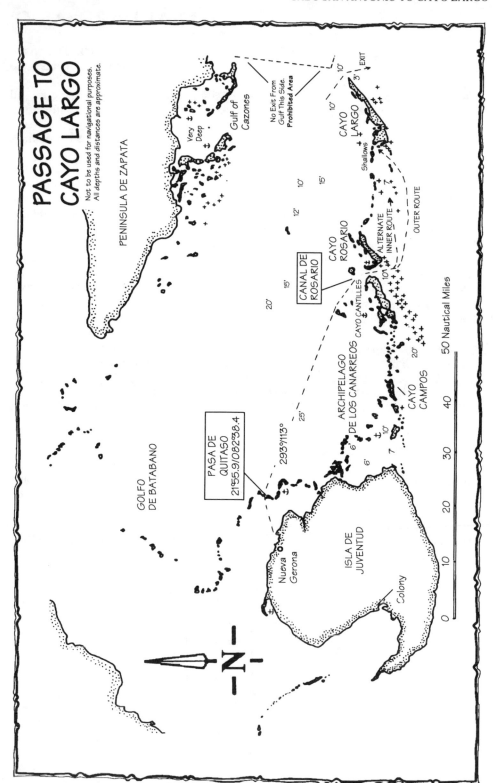

PASSAGE TO CAYO LARGO

Not to be used for navigational purposes.
All depths and distances are approximate.

PENINSULA DE ZAPATA

Very Deep

Gulf of Cazones

No Exit From Gulf This Side. **Prohibited Area**

EXIT

CAYO LARGO

Shallows

ALTERNATE INNER ROUTE

OUTER ROUTE

CANAL DE ROSARIO

CAYO ROSARIO

CAYO CANTILLES

ARCHIPELAGO DE LOS CANARREOS

CAYO CAMPOS

PASA DE QUITASO
21°55.9/082°38.4

293°/113°

GOLFO DE BATABANO

Nueva Gerona

ISLA DE JUVENTUD

Colony

50 Nautical Miles

0   10   20   30   40

155

CANAL DE ROSARIO:

This is the main entrance/exit through the cays along the southeast gulf. Due to the shallows further east the only way to Cayo Largo is via the outside of the reef, so this is the last chance to anchor overnight.

A course of 113°M from Quitasol should take you a mile north of Cayo Tablones and 5 miles further southeast the Rosario Canal marker will begin to show just southwest of Cayo Pasaje.

The main inner light is at pos.21°40.8N / 081°58.3W, but despite its size bird droppings make it difficult to see from the northwest when the light is not working.

If the wind is east or northeast then anchor overnight in the lee of Cayo Pasaje but as before check the anchor carefully. Again, the bottom here is a mat of poor-holding grass and I have had to swim down to forcefully reposition the hook in a gully for additional grip.

Note: The current through the canal can change direction 180° according to the tide, so make sure the hook cannot wriggle loose.

In the more unusual event of a southeast wind then you can enter the Media Luna lagoon inside Cayo Rosario itself. There is good bone-fishing to be had there, but be careful about the wind swinging later, and pay close attention to your depth.

A few years ago we came in here to anchor overnight in this lagoon and encountered a large flock of pink flamingos wading in the shallows just south of Pasaje! The only other flamingos I'd seen before that were plastic and lived on blue-rinse suburban lawns in Miami.

The final 26-mile run to Cayo Largo can be accomplished only via the outside of the keys, so follow the lights out through the wide canal and turn east. The canal itself is quite wide, but the inner entrance/exit marks denote a reef on either side and are set closer together, with the red inner marker on the eastern side standing directly on the reef.

Go through the middle along 175°M to the two outer buoys 500 yards further on at 21°35.6/081°56.2 before making your turn.

GENERALLY CALM SEAS

Under normal conditions the sea will generally be quite calm and you can make the entire run in deep water, but in the event of a southeast wind the waves can easily be steep enough to persuade you to make this passage through the shallower waters above and inside the wall.

In the latter case you should exercise caution all the way. Although this is an easy run over sand, it *is* shallow in places and there are occasional coral banks, usually quite visible through the water.

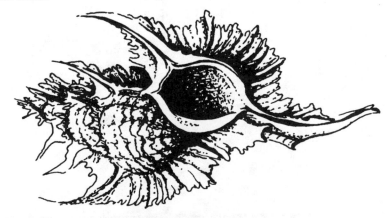

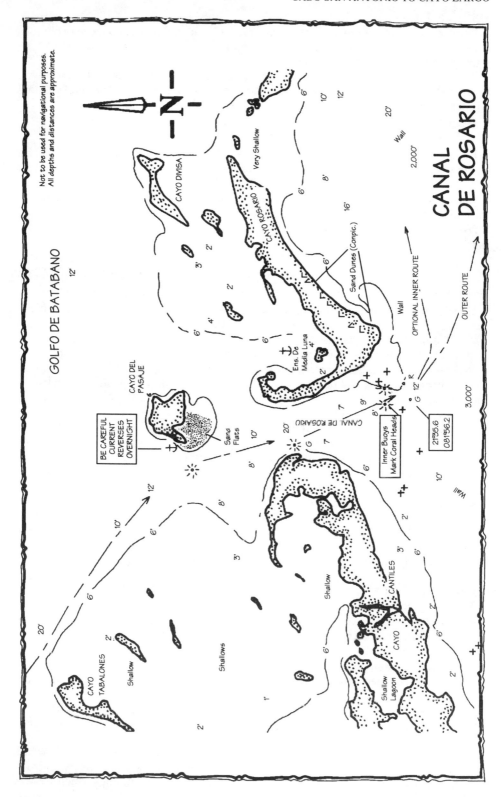

CANAL DE ROSARIO

Not to be used for navigational purposes.
All depths and distances are approximate.

GOLFO DE BATABANO

CAYO DIVISA

Very Shallow

CAYO ROSARIO

Sand Dunes (Conspic.)

Wall

20'

2,000'

12'

10'

6'

8'

6'

16'

6'

OPTIONAL INNER ROUTE

OUTER ROUTE

Wall

Ens. De
Media Luna

4'

2'

3'

2'

6'

4'

6'

2'

CAYO DEL PASAJE

BE CAREFUL
CURRENT
REVERSES
OVERNIGHT

Sand
Flats

10'

20'

8'

CANAL DE ROSARIO

Inner Buoys
Mark Coral Heads

G 12' R

6'

7'

8'

2135.6
08156.2

3,000'

10'

12'

10'

6'

20'

6'

8'

3'

G

7'

6'

8'

2'

2'

3'

6'

CANTILES

CAYO

Shallow

Shallow
Lagoon

2'

1'

2'

Shallows

6'

Shallow

CAYO
TABALONES

2'

Shallow

157

INNER ROUTE:

Remain about a mile or two off the beaches but look out particularly for the very obvious shoals south of the two small islets on the western tip of the Perases keys. Just stay in the light green stuff, but avoid it if it gets *too* pale.

As you begin to see huts, cabanas, and semi-naked bodies, you are nearing the resort area. Turn north when you approach the western shores of La Sirena beach and the marked canal will take you in to the marina.

OUTER ROUTE:

Parallel the wall at anything around 21°32.5N until you come to the light at the western end of Cayo de Los Ballenatos. The main channel-markers are 1.5 miles east of the light and consist of two R/Gr lighted buoys at 21°35.0 N / 081°36.7W.

Enter along 330°M to a large floating yellow buoy, then steer 50°M for 2 1/2 miles to the end of the dredged channel leading in to the marina.

Note: There is another easy entrance just a bit further to the east, but it's not so well marked.

CAYO LARGO

Cuba's premiere foreign tourist resort along the southern keys, this is unfortunately not the place to go if you want to get a taste of mainstream Cuban life. Completely isolated some 25 miles from the mainland, it consists of a full-service marina, an airport, three or four hotels, and little else apart from superb white beaches and sparkling blue seas.

What it does offer to the cruiser is possibly the best marina-docks in Cuba, making it an extremely civilized base for further exploration and a jump-off point to the eastern half of the country.

CONVENIENT FOR CLEARANCE

Customs and immigration are represented here and the authorities are thoroughly familiar with all aspects of international documentation making it a convenient spot to clear in or out of the country.

So efficient are they here that we once managed to clear into Cayo Largo and out of Cuba, *both* at the same time, and in less than 10 minutes!

The marina answers the VHF on channel 06. They will send a boat to escort you through if you are not familiar with the reef, and if coming from abroad they will arrange for the officials to be ready when you dock.

Not clearly shown on the normally precise ICH charts, the final short entrance-channel is somewhat hidden from sight amongst the vegetation of the cays, but is marked along its length by the usual sentry-box lights beginning at pos. 21°36.9N / 081°34.4W.

Follow the channel northeast through to the basin in front of the neat white dock and come alongside just east of the open bar/restaurant. There will usually be someone to take your lines and the marina will probably have a representative at dockside to assist you with any inquiries or paperwork.

Electricity and water hook-ups are supplied with the usual proviso that you will have to improvise your connections, and fuel is also available. Dock charges are .35 cents/foot per night.

Amazingly enough there is a small, newly-established boat's chandler opposite where you might just be able to get that cleaning-agent which claims to remove black rubber-marks from your topsides... Very important in Cuba.

As well as the cafe-bar on the dock there is a surprisingly good restaurant just to the left, so if you wish to be serenaded all night over an excellent meal, by all means patronize it.

In the immediate surrounds of the dock there are a number of buildings which serve in

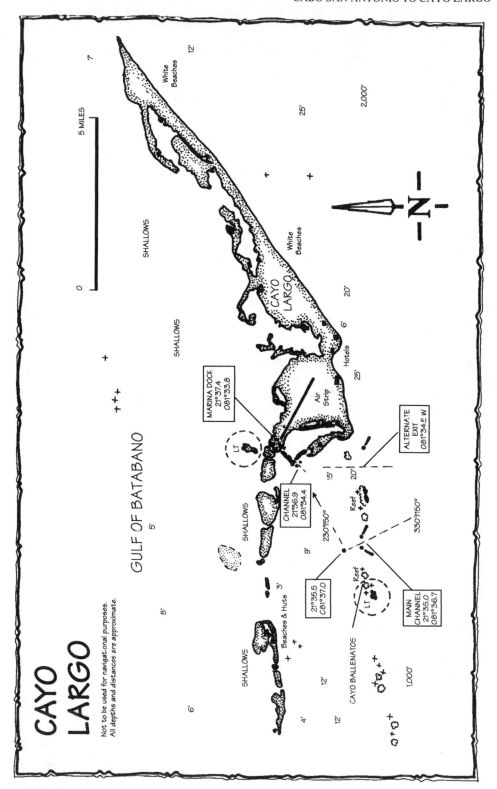

CAYO
LARGO

Not to be used for navigational purposes.
All depths and distances are approximate.

GULF OF BATABANO

N

5 MILES

0

SHALLOWS

SHALLOWS

SHALLOWS

SHALLOWS

SHALLOWS

White
Beaches

White
Beaches

CAYO
LARGO

12'

25'

2,000'

20'

6'

25'

Hotels

Air
Strip

LT

MARINA DOCK
21°37.4
081°33.8

CHANNEL
21°36.9
081°34.4

ALTERNATE
EXIT
081°34.5 W

15'

20'

230°/50°

330°/150°

Reef

9'

5'

3'

Beaches & Huts

21°35.5
081°37.0

Reef

LT

MAIN
CHANNEL
21°35.0
081°36.7

CAYO BALLENATOS

1,000'

6'

4'

12'

12'

8'

various capacities. On the right, past the usual tee-shirt/art shops you may visit a turtle-farm, and just north of that there is a medical post and pharmacy which we have had occasion to use in the past (thank you, socialized medicine).

If you wait for the hourly ferry to return to the dock, free open buses collect tourists from the dock and take them to any of the hotels 5 miles along the southern beaches.

The bus runs east alongside the airport (complete with disco!) and if you wish to stop anywhere along the route just shout up to the driver. Likewise, when he delays too long after stopping.

At the hotels there are hard-currency shops where prices are surprisingly competitive and we have been able to purchase some beautiful books here.

Tours to other parts of the country are advertised in the hotel lobbies and if you fancy a ride in one of the huge radial-engined Russian biplanes which drone overhead then this is the place to get it. There is no reason to come all this way and not see as much of Cuba as possible, so for what in the greater scheme of things is really little additional cost (e.g., U.S. $25 to Havana) you might wish to fly on to parts of the mainland you would otherwise miss.

All varieties of watersports are available in Cayo Largo, and at the dock you're ideally placed to take advantage of scuba diving, jet-ski rentals, and boat-tours to various beaches for barbecues and booze.

Bonefish (macabí) and tarpon (sábalo) can be fished amongst the cays to the west, and if you want to use your dinghy then arrange with the resident Guarda Frontera at the dock for a despacho. Fishing guides (not very professional ones) can be arranged if you'd prefer to merely scare-off the fish.

ARRANGE CLEARANCE IN ADVANCE

Clearing out should best be arranged in advance as the officials actually have to come from the nearby airstrip, and there is the question of paying your bill.

If you are heading on for somewhere like Casilda to the east you will still need to clear with immigration.

A large yacht, once reportedly utilized for Fidel Castro's pleasure, is tied to the docks at Cayo Largo in the Cuban Cays. (Photo by Simon Charles)

SOUTH CUBAN BONUS:
A SIDE TRIP TO THE CAYMAN ISLANDS!

Okay, so you didn't know about this when you bought the book, but by now you're as close as you'll ever be to these islands. This could be the only opportunity you'll get.

Clear immigration in Cayo Largo, spend a week in the three small British-administered islands to the south, and come back into Cuba (at Casilda or Cienfuegos) without having travelled much out of your way... Sounds good, eh?

If you have any mechanical work to be done then this is a good place too, as there is a boatyard which can handle all aspects of maintenance, and parts are more easily obtainable than in Cuba.

An excellent place to become properly certified, scuba-diving is the main attraction in the Caymans.

GRAND CAYMAN
CHART NO.DMA 27241 (US)

A direct course from the exit at Cayo Largo to Georgetown Harbor along the west coast of Grand Cayman is 177°M, and the journey is 138 miles, assisted slightly by the counter-current looping south.

You may aim towards the middle of the island on 175°M if you prefer not to miss, but time your journey for a night-arrival, and you'll have the lights to aim at from well out to sea. Just be aware that there is a reef all along the north coast, and what lights you see are well inshore from this, sometimes 5 to 6 miles inshore.

If you come in by night you will be permitted to moor amongst the other craft in front of the city, and you can thus get a good night's rest before clearing in.

All arrivals in Grand Cayman must be made at the harbor (19°18.0N / 081°23.1) and the best times to arrive are Sundays and Mondays as cruise-liners visit most of the other days. You can contact the authorities at any time on channel 16 by calling Georgetown Port Security.

At night be careful to avoid the unlit dive-boats (and the yellow mini-submarines) which are moored up to 200 yards offshore, and use a flashlight to find a sandy patch for your anchor. The water is perfectly transparent, so you have no excuse for doing otherwise. This law is strictly enforced everywhere in the Cayman Islands, and to this end there are permanent dive-moorings (free on a first-come basis) situated along the wall offshore on all the islands.

These moorings must also be carefully avoided when making an approach, so pass just off the wall at night.

The coordinates given will put you 300 yards off the town's bakery and you will usually be expected to clear in 1/2 mile to the southeast, alongside a sloping concrete ramp on the northern side of the larger container wharf.

Due to the maniac activities of the water-taxis serving the cruise-ships there can be a lot of violent swells present and the slope will make for a tricky mooring, so leave your lines slack, and have someone fending off all the time you are alongside. Better yet, avoid the days on which the cruise-ships visit.

In an unfortunate contrast to Cuba, only the idle or curious will help with your lines here.

You will have to present your Cuban clearance-papers, fill-in customs and immigration forms, and receive a perfunctory spraying down by the Mosquito Research official who charges you $25 for the privilege. This gentleman never has any change, so if you don't want to get stiffed have the exact money ready.

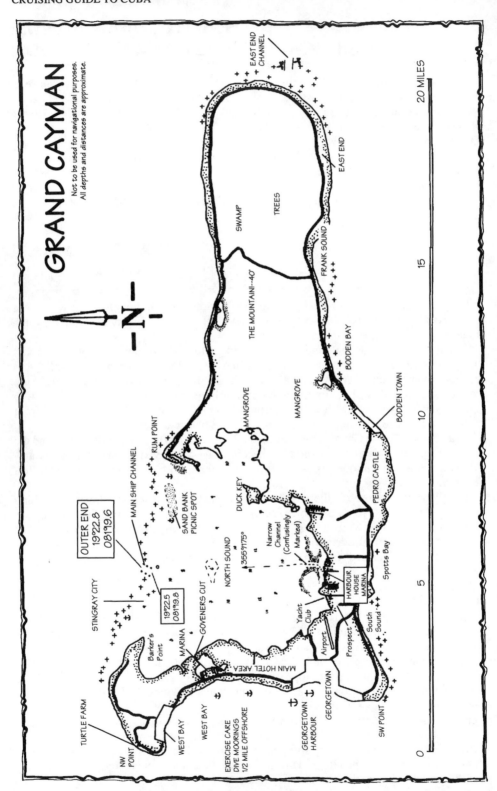

GRAND CAYMAN

Not to be used for navigational purposes.
All depths and distances are approximate.

N

EAST END CHANNEL

EAST END

SWAMP

TREES

FRANK SOUND

THE MOUNTAIN---40'

BODDEN BAY

MANGROVE

MANGROVE

BODDEN TOWN

RUM POINT

PEDRO CASTLE

MAIN SHIP CHANNEL

OUTER END
19°22.8
081°19.6

SAND BANK
PICNIC SPOT

DUCK KEY

Narrow Channel
(Confusingly
Marked)

355°/175°

Spotts Bay

NORTH SOUND

19°22.5
081°19.8

GOVENERS CUT

STINGRAY CITY

HARBOUR
HOUSE
MARINA

Barker's
Point

MARINA

Yacht
Club

South
Sound

Prospect

Airport

MAIN HOTEL AREA

TURTLE FARM

NW
POINT

WEST BAY

WEST BAY

EXERCISE CARE
DIVE MOORINGS
1/2 MILE OFFSHORE

GEORGETOWN
HARBOUR

GEORGETOWN

SW POINT

0   5   15   20 MILES

You may remain at anchor in the bay for the duration, or seek out a berth inside North Sound by coming round the island and entering the 1/2 mile marked channel at a position of 19°22.8N / 081°19.6W.

This large sound is relatively shallow in places but largely navigable across its area. Berths are available at Governors Harbour and a recent Japanese-funded development, both in the northwest portion of the bay. Or a course of 175°M will take you to Harbour House marina on the extreme southern edge of the sound where all maintenance work can be carried out.

The marina at Harbour House (channel 16) is in fact a proper boatyard equipped with two Travel-Lift hoists and facilities for hull, propeller, and engine work. Expensive to be sure, but at least available.

You will have to go through markers showing a dredged channel (6-foot max) just east of the marina as the sound is shallow along there, but don't be confused by the earlier floating marks which merely denote the limits to the Marine Replishment Zones in the sound.

Go berserk in the supermarkets.... After so long in Cuba you deserve it. Everything you were accustomed to before is once again on the shelves, but be careful not to blow your budget as prices are generally higher than elsewhere.

Get your scuba training done here too. You'll never encounter a better place for it and in any case you really should be properly trained (they even offer courses run in Japanese!).

Note: Rental cars are cheaper here, but cigarettes and booze are much cheaper in Cuba.

DEPARTING FOR THE SISTER ISLANDS

If departing Grand Cayman for the sister islands it will probably be best to travel overnight, in which case arrange your papers the day before in the offices downtown near the cruise-ship terminal. Your clearance is valid for 24 hours and you may leave directly from North Sound if you wish, but be extremely careful about the exit channel through the reef at night.

The *inner* end of the short channel is at 19°22.5N / 081°19.8W, but the course through the reef is 25°M and *not* north/south as might otherwise appear. The markers are indistinct at night and more than one yacht has been lost coming through on the wrong course, so it might be wisest to leave in the last light of the day.

Note: If going back to Cuba from North Sound then the course to Cayo Largo is 355°M for 133 miles.

The course to Cienfuegos is 019°M for 167 miles (see later notes about the Jagua Bank), and if going to Casilda head 030°M for 157 miles.

163

LITTLE CAYMAN & CAYMAN BRAC
CHART NO. DMA 27241 (US)

This can be a rough passage against both the prevailing winds and currents, so wait for settled weather (go to the airport for an up-to-the-minute forecast) and favorable winds before departing.

These twin islands both lie along the same course and due to their shape make a narrow target, but 076°M for 77 miles will take you from the reef exit in North Sound to the entrance at Owens Sound on the southwest coast of Little Cayman.

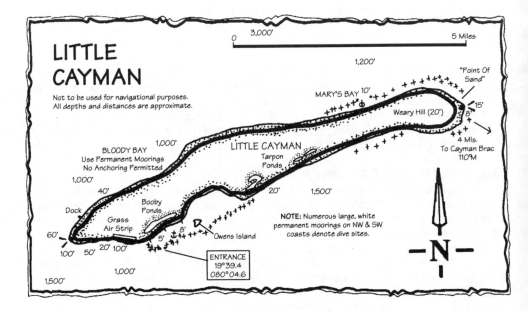

This is a narrow entrance, and due to its position relative to the prevailing swells should not be attempted in a southeast wind of any strength at all. Review the section on Reef Entrances if you have to do it under these conditions, and be careful. Many boats have been lost here to incautious skippers.

There are markers on the reef and also range-marks ashore that will guide you through (0°/180°M), but the sound is rather shallow, so turn right once inside and pick up the permanent mooring about 1/4-mile east near the reef. On no account attempt to approach the docks onshore as they require local knowledge and a draft of less than 4-foot.

Note: If there is any doubt, go round to the north side where you can tie up to any of the strong permanent dive-boat moorings along the wall in Bloody Bay. Except temporarily, don't trust the exposed concrete wharf there.

Even though you are coming in from Grand Cayman you will still require clearance here so you should contact Little Cayman Customs on channel 16 before arriving. Don't worry, the process is friendly and extremely quick. The officer will come out to you in his boat if you're in the sound, and if you're in Bloody Bay you can skip it until you get ashore.

It may appear on first glance that Little Cayman presents too many difficulties to be worth it, and to a visitor it may seem that all they do here is drink and dive, but the diving along the northwest coast in Bloody Bay really is superb.

If you visit any of the four small hotels ashore they will be pleased to include you in their regular organized dives and I'll admit to bias here, but if I wanted the absolute best I'd dive with Gaye at Pirates Point Resort (on channel 16).

Little Cayman is also famous for its iguanas who have the run of the island and can often be seen mooching about near the small terminal at the eastern end of the grass airstrip. If you do rent a car from the island's one shop remember that both iguanas and aircraft have right-of-way on the road!

Excellent food is also to be had at Pirates Point Resort, whilst the eccentric proprietor, Gladys Howard, takes guests on nature-walks every Sunday morning.

LEAVING FOR CUBA FROM THE CAYMANS

If you are leaving for Cuba you must clear out from the slightly larger and considerably more organized island of Cayman Brac, just east of Little Cayman. This can be done from the immigration offices in Stake Bay (19°43.0N / 079°50.0W) in front of the prominent radio tower 4 miles along the northwest coast.

There are permanent moorings just off the small concrete landing so you can dinghy ashore with the ship's papers to clear in or out. The offices are 200 yards along the road.

Clearance only takes 15 minutes, and there's a supermarket just opposite the government offices where you can stock up on ice and whatever else you've managed to forget.

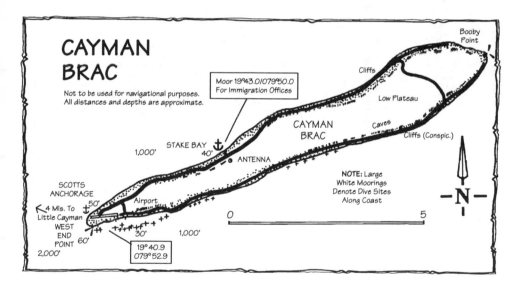

Equally supplied with dive-sites (even if they're not quite as good) the Brac also has a sound in the southwest corner of the island where most of the dive-boats moor.

The entrance at 19°40.9N /079°52.9W is marked, but this sound is also shallow so you will have to pick your way carefully once inside... Call the Brac Reef Resort on channel 16 (or any one of the multitude of dive-boats) for up-to-the minute advice on mooring.

There are no surprises clearing back into Cuba from the Cayman Islands, especially if you have retained your previous Cruising Permit/Safety Inspection Certificate.

The course to Cienfuegos from Stake Bay is 349°M for 143 miles, and if you prefer to go direct to Casilda set 359°M (I use the north-star) for 119 miles. Both these courses will put you a safe mile or so west of the main entrance channels.

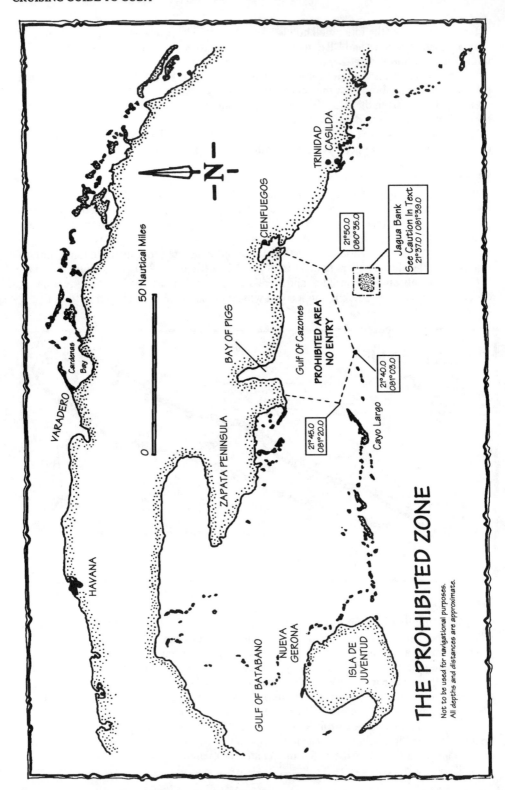

THE PROHIBITED ZONE

Not to be used for navigational purposes.
All depths and distances are approximate.

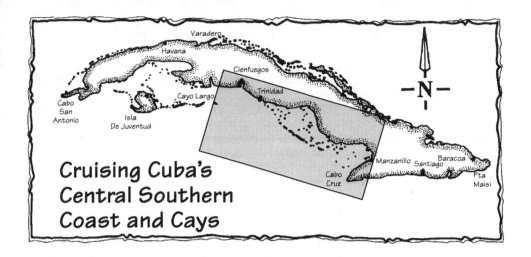

Cruising Cuba's
Central Southern
Coast and Cays

CAYO LARGO TO CABO CRUZ

ROUTES

At the western end of this section there is a large area surrounding the Bay of Pigs to the east of the Gulf of Cazones. For various reasons, strategic, political, and historic, this area is a prohibited zone and is marked as such on all Cuban charts. If using any of the foreign chart issues, then it will probably not be shown. If so, draw it in.

As you can see, there's still room to go round if you're transiting the coast and wish to enter Cazones (Chart No. ICH 1160), but do not pretend innocence if you're found inside the Zona Prohibida. The history of this area is too symbolic to the military for them to resist giving the unwary a rough ride.

Between Cienfuegos and Casilda there isn't much in the line of strategy to consider, but going eastwards over the next 150-200 miles you may choose to take either an inside passage, along a low lying coast, or an outer route through the cays which angle progressively further offshore.

THE INNER ROUTE

The inner route is plied by commercial vessels delivering cargo up and down the coast, and is thus extensively marked. You can do the entire route along major channels signposted by a familiar mixture of large concrete box-structures, floating buoys, and rust-streaked pylon affairs camouflaged by a fertile mixture of bird feathers, droppings, and dried fish-heads.

This route will take you past Casilda and into the gulfs of Ana María and Guacanayabo (another name which requires practice) where the only townships deal more or less exclusively in the export of sugar, then it runs up against the jutting peninsula of Granma province where the cities of Manzanillo and Niquero offer a better chance of resupply.

THE OUTER ROUTE

The outer route will take you, as before, to Casilda and the inland city of Trinidad, but here it diverges along the line of the cays, following them through the Gardens of the Queen and the Twelve League Labyrinth before linking up again with the inner route at Manzanillo.

The prevailing easterlies are much modified by the considerable land mass of the island

and it's more likely that you will have favourable winds for easting along this stretch than the exposed Bahamas-side of Cuba. There is also a convenient southeast counter-current which can assist if you chose to cruise outside of the cays and along the wall.

The very nature of this almost totally deserted and untravelled multitude of islands, makes it almost impossible to give an extensive cay-by-cay guide except for a few selected anchorages along our route. Certainly you will discover others off to the side, and even find that some reported here are supplanted or made redundant by your own discoveries. That's only how it should be, and out of all the cruising areas in Cuba this one offers the most opportunities for further experimentation. After all, the area enclosed by the cays here is approximately 5,000 nautical square miles!

In addition, there are no inhabitants here, and while you may occasionally run across tourists in the various halts prior to the southern cays you most assuredly will not come across any here. Apart from the occasional fishing boat you will be as isolated from your fellow man as you've ever been.

PASSAGE PLANNING CONSIDERATIONS

Regarding passage planning, along the outer cays your courses should be set only after consulting adequate charts, and you should be prepared to abandon fixed courses when necessary. Along here there are numerous passes, occasionally calling for six or seven course changes in a relatively short distance and precisely detailed descriptions can be mind-numbingly complex.

You may prefer therefore, to lay out your own courses through the cays following only a general description of the route. For this you should be prepared to use both the experience you've already gained in reef-navigation, and proper charts.

If, on the other hand you're taking the inner route, then the main ship channels between the major ports along the coast are well-marked along their length and need little description.

Oxen are utilized in the fields for transporting the harvest and other agricultural purposes. (Photo by George Halloran)

There are a variety of charts on the market dealing with this section of Cuba. When we first travelled here we had a disparate mixture, including a few older photocopies obtained from different sources, and it was only much later that we obtained a complete matched set of original Cuban charts.

While we still maintain that the best are the ICH series (black and white or colored), if they are difficult to come by then by all means use from among the others but be prepared to feel your way through the smaller passes. Everyone else does.

Note: The magnetic deviation which has been sneakily increasing as you've progressed from Cabo San Antonio in the west is now going to grow from 2° at Cienfuegos to 3.5° at Cabo Cruz, so don't forget to factor this into your courses.

CAUTION!

You may be planning to arrive direct from Cayo Largo taking the direct route across the Gulf of Cazones to Trinidad. If so, consider carefully the shallow Jagua bank along your path. This isolated area of reef leaps vertically up from the depths to within a few feet of the surface and contains several wrecks perched atop a 36-square mile submarine pedestal some 5,000 feet high. It would be best to avoid an area 3-5 miles in all directions from position 21°37.0N / 080°39.0W, unless passing by during the day and considering a dive along its undoubtedly promising walls.

The waters in the gulf can also be rougher than expected (perhaps due to this obstruction and the currents swirling through) so have the boat well prepared for what is in any case an open offshore run.

We have moreover come across heavy squalls, making for such an uncomfortable passage that the crew had to be brought below for safety in the confused seas.

CIENFUEGOS
CHART NOS. ICH 1142, 1158, OR 1840 (CUBAN)

The city of Cienfuegos, one of the oldest in Cuba, is somewhat marred visually by large cement works and a naval base, but work on the imposing nuclear generating station has been suspended in the last few years and for the cruiser there are spendid views along the entry routes and past the castle guarding the splendid harbour. It is also one of the largest cities in Cuba and any marine repair work one might desire can be carried out within the usual confines of parts availability.

The narrow entrance to the enormous bay is deep and free of any outstanding dangers and may be made visually from anywhere around the outer buoys marking the channel. There is a Guárda Frontera post one mile in and some 600 yards before the old fort high on the western shores of the entrance channel, so you must stop here for clearance before continuing onwards.

If already legitimately in the country, the Guárda Frontera may allow you to continue on to the marina inside the bay for later clearance, but don't count on it.

Whatever, you will be probably pressured to take a pilot on board but resist this by saying you already know the way to the Punta Gorda Base Nautica and avoid paying a perfectly unecessary $30 fee.

Passing west of the small cay at the inner entrance to the bay, from the No.15 buoy head 014°M to the No.18 mark just west of the peninsula at Pta.. Gorda where the yellow and grey docks of the Base Nautica will be on your starboard, north of the hotel and close to the public beach.

The moorings more or less radiate outwards from a central dock parallel to the shore, and due to the real danger of swim-aboard crime it will be wisest to berth at one of the northernmost docks so as to be as far as possible from the beach. We know of at least one foreign yacht which lost its dinghy here, so secure yours well.

There were several yachts damaged here during the storms of early 1993 and those that fared best were also on the northern docks facing into the swells.

MARINA IS NEAR HOTEL

Once ashore, the marina offices are to the left while the hotel Jagua is over towards the right at the beginning of the peninsula. Being so close, the hotel can be utilized for phone calls, tour inquiries, car rental, taxis, casual supplies and so on, while there is a source of wholesale provisions for the boat by asking for Cemex at the marina.

When in search of the social scene go north along the Malecon (the waterfront road) until past Av.46 where the road changes into the Paseo del Prado.

If you're looking for the older parts, then Pueblo Nuevo just west of the Paseo is where the most interesting places such as the José Martí Square, museums, and historic buildings are located.

An example of a Cuban navigational marker. (Photo by Simon Charles)

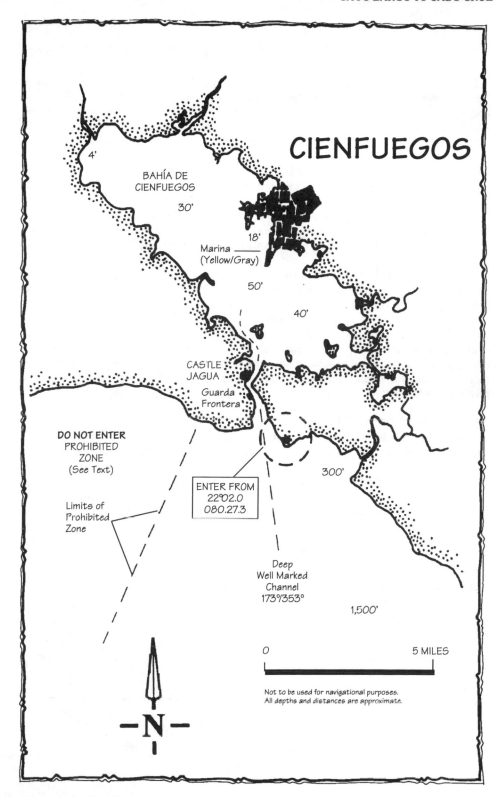

CIENFUEGOS

BAHÍA DE
CIENFUEGOS

4'

30'

18'

Marina
(Yellow/Gray)

50'

40'

CASTLE
JAGUA

Guarda
Frontera

DO NOT ENTER
PROHIBITED
ZONE
(See Text)

Limits of
Prohibited
Zone

ENTER FROM
22°02.0
080.27.3

300'

Deep
Well Marked
Channel
173°/353°

1,500'

0   5 MILES

Not to be used for navigational purposes.
All depths and distances are approximate.

— N —

CASILDA
CHART NOS. ICH 1141, 1432 OR 1431 (CUBAN)

Despite the limited appeal and downright ugliness of this port, it does serve the city of Trinidad some six or seven miles inland. There is absolutely no excuse for visiting Cuba and neglecting that jewel of a city, so beautiful that UNESCO has declared it part of the World Heritage list.

In addition, it's the gateway to the southeastern cays and the inland mountains.

THE CITY THRIVED ON SUGAR

One of the original seven colonial villas (garrisons) in the era of the Conquistadores, the city once thrived on sugar. Thousands of slaves were imported to till the fields of the rich families who built their majestic dwellings around the cathedral of Santisima Trinidad off the main square. Interestingly, some of the streets have old cannons buried muzzle-down to protect the corner-houses from being damaged by wide-turning horse-drawn vehicles and the like.

The old mansions in the cobbled streets have largely been preserved and tourists are encouraged to visit these. For a dollar or two you can stroll about opulent rooms filled with their original furniture, all the time followed by an informative middle-aged matron who precisely describes (or makes a wild guess at) any of the objects you might wish to pause over. One of the museums here, devoted to the years of CIA destabilization campaigns, even has a hands-on exhibit of a captured "pirate" vessel used to prey on official or unofficial Cuban boats and to land agents in the area. A fast cabin-cruiser painted strangely matt-black and converted to fire heavy machine-guns from fixed mounts... Many's the time I've wished for one of my own.

THE ROUTE INTO CASILDA

Whether approaching from the gulf of Cazones or from Cienfuegos, the way into the sheltered gulf of Ana María at Casilda is through the Pasa de las Mulatas a few miles south of Casilda.

This pass through the reef is used by major vessels and is consequently marked by a large light at position 21°41.7N / 079°58.6 although you could safely enter anywhere up to a mile north of this. Go through along a course of 83°M and turn due north at the following marker 2/3 of a mile in.

This will take you to a channel light at the eastern end of the Ancón peninsula some 2 miles away, fine on the port bow. There is a shallow bank either side of your course as you get within half a mile of the light so don't stray off-line, but the sand-bank on your starboard is marked by a stake so you will be able to see whether you're on line.

There is usually a motley collection of small fishing boats at the reef so go slowly past them as they don't have a lot of freeboard. Usually powered by simple sails made of crudely-stitched canvas and sackcloth, these tiny affairs are solely balanced by the crewmembers' precarious seating-position with little in the way of ballast to help. If they don't wave back it's probably because they're scared to let go.

The port officials here, unusually enough, will actually answer repeated VHF calls to "Seguridad Marítima" on 16 and

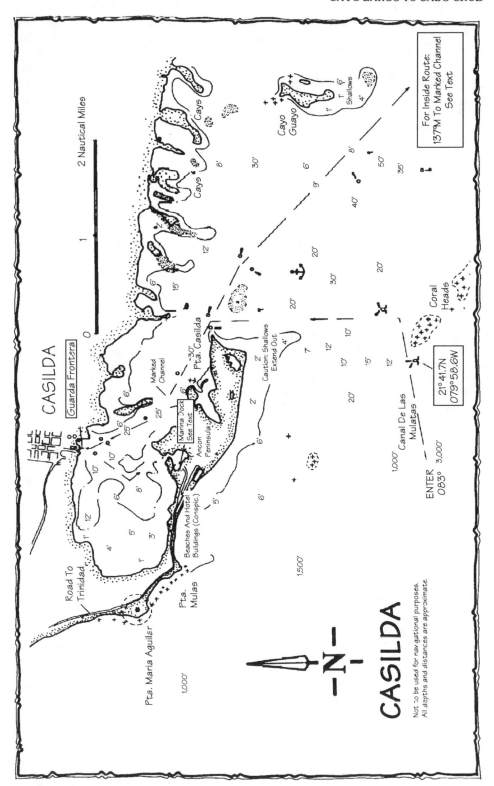

CASILDA

Not to be used for navigational purposes.
All depths and distances are approximate.

For Inside Route:
137°M To Marked Channel
See Text

21° 41.7N
079° 58.6W

will offer instructions if you are unsure, but in any case you should proceed in as described.

Once at the tip of the peninsula, the main channel will open up along a properly marked and maintained passage WNW into the inner bay harbour and whether you're coming in from Cayo Largo, Cienfuegos, or the Cayman Islands you will still have to put up with approximately the same formalities when docking.

DOCKING

The well constructed wharf northwest across the basin to the right, inviting though it may be, is not your destination. Instead, you proceed north towards a closer sagging wooden affair crowded by fishing vessels of all descriptions, and containing a small sentry-post/ shack halfway along its length. There are some dangerous pilings barely protruding from the surface directly off the end, so come in from the right where there is 8-9 foot depth and find a gap into which you can manouver. Be flexible in your attitude towards fenders here as the top of the wharf is irregular to say the least, and it may be better to have crewmembers permanently assigned to fending-off once secured at the dock.

We have had endless delays when checking in as the officials have to come from the ship's terminal across the basin and even when they arrive they tend to be somewhat picky.

This is the only place anywhere on the coast of Cuba where we have been sniffed over by a dog, who looked most unhappy as he wildly scrabbled for grip on deck and further made clear his absolute refusal to visit a hot engine-room.

Things can be even slower on a Sunday so avoid this day like the plague, and you won't have to pay extra dues for the priviledge. Mind you, you can pass the time watching the small fishing dinghies being searched too when they come in.

AFTER CLEARING CUSTOMS

Having cleared customs and immigration (both of these august bodies will require their pound of flesh), it will be suggested that you proceed to the Base Nautica across the bay south where you can see the top of the hotel over the mangroves. Translated literally into "Nautical Base", this is an airless, ugly, mooring between mosquito infested cays behind the Ancón Hotel complex. The various boats serving the tourist industry anchor there at night but the entrance is shallow and not shown on all charts, so I would advise care and a sharp eye on the depth-sounder. The bottom is soft mud, so no harm can come to you, but in any case the base is a charmless place to spend any time and it may be better to anchor off to the side of the main Casilda entrance channel.

You will, even moored inside the base, have to use your dinghy to come ashore so the additional inconvenience will be minimal.

The one advantage offered by the Base Nautica is that it does have a dirty concrete wharf alongside which you can draw if purchasing fuel, and there is a stand-pipe for water too.

Fuel prices in 1993 were 90 cents a litre for diesel ($3.40/gal. U.S.). We have also obtained ice there by requesting it well beforehand and including it in a deal for provisions.

MOORING YOUR DINGHY

Your dinghy may be moored at the low concrete dock inside the Base Nautica, a short red-dust walk from the hotels fronting the beach on the other side of the peninsula. A new hotel, with an emphasis on scuba-diving, was being constructed in 1993 and this may well be finished by the time this book is printed, but at time of writing there was only the Hotel Ancón next to the base and two other hotels about two or three miles along the beach.

The Ancón seems marooned in the 1950's and 60's and luckily this ghastly object is crumbling at a goodly pace, so with luck it may no longer blight the beachfront when you arrive. The dimly-lit lobby is crowded with package-tourists looking emptily at the dust covered walls and wondering what there is to do except hang out on the beach or take even more package-tours to other parts of Cuba. They wear coloured wristbands to denote their group (and rate), eating at prescribed times in prescribed refectories... Horseman, pass by.

Better spend your time in Trinidad, or if you wish to experience a more typically Cuban day out then spend Sunday afternoon on the beach at La Boca just down the coast-road on the way to Trinidad. This beach, at the mouth of a narrow river is where the inhabitants of the area meet to relax in a lively congregation of music, flirting, and fistfights. They're far more interesting than the dowdy crowd of pale visitors from the north along the Ancón Peninsula, and you'll be made more welcome too.

As you're moored close at hand, the unfortunate hotel Ancón will have to be your base of operations for renting cars (in spite of the notices there may not be any available just when you want) or obtaining taxis into the city. A trip into the spectacular Escambray Mountains will be a welcome diversion after having been aboard for some days, so explore this possibility with regards to the rental car question, combining it with your visit to Trinidad. If driving, beware of the hordes of local cyclists wobbling two-up along the beach roads, and the additional hazard of enthusiastic looking foreigners on cycling tours!

There are a couple of hard-currency shops on the premises too, and although the range of goods sold is limited you may be able to re-provision somewhat if you've used up your roasted peanuts and bottled olives. The liquor racks are always full though, and you may find cosmetics and skin-diving equipment at competitive prices.

As in other hotels in Cuba, there is always a cigar-maker rolling his products by hand in the lobby.

One of our crewmembers got ill on a passage once and received excellent attention at the medical post under the hotel, so don't forget this service.

LEAVING:

If planning to go far afield from Casilda you will have to return to the Guárda Frontera post on the dock and await clearances and your despacho. They'll even give you a Guía de Recala (list of stops) extending all the way to Santiago, so avail yourself of this facility emphasizing that you're going by way of the cays and will be anchored out most of the way.

If you're only going out for a day or two among the cays here then Victoriano the local Guárda Frontera soldier at the Base Nautica will be able to issue you with the despacho.

For the inside passage along the coast, follow the large markers out but do not turn south at the tip of the peninsula along your original entry route. Instead, continue on to the end of the markers, go southeast 4 miles along 137°M to pass Cayo Guáyo well off to your port side, then on into a marked channel turning back NE at 21°40.6N / 079°54.2W at the Canal de los Guáiros. At the other end, go ESE following intermittent marks to the Pasa de los Machos, another well signposted northeasterly channel at 21°39.1N / 079°48.3W.

From here you can easily navigate eastward down the coast towards the port of your choice. It's mostly marked all along the way.

CAYO BLANCO

Near Casilda and deserving of a visit even if you're going to take the inner route. You can snorkel for lobster close off the eastern tip in the elkhorn-coral forests, and follow that up with a midnight barbecue on the beach.

To get here, you retrace your entry route, but instead of actually exiting the pass out through the reef at the Pasa de las Mulatas merely proceed from the inside marker along a course of 132° M to the wreck on the coast of Cayo Blanco some 5.5 miles away. You might alternately parallel the reef along the outside on a similar course.

Be careful when mooring here, as there is an underwater-bank east of this point which can cause problems if the Kabatic effect causes a wind shift (as it surely will around here) in the night.

We've found it best to remain a hundred yards north of the wreck and to make sure the anchor is well dug in as the early morning winds can be strong here.

This cay is the very occasional destination for boat tours from the hotel Ancón and they like to moor to the wreck itself but don't stay long. You on the other hand can spend the day lobstering from the dinghy, or wandering along the beach and through the middle of the cay to the other shore. On that side there is evidence of a long-ago cataclysmic storm which has heaped up enormous mounds of dead coral, ripped from the depths to bleach in the sun.

At Cayo Blanco the aforesaid wind-shifts once caused us to seek out shelter across the bay in the **Fondeadero** (anchorage) **Jobabo** close in to the mangroves. Say 3 miles away on 30°M

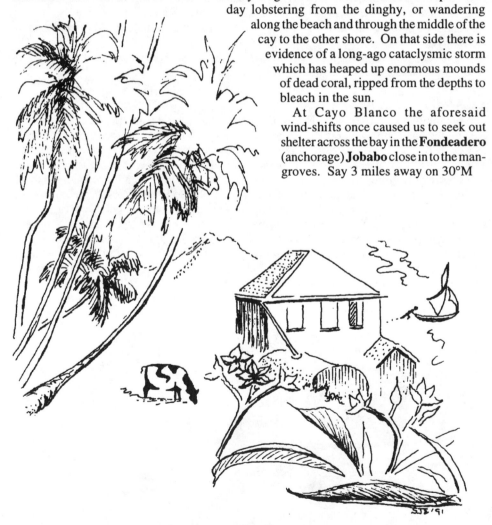

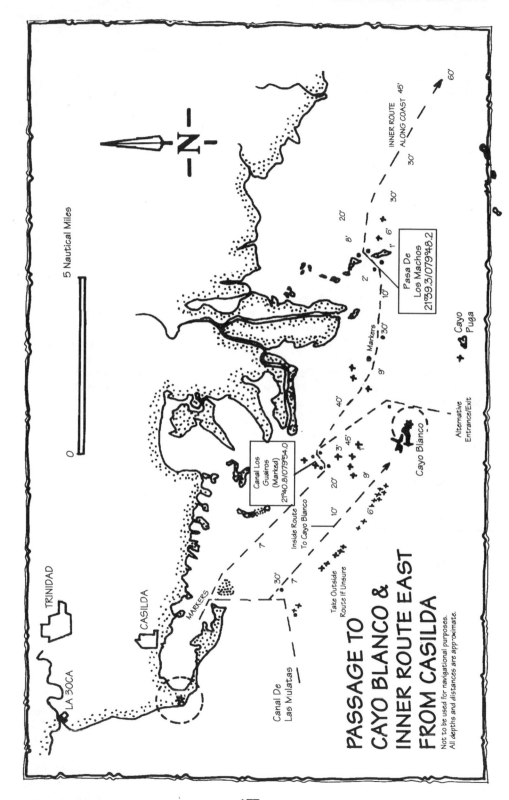

PASSAGE TO
CAYO BLANCO &
INNER ROUTE EAST
FROM CASILDA

Not to be used for navigational purposes.
All depths and distances are approximate.

5 Nautical Miles

Canal De
Las Mulatas

Take Outside
Route If Unsure

Inside Route
To Cayo Blanco

Canal Los
Guairos
(Marked)
21°40.8/079°54.0

Pasa De
Los Machos
21°39.3/079°48.2

INNER ROUTE
ALONG COAST

Cayo Puga

Cayo Blanco

Alternative
Entrance/Exit

Markers

TRINIDAD

CASILDA

LA BOCA

MARKERS

CAYO ZAZA DE FUERA
CHART NO. ICH 1431 (CUBAN)

Travelling southeast along the outer cays we need places to rest up overnight and the first of these could well be Zaza de Fuera at 21°27.5N /079°34.8W, easily attainable from either the inner or the outside routes.

If coming from Casilda along the inner route: Proceeding from the last pass at Los Machos, take up a course of 113°M some 10 miles towards the light on Cayo Blanco de Zaza with its odd structures nearby, then a further 8 miles along 168°M (or visual if you can see that far) to the tip of the island.

If coming here from an earlier halt at Cayo Blanco: The easiest route is outside the reef via the passes at either end of that cay, and back in past the light at the Canal de Tunas about 11miles SE. From here it's visual (117°M) approx. 7 miles to the anchorage.

At first we anchored here on the west side of the island amongst the shallows in 5-7 feet but later found a secluded inner lagoon with an entrance on the west side of the island, north of the wreck and the stake.

You can manouver into this facinating bayou to find yourself totally surrounded on all sides by a protecting wall of tall mangroves and with passages out the other side for the dinghy. Inside this secure anchorage you will see fish leaping, birds nesting, and taking the dinghy through to the other northeast side of the island you can trail a hook or take your spear for even better luck over the coral there.

Speaking of which, the bottom on the east side is a lot shallower and sharper, so leave the way you came in.

From Cayo Zaza de Fuera heading further along the inner routes, give the northwest tip of the cay a wide berth and proceed north to Tunas, or 98°M to pick up the channel markers north of **Manati Bank** some 14 miles away.

On the other hand you may be continuing along the outer passages to the beautiful archipelago of cays and reefs called The Gardens of the Queen and the Twelve-League Labyrinth.

CAYO BRETON & LOS JARDINES DE LA REINA
CHART NOS. ICH 1141 & 1430 (CUBAN)

Directly between Zaza and Cayo Bretón, the direct line from the southwest tip is closely proscribed by the presence of a long bank on the starboard side of the boat. Your route therefore should aim to leave adequate clearance over to that side by taking your vessel round the shallows and northeast of Zaza, to enable a course of 170°M over the 27 miles to the lights at the inside of the Bretón reef entrance (21°11.4N / 079°28.9W). Here you can visually steer in a gentle parabola into the lee of Cayo Bretón.

At the southwest tip of the cay there are more of the Acopios or fishing-service docks as described in chapter five (Cayos de la Lena), where you can obtain ice or any other services you wish to beg, borrow, or buy. This is a good place to put up for the night and from which you can explore on dinghy.

We have in the past picked our way in between the reef and Cayo Bretón, endeavoring to find a way into the lagoon between Cinco Balas (Five-Bullets Key) and Alcatraz Grande. But this is a tricky prospect, and although we got there we couldn't actually enter the lagoon in the end. We did find an entry through a gap in the reef 240°/60°M at position 21°02.4N /079°19.7W, which you might use if you wish to anchor overnight in this area as we have done peacefully at Alcatracito. Gosh, I just love the names of these cays.

Having headed out the gap in the reef again after anchoring overnight, you can parallel the shore off any breakers along the cays (Cayos Las Doce Leguas), or come in almost immediately through Boca Grande (Big-Mouth canal) to a safe anchorage worth investigating just round the corner at Estero Inglés.

Rolling hills in this countryside scene are dotted with rural homes. The hills extend nearly to the water. (Photo by George Halloran)

CAYOS CABALLONES, ANCLITAS & THE INNER KEYS
CHART NOS. ICH 1139 & 1428 (CUBAN)

Some 13 miles to the east (80°M) of Boca Grande canal on the inside section there is a wonderful group of cays where good sheltered anchorages are easily available. You may proceed along a course of 75°M into the crescent of Cayo Cuervo (Crow Cay) or even continue a further 7 miles to Manuel Gomez entering 75°M to a position of approximately 21°03.0N / 078°50.5W.

The fishing fleet hangs out around here with their Centros de Acopios for ice, water, stores etc.and over at Algodon Grande nearby a hotel is being constructed too. But in the main the place is pretty well deserted and this group of cays with their smaller cousins could well be deserving of a week or so. If you wish to enter Algodon Grande then you should approach from below to come in at the gap behind the reef over on the southwest tip.

These cays also make for a convenient jump-off point for the inner ship-canal towards the southeast or if visiting the town of Jucaro 30 miles to the north.

You may on the other hand, prefer to travel along the outer cays where the two contrasting sides present themselves as passages for coasting.

179

Both these routes offer a convenient route depending on your preference as to the wind, with the outer passage offering more beaches and the inner route more tempting if it's rough outside.

Do not imagine that the inner passage will always be calm, as within this large gulf a stormy northeast wind will have quite enough time to reach a goodly velocity, and can whip up large waves thank you, in spite of the ostensible shelter of the mainland.

On the northern side, trailing southwest after the Boca Grande canal as far as Caballones, there is a long mostly-submerged inner reef separated from the cays by a half a mile and in a northeasterly blow this might appear to offer some shelter from broadside waves on the inside route. Don't be tempted, as we've found that the reef for some reason or the other does not in fact abate much of the seas; it's shallow between the reef and the cay, and you need to be constantly on the lookout for coral heads.

If it's rough inside the gulf, go along the outside instead where an interesting anchorage may be found inside Las Auras behind Punta Escondida on Cayo Caballones. In spite of it not being shown on chart No. 1139 there is a reef entry from outside at 20°50.5N / 070°03.9W along a heading of 72°M.

From the above position there is excellent scuba-diving all along the outer wall just where your depth-sounder suddenly drops off the scale.

The presence of the wall, even if a bit intimidating to the novice diver, does make for easy underwater navigation. Just head one way along the edge, and come back following the same route. You should do the deeper portion first, down the drop-off to your comfort/ skill level and come back along the shallower top edge where you will be able to pick up on the anchor, or the boat bobbing overhead.

PLEASE, ANYTHING BUT LOBSTER...

Passing the fishing boats rafted together for company at the Canal de Caballones we come to Cayo Anclitas where there's even a turtle rearing station on the eastern end. You may enter the Piedra Grande or Piedra Chiquita passes to anchor in the flats there and to stock your freezer compartment, or alternatively continue on the outside for six more miles to Cayo Cachiboca where you can anchor in the western part of the pass.

Be careful, my crew have complained bitterly about being served lobster for breakfast, supper, lunch etc., for a week and a half!

That trip, we even made lobster *soup* for a change.

Having left your overnight anchorages to continue along the coast you can again take a mid-morning break to scuba dive in beautifully clear waters over the coral reef and then continue your journey two hours later in the afternoon, cooled, refreshed and thrilled.

As before, lower the anchor near the wall for the best dives. Sometimes there are two distinct walls, say one at 20-30 feet and a further one at 70-80 feet going straight down. I've been repeatedly buzzed by an inquisitive tarpon off the coast here at 60 feet, just above the second ledge. It's very startling!

BEACH FRINGED CAYS

Proceeding along the coast in any wind north of east, the seas will make for relaxed cruising. The tiny cays are fringed with beautiful white beaches, and coming in over the wall it'll take a strong will or a tight schedule to resist pausing somewhere before Cayo Caguamas 20 miles on. There is evidence of hotel construction along the coast there just before the light tower halfway along but this appears abandoned now, perhaps testimony to the difficulties of investment in Cuba.

Doubtless thoughts of retiring to a cay somewhere along the southern rim will have already come to mind, but take note of such signs. Many are the foreign investors in Cuba who've confessed disenchantment with local business practices, and broken promises.

Perhaps this is why the coast here will be so rewarding to cruise for so many years to come.

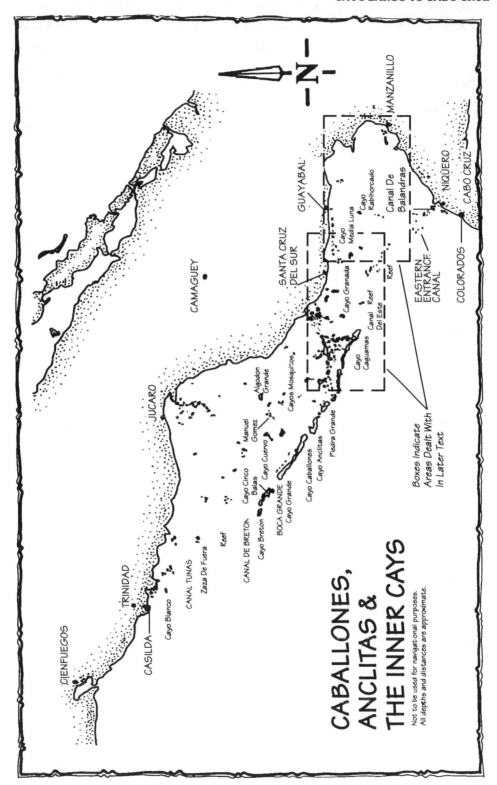

CABALLONES,
ANCLITAS &
THE INNER CAYS

Not to be used for navigational purposes.
All depths and distances are approximate.

181

THE INNER KEYS & CHANNEL TO MANZANILLO
CHART NOS. ICH 1138 & 1426 (CUBAN)

As before, you will have noticed your courses needing still further adjustment to compensate for the growing magnetic deviation. Refering to my old charts, still pencil-marked with unerased courses I see the notation. " Mag Dev seems to have grown to 3-4 deg".

Figure it in when deviating from those headings shown here.

TOWARDS CAYO CAGUAMAS

From the outside passage you can come in through the buoyed-channel at Cabeza del Este on the eastern tip of Cayo Caguamas where the fishing fleet has a small hideout. If the light still allows it there's a wonderful sheltered inlet located at **Cayo Granada** (20°37.6N / 078°14.8W) some 8 miles away approx. 30-35°M, and it's well worth making for here if you expect any trouble from the east or northeast.

This is a sickle-shaped cay with good water anywhere inside its bay, and apart from an area of shoal waters on its northwest tip you may enter anywhere on the western side. There's a small and perfectly visible obstruction (a pile) in the bay just south of the middle but apart from this you should have no problems here. We've used this cay to shelter from a violent cold front which swept in from the east, but in any case it makes an excellent jumping-off point for any of the the coastal towns like Santa Cruz or Guayabal along the route to Manzanillo.

From here, it's an easy 8-mile run 107°M to the Outer Mate Passage, a well marked pass off the southern tip of the cays reaching out from the mainland. You are now back in the main commercial channel inside the cays and heading generally towards the ports on the peninsula of Granma Province. The channel bears 139°M along a string of marks to the next pass 6 miles on at Juan Suarez whereupon you can head some 30 miles towards the Chinchorro Pass through the shallow banks and coral heads obstructing the eastern central portion of the gulf.

WORTHWHILE FOR SHELTER

Along the way to the pass (90°M) you'll pass closely by two other cays worth using for shelter or pleasure. **Media Luna**, and **Rabihorcada**. (See chart on page 184).

If using photocopies, or even original black and white charts, be careful not to misinterpret them and think that the reefs comprising the misnamed Esperanza Buena (Good Hope) bank to the southeast are really cays; they're not.

If light is a factor, then halt along the way at one or the other cays named above. They both offer better hope.

The first time we passed here, using photocopies of photocopies, we made this elementary mistake and headed for what we'd assumed was shelter 10 miles away. Only when the expected cay failed to pop up over the horizon did we realise our error, and it was a bit of a scramble to get back to Rabihorcado before nightfall. Mind you, we did thereupon discover a strange inner-world inside the cay, and entered through a narrow stick-marked channel on the western side.

This channel, not at all obvious and only 15 feet wide, lies in the second shallow bay from the northwest tip and progresses east/west from approximately 20°31.1N / 077°38.2W into a series of secret lagoons splitting the cay.

If the entrance is a bit tricky, the deep and totally hidden anchorage is more than worth the trouble and really sums up what cruising the southern cays is all about. Clear, black, limpid waters, creepy with presence. Of what, we can only surmise.

NOTE: THIS CHART ADJOINS THE CHART ON FOLLOWING PAGE

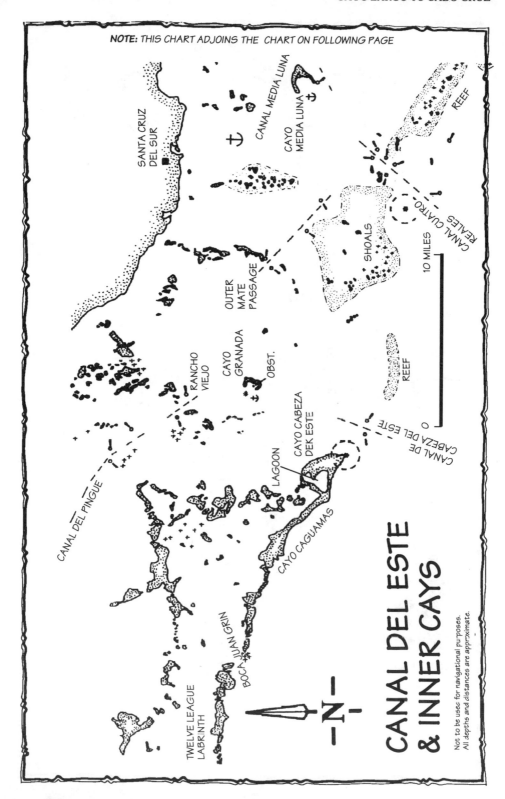

CANAL DEL ESTE
& INNER CAYS

Not to be used for navigational purposes.
All depths and distances are approximate.

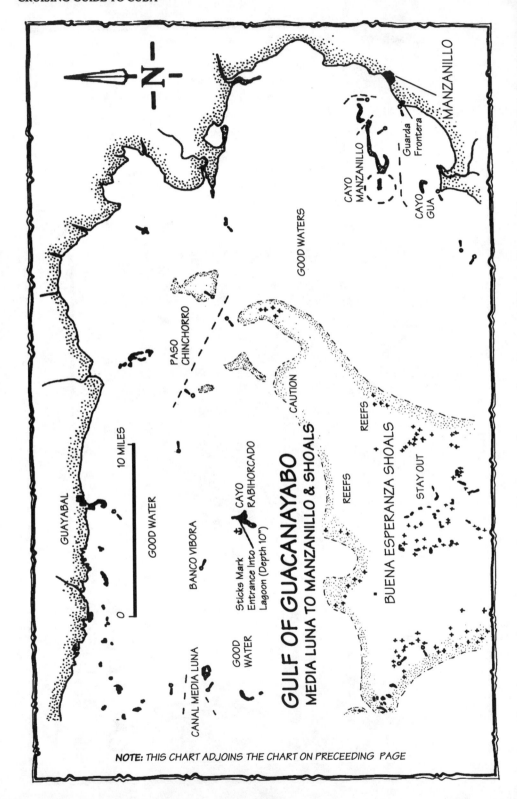

GULF OF GUACANAYABO
MEDIA LUNA TO MANZANILLO & SHOALS

MANZANILLO

CAYO MANZANILLO

CAYO GUA

Guarda Frontera

GOOD WATERS

PASO CHINCHORRO

CAUTION

REEFS

REEFS

BUENA ESPERANZA SHOALS

STAY OUT

GUAYABAL

10 MILES

GOOD WATER

BANCO VIBORA

Sticks Mark Entrance Into Lagoon (Depth 10")

CAYO RABIHORCADO

GOOD WATER

CANAL MEDIA LUNA

NOTE: THIS CHART ADJOINS THE CHART ON PRECEEDING PAGE

Passing through the canal at Chinchorro it's a straight run (126°M for 17 miles) to Manzanillo on the mainland coast and guarded by cays right in front. If you wish, you may go round the cay to the north (the main commercial route), but there is a 140/320° passage between the cays at Pasa Honda (enter from 20°22.5N / 077°10.7W) which is just as easy.

We've never been able to get a reply from any of the harbour authorities here (and if we did the static on the VHF all along this part of the coast would make them unintelligable), so do like us and show up unannounced.

MANZANILLO
CHART NO. ICH 1138 (CUBAN)

This provincial city seems to have seen better days but still retains a certain charm with its malecon (sea-wall) edged with tiny public parks. The potholed main street runs parallel and at its northern end is lined with wide sidewalks sheltered by sagging, overhanging roofs. Supported by pillars, these roofs give it an intriguing if rundown colonial aspect. In addition, further in there are several older buildings around the main square where there is another museum.

Originally a smuggling port and now dealing mainly with the more legitimate transport of sugar and general cargo, this is the best chance you will have for reprovisioning along the coast here and for touring the mountains to the southeast.

If coming in from an extended cruise amongst the cays you're probably out of the habit of checking in, but this is one of the more major cities along the coast so they'll insist on proper documentation. Entering from the north, the Guárda Frontera post is partially concealed from view, and the first time we entered we had to adopt our standard tactic of approaching an occupied wharf from which a crowd of small boys shouted out conflicting directions. Suffice to say the post is at the southern end of the town, past the large hotel and the apartment blocks on the hill.

Next to the prominent Punta Caimanera light (Fl.R 4s) you will find the entrance to a small enclosed harbour 20°19.8N / 077°09.3W. At its mouth, there's the wreck of one more unwary vessel and the concrete-fronted Guárda Frontera barracks with a good wharf and lots of cleats.

The harbour is filled with a motley collection of fishing vessels the crews of which will stare in fascination as you attempt to turn round. For the honour of all yet to come, do it right... Don't worry, there's plenty of room.

LOCATE THE PORT CAPTAIN
Having cleared in, if the Guárda Frontera can't locate the port captain for instructions then you may well be asked to anchor off a slipway ("Grada" in Spanish) about a mile back towards the town to await directions. If so, you should be careful about the swimmers milling about in the water off the small town beach to the left of the dock. They will swim out, surrounding the boat and engaging you in friendly conversation, but the officials will take a dim view if you permit any on board.

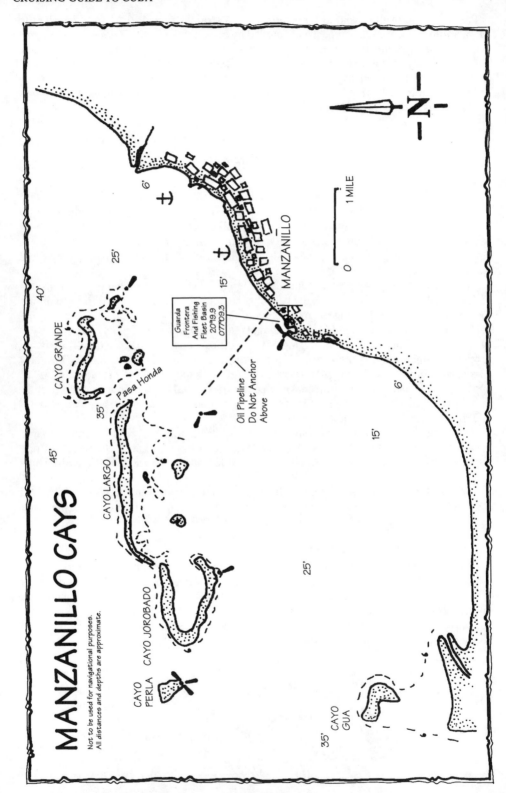

MANZANILLO CAYS

Not to be used for navigational purposes.
All distances and depths are approximate.

CAYO GRANDE

CAYO LARGO

Pasa Honda

CAYO JOROBADO

CAYO PERLA

CAYO GUA

Guarda Frontera
And Fishing
Fleet Basin
20°09.9
077°09.3

Oil Pipeline
Do Not Anchor
Above

MANZANILLO

1 MILE

0

40'

25'

35'

45'

35'

15'

15'

25'

6'

6'

6'

The wharf here, used mainly by tugboats and protected by large dirty black tires suspended by chains makes a handy dock if you can wheedle permission from the Harbour Master when he arrives. Just be careful of the submerged ferrocement wreck just alongside the outer southwest corner.

The shipyard consists of a slipway where large tugs and steel pontoon-barges are repaired by arc-welders, or otherwise attended to by muscular men wielding large sledgehammers. If you are allowed to remain here you will be close to the only hotel which accepts foreigners. It's up the hill at the southern end of the town and can be reached on foot by taking a long narrow set of steps up the hillside.

The Hotel Guacanayabo is a pretty depressing place sometimes, especially when it's darkened by electricity cuts in the off-season, but it does have a swimming pool which may tempt those who've had it up to here with saltwater for the time being.

Be careful about what you say to people in the bar and don't get involved with shady characters who may well be a lot more official than they pretend.

It was here that my good friend Brendan (a droll Irishman) offered the advice, "Don't ever trust a Cuban without biceps!". And he may well be right.

PROBABLY YOUR BEST OPTION

The wharf may be noisy at times, but will probably be the best option unless you're allowed down at the other end of town, and you will be able to pick up all kinds of advice on coastal passaging from the tugboat crews here. A casual armed guard will constantly patrol the yard and you will have to shout through the gate to get in, but you'd have to do the same sort of thing anywhere else in the hemisphere.

Unlike most other places in the hemisphere however is the welcome you'll find aboard the other local vessels alongside the wharf.

The town does have a Provedora de Buques (ships store) downtown which supplies provisions direct to your boat at wholesale prices. Operated by the Empresa Consignataria Mambisa (the excellent coastal pilotage organization) this service is worth every penny, so ask the port authorities about it when you dock.

If you are not actually at anchor, but rather alongside a dock, you will not be expected to return to the Guárda Frontera post when leaving. Instead, someone will come down to your boat .

But whatever, be prepared to face lots of paperwork.

SOUTHWEST TO CABO CRUZ
CHART NOS. ICH 1138 & 1137 (CUBAN)

Heading out of Manzanillo there are are two routes to Cabo Cruz in the southwest.

The **inner passage** takes you close to the coast and is visual all the way with a couple of tricky wriggles through more or less vaguely marked channels. (See chart next page).

The **outermost route**, tending out of sight of land, is better marked but unfortunately does not allow a convenient resting place for preparing for the trip round the cape. It is perhaps more suited to larger deep-drafted vessels which might not need or wish to rest up overnight.

Interestingly enough, the official south coast pilots (the service is called "Practicos" if you should ever require it) receive their training in these waters.

CHOOSING THE OUTERMOST ROUTE

Taking the outermost route first, leave your mooring and approach the western tip of the cays fronting Manzanillo. There is a light on the end, and a 22-mile course from here along 247°M will run you into the light at position 20°11.2N / 077°35.6W near the Madrona Channel 8 miles off the town of Niquero.

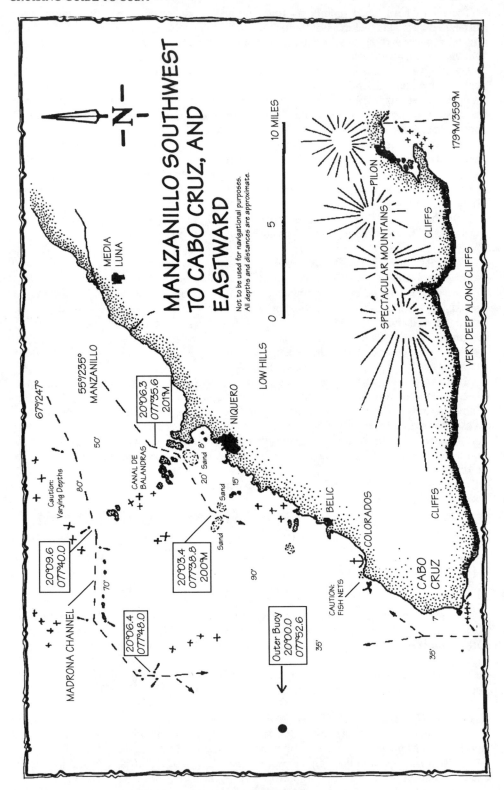

MANZANILLO SOUTHWEST TO CABO CRUZ, AND EASTWARD

Not to be used for navigational purposes.
All depths and distances are approximate.

10 MILES

0   5

67°/247°

55°/235°
MANZANILLO

MEDIA
LUNA

20°06.3
077°35.6
201M

CANAL DE
BALANDRAS

Caution:
Varying Depths

50'

80'

70'

20°09.6
077°40.0

MADRONA CHANNEL

20°06.4
077°48.0

20°03.4
077°38.8
200M

Outer Buoy
20°00.0
077°52.6

CAUTION:
FISH NETS

35'

90'

20' Sand

8'

15'

Sand

Sand

NIQUERO

LOW HILLS

BELIC

COLORADOS

CLIFFS

CABO
CRUZ

7

35'

SPECTACULAR MOUNTAINS

PILON

CLIFFS

1799M/3559M

VERY DEEP ALONG CLIFFS

Give the light a safe berth (pass it on your right, as it sits atop a coral head), and take up a course of 73°M towards the beginning of the 10-mile channel which will tend west and then southwest. Finally, leaving the channel you can now set course 15 miles due south to Cabo Cruz, on the other side of which lie the cliffs of the southeast coast.

THE INNER ROUTE

If you prefer to take the inner route, then clear Cayo Guá southwest of Manzanillo by a couple of hundred yards and continue visually, southwest along the coast in comfortable water. A 25-mile run will bring you to the Balandras Keys jutting out just before you come to the town of Niquero. There is a narrow channel through the cays running 21°/201°M which although marked will require some care. Look for the channel entrance around 20°06.3N / 077°35.6W avoiding a rather conspicuous sandbank to your port immediately upon leaving.

At the exit to the Balandras Channel go past the town of Niquero, continuing instead 240°M to the next pass some 3 1/2 miles on at Azagua. This pass is marked only on its northern side, by two stakes, but this may change with time or opportunity. Just be prepared with a sharp lookout for sandbanks on either side even though the channel itself is deep.

From here a course of 204°M will take you 7 1/2 miles to the overnight shelter of the bight at Colorados beach where you can anchor in good water around 19°55.7N / 077°41.9W.

Note that some halfway along this final route there is an obstruction off the cays near Limones a mile or two up from the village of Belic, so once again watch for the mark.

At the beach, while it is still daylight, take note of any evidence of nets strung out from poles in the water. There are usually some off the point at Colorados and you will likely be leaving in darkness for the trip round the Cape, so plot them on your charts for later avoidance.

This is an interesting spot, not merely for the abundance of life below the surface amongst the turtle-grass, but for more serious reasons.

You are now anchored off one of the more historic sites of the western hemisphere. No matter what your political persuasion, you cannot help but feel moved by the sight of the beach and the mangroves where Fidel Castro, his brother Raoul, Ernesto "Che" Guevarra, and their compadres landed in the darkness of Dec 2nd 1956. By the time the smoke of ambush had cleared only 12 of the original 81 were still alive or uncaptured, and those survivors could only flee through swamp and bush to the nearby hills, starvation, and struggle.

From such inauspicious beginnings have enormous changes come and their worst enemies cannot but salute their bravery.

Courtyards are common to many Cuban homes. Here a woman pauses below her drying laundry. (Photo by George Halloran)

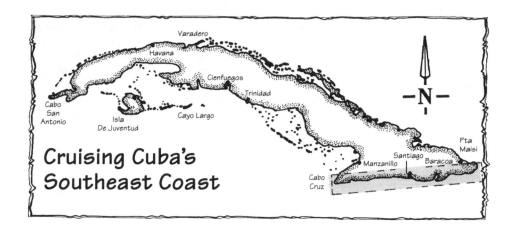

Cruising Cuba's
Southeast Coast

CABO CRUZ TO PUNTA MAISÍ

GENERAL

This chapter, albeit smaller than the rest, is nevertheless going to introduce you to the most spectacular coastline in Cuba. Between the two acutely angled capes at either end, this arid coast is bordered for the next 220 miles by rocky cliffs and awesome scrub-covered mountains, some visible from as far away as Jamaica. Having coasted the Cuban cays, or perhaps come down from the U.S.A., this dramatic change will require a different technique, the key to which is avoiding travel in any strong winds with a southern component.

NOTE MAGNETIC DEVIATION

Once again, we note that the magnetic deviation varies from about 3 degrees at Cabo Cruz to 5 degrees at Punta Maisí, but this has little effect on courses so plotting your position is fairly easy. In general, this revolves around taking a quick look at the shoreline a couple of hundred yards away, then putting a nice neat cross on the chart just a little ahead of the last one. As the coastline runs almost dead east-west you can more or less forget about latitudes and navigate as close in as you feel comfortable.

There won't be much in the way of outlying dangers off the coast and there's sometimes even a little counter-current near the shore running east along your route, especially in early summer. The main western-setting current through the windward passage between Haiti and Cuba runs too far offshore to be of much hindrance, so don't worry about that either.

The coast is evenly spaced along its length with secure harbours, each about a day-sail away from its neighbor. Once embarked on a passage however there are few alternate shelters, so your preparations must be careful in this regard. Luckily the winds along the coast are usually quite predictable and can be calculated according to the time of day with some accuracy, thus leaving the question of passage planning to revolve around scheduling and mechanical efficiency, i.e., leaving in good time, and not breaking down along the way. As a matter of fact, the median wind velocities vary between 7-11 knots in summer and 5-7 knots in winter, except for the eastern tip where the winds can sometimes be stronger. If you don't go berserk you'll more than likely have a nice gentle sail along what otherwise appears on the map to be a difficult stretch.

STRATEGY

Regarding general passage-planning, the time of the day will determine your comfort level coming round the western corner, and early departures are called for to avoid an uncomfortable swell broadside on to your route. As a rule, we find that the daylight winds at the extreme west (Cabo Cruz) oscillate between northeast in the very early hours and southeast for the rest of the day; so it's best to round the cape before daylight and to anchor in Portillo by midday after what can be an uncomfortable passage if the wind is strong. Happily the view is best at this time of the day, and you've not yet been drugged by alcohol or the motion of your craft.

KABATIC EFFECT IS PRONOUNCED

Along the mid-section (either side of Santiago) where the land-mass is greater, the Kabatic effect is considerably more pronounced and winds usually start off anywhere around north northeast at daybreak, veering clockwise to south southwest by afternoon. The distances again call for early starts, but in general the wave motion is not going to cause any problems and you can coast as close as you dare. In any case, if you are motoring close-in under an onshore breeze you should have an anchor ready to deploy instantly in the event of engine failure.

Finally, at the extreme east (Punta Maisí) the prevailing winds overcome any local effect and are more or less constantly east northeast, veering or backing only as dictated by larger weather patterns.

Having said that, do not be worried by what might seem to be a difficult time ahead as severe weather is rare, and only a third (the weakest third) of the cold fronts reaching Cuba actually get down this far, and only the most determined of tropical systems will affect the coast.

ROUNDING CABO CRUZ
CHART NO. ICH 1137 (CUBAN)

The night before rounding the cape, after your swim and before the weather forecast, should be devoted to plotting and noting your courses. You need to be leaving well before dawn and if on the way into your overnight anchorage you saw any nets (generally set at the western tip of the bight) they should be plotted onto the charts as you won't see them in the morning.

The engine and other inspections can also be done the night before, laying out your navigation instruments ready for use so nothing delays your departure once conditions are right. This passage can be rough and you might have to hang on, so prepare sandwiches in foil to avoid going below, set the alarm for two o'clock, take a stiff drink and get an early night... Wake and leave while it's still dark.

A STRAIGHTFORWARD ROUTE

This is likely to be the last time you use your compass for the next 200 miles, but just for now remember the 3-degree variation, and it'll be a pretty straightforward route to the cape where there's a pilot station if you need advice. Note that there seems to be a confusion of lights just off the tip, so give them a wide berth and head into the growing swells where the currents swirl off the point. Aim to be well south before making your westerly turn at about 19 °49.0N to miss the anchored fishing-boat sheltering just off the point and the darkened headland. The swells along here will grow hugely during the morning as the winds usually shift round to the southwest by ten o'clock, so you will probably be glad to make your first stop at Pilón or Portillo some 30 miles along an increasingly spectacular coast.

A balcony provides an excellent vantage point for viewing a street festival in Santiago.
(Photo by Simon Charles)

PILÓN
CHART NO. ICH 1137

Pilón, a sugar and fishing community of some 10,000 inhabitants is well guarded by reefs and numerous coral heads. These reefs in fact offer good protection to the vessels within so you might wish to enter, but if you have been closely hugging the coast then hang at least a mile offshore as you come up to the bay of Pilón. There are range lights to bring you in north from approximately 77 °17.0W and further buoyage will direct you along the way. There is one long wharf inside the port but in reality it is in bad repair and little used, with the majority of fishing boats using their own L-shaped wooden dock a little further in. Although times change, if you are not desperate there is little to recommend the port at this time.

A handcarved, wooden sculpture for sale in a street market. (Photo by George Halloran)

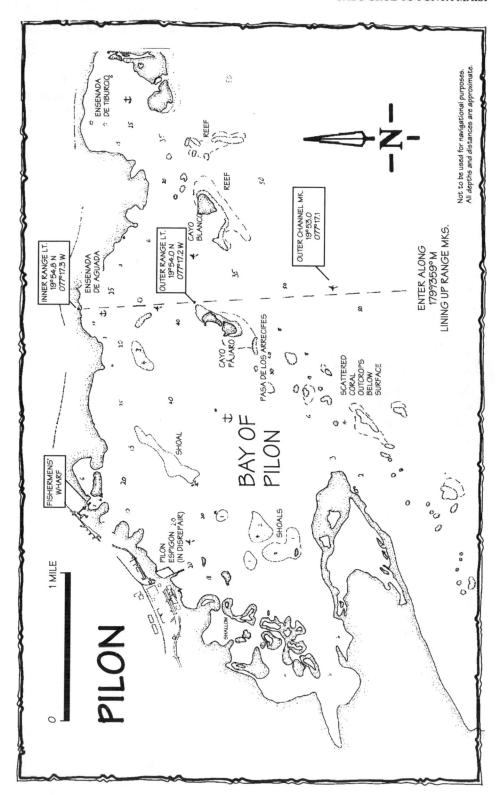

PILON

1 MILE

0

FISHERMENS' WHARF

INNER RANGE LT.
19°54.8 N
077°17.3 W

ENSENADA
DE AGUADA

ENSENADA
DE TIBURCIO

REEF

REEF

OUTER RANGE LT.
19°54.0 N
077°17.2 W

CAYO
BLANCO

OUTER CHANNEL MK.
19°53.0
077°17.1

ENTER ALONG
179°/359° M
LINING UP RANGE MKS.

CAYO
PAJARO

PASA DE LOS ARRECIFES

BAY OF
PILON

SHOAL

SCATTERED
CORAL
OUTCROPS
BELOW
SURFACE

SHOALS

PILON
ESPIGON
(IN DISREPAIR)

SHALLOW

Not to be used for navigational purposes.
All depths and distances are approximate.

N

MAREA DEL PORTILLO
CHART NOS. ICH 1137 & 1136

Altogether easier to enter than Pilón, you will find Portillo only 5 miles further at around 077 °11.5W. This tiny bay makes for the first of our two planned halts along the route to Santiago.

The deep channel entrance, open to the sea, is visual directly through the markers but once inside you are presented with a widening bay with two largish hotels to the northwest and a flimsy dock reaching out between them. Just be sure you don't approach too closely to the final inner channel mark as it sits on a bank which suddenly alters the depth and heaps up the waves. As the beaches fronting the hotels are right in front of the entrance you will probably be better off turning right as soon as you pass the point inside. Over to the northeastern corner of the enclosed bay there is a tiny fishing village and you can find a beautifully calm, protected anchorage close to the mangroves opposite. You're not missing much by mooring over here as the hotel beaches are a fine mix of sand and silt, and unless you've come for some sort of weird cure I'd stay off them.

Exhaustion will have taken over, so you might as well get some sleep before going ashore later, but do not be surprised if a visitor in the form of a Guarda Frontera official is rowed out to you to inspect your documents in the afternoon. There isn't much in the way of official presence and it's likely that he's been dispatched from Pilón, so offer a soft drink and sympathy. He's probably hot and bothered, and the unfortunate fisherman who's just finished rowing him will likely be similarly afflicted too.

DINGHY TO THE SCUBA SHOP

The closer of the hotels has a scuba-shop just to its left where you can leave the dinghy, and if the more sheltered hotel further to the west has still not been completed (or the dock has collapsed) you can practice making beach landings when you go ashore.

British or Northern U.S. divers will already know the technique as they use it all the time with their inflatables. Take up a position outside the surf line and release the engine tilt-lock while (just like your big-boat entrances) waiting for your moment. Now go hard at the sand, trying to keep ahead of the surge, then just before driving onto the shore **cut the motor** and leap into the surf alongside. With any luck the engine really will have stopped and you won't lose a toe while grabbing the sides of the boat, and you can still physically drag it up as high as it'll go. They'll love you for the entertainment as you realize you've done it all in your dress-shorts (the ones with the crease), and your wallet's floating away alongside one of your flip-flops! So much so, that they'll even watch your dinghy for you.

Later on when you leave, you will have to wade the dinghy out into the waves and start the motor (in neutral) from alongside before leaping in one at a time.

THE ONLY FUNCTIONING HOTEL

Portillo's only functioning hotel in 1993 took foreign visitors in winter and Cubans in summer, so what you get depends on when you arrive. Either way, there are a couple of bars, a restaurant, telephone facilities and the usual stuff from the front desk (the carpeta) You can also obtain rental cars if you wish to tour the mountains where Fidel and the survivors of the landing at Los Colorados beach hid out during the first year of the revolution.

Remember, if you're going to eat or drink during the afternoon that it's going to be getting dark later and this may have a bearing on your trip back in the dinghy. Try not to drown just to entertain the curious. Believe me, a friendly throng of Cuban holiday-makers can cause a serious miscalculation at the bar.

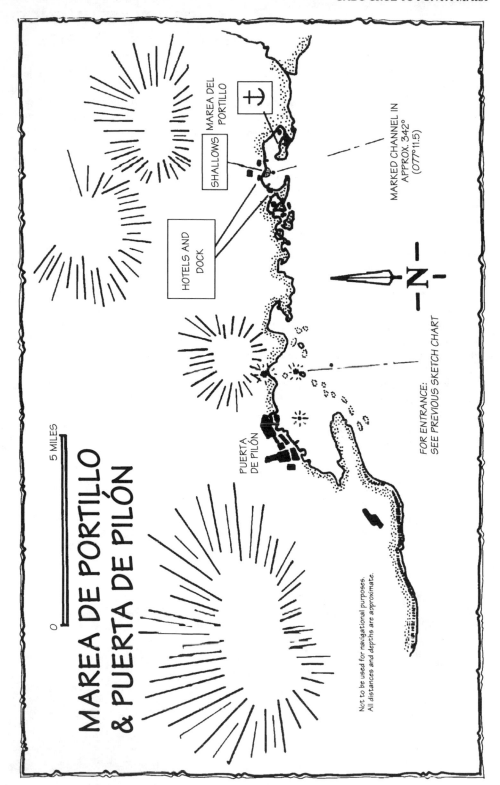

MAREA DE PORTILLO
& PUERTA DE PILÓN

5 MILES

0

MAREA DEL PORTILLO

SHALLOWS

HOTELS AND DOCK

PUERTA DE PILÓN

MARKED CHANNEL IN APPROX. 342°
(077°11.5)

N

FOR ENTRANCE:
SEE PREVIOUS SKETCH CHART

Not to be used for navigational purposes.
All distances and depths are approximate.

ROUTE TO CHIVIRICO
CHART NO. ICH 1136 (CUBAN)

In pleasant sunny weather this passage will be the highlight of the cruise. The route is about 48 miles long so you'll have to get up early, leaving at or before first light, but you will be rewarded by the most amazing views and the best scenery of the whole trip. There may not be much in the way of shelter if the winds were to come strongly out of the south, but unless you've made a serious error in forecasting there's no reason to worry overmuch.

Leaving around 6 a.m. will allow you to see the marks on the way out, and as usual the winds will be light early in the morning. Later on as the sun gets high, you will be well away from the influence of the cape, so although the swells offshore may be large, they'll be slow and easy. Inshore the swells diminish, so provided the surge is not too great the absence of outlying dangers along the coastline means that you can cruise as close to the hard bits as you feel safe.

Along the way you will pass tall cliffs, rock-faces undercut by pounding surf, beaches, secluded valleys like oases filled with royal palms, and huge mountains sweeping right down to the waterside.

AN UNMISTAKABLE LANDMARK

Although it is by no means the only enormous landmark along this awesome coast the tallest of these mountains, the **Pico Turquino** at 6,500 feet is visible on a good day from as far away as Jamaica 90 miles away and if you have time and the water is calm you may even wish to make a rare dive on a perfectly preserved wartime wreck at the base of the mountain.

This seldom visited relic of the Spanish-American war is the cruiser *Colón*, sunk during a naval engagement in 1898. The wreck lies below the surface on a submarine ledge, with one half suspended at 50 feet and the rest hanging crazily down the slope as far as 150 feet.

To find it you need to pass the village of Ocujal and locate the Ensenada Turquino east of the peak, between the rocky point and the bridge over the river. Just east of the point and halfway up the slopes behind the shoreline there is a fence pointing directly at the wreck some 100 feet offshore at a position approximately 019 °56.1N / 076 ° 46.6W.

You will find that the visibility gets considerably better once below the first 10 feet but nevertheless it will pay to take along a good dive-light to explore this fascinating iron wreck, complete with engines, turrets, steel plate and girders. A serious note of caution: If there is any danger of your boat being swept onto the shore by the surge then it will certainly be better to do a swim-out beach-dive, by road, from Chvirico 20 miles further on.

A charcoal maker pursuing his trade. (Photo by Simon Charles)

CHIVIRICO
CHART NO. ICH 1136 (CUBAN)

This wonderfully enclosed little cove 45 miles west of Santiago at 076°24.0W, makes for a convenient overnight stopover. Even were it not so, the harbour would be worth a stop just for the view only 5 minutes walk from your anchorage.

Immediately east of the protruding hill with the red-roofed hotel and 2.25 miles west of Punta Tabacal the entrance is marked by two range-lights along a course of 340°M . The course along which you come in is closely guarded, both east and west by coral heads, so you should turn to come in from a fair distance out and be careful to keep on line. There are some outer banks of coral to be aware of too, and after a welcome break in the southeastern outer cays we are now going to be threatened once again with the "Curse of the Submerged Snorkeller" so keep your eyes open.

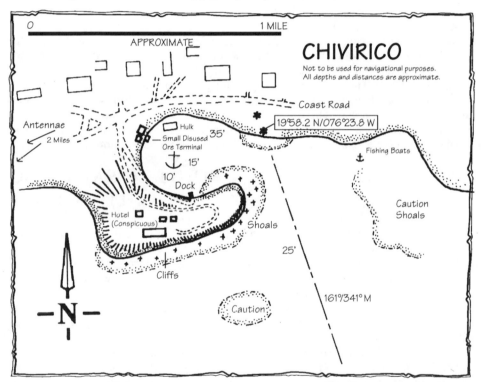

As you come in, you will see the coral banks submerged alongside the point to the west clearly visible in the midday sun and protected from the evening reflections by the hill, so approach the onshore range-marks closely and make a sharp turn to the west once the channel opens there. Here you'll find yourself inside a small cove enclosed on all sides by sheer rock walls and with adequate water for even the most demanding keel. You can drop anchor wherever you see fit but it's best to set up near the small floating dock serving the scuba boat on the south side, not the abandoned old ore-facility on the northwest. Perhaps you may even be permitted to moor alongside if your craft is small enough.

I have come across a Canadian yacht there which used the basin to anchor in while the owner returned home to tend to a sick parent. No-one molested the boat which bobbed happily at anchor for more than three months, and it's unlikely that anything short of a slap-bang head on full force direct hit by a hurricane could disturb you once inside. Mind you, there would be a press of small fishing-boats which more usually moor over to the northeastern side of the entrance to the bay where they have their own facilities.

Sometime later, as you finally have everything put in its place, a perspiring soldier will cycle over from the Guarda Frontera post near the fishing boats and you can dinghy your documents over to him at the floating dock. Once again it won't take any length of time, and you can take a walk along the track from the dock and up the steep road to the Hotel Los Galeones on the hill. If he doesn't show up before you leave then he'll probably track you down at the bar later.

Take your camera and a good long lens to get some really nice shots of your own boat below, completely framed by trees, banks, and cliffs.

At the hotel you can rent cars, make phone calls, eat at a rather uninspired restaurant, swim in the pool, and do a deal with the scuba dive-master to take you out to some hidden submerged banks or even back to the wreck of the Colón. On the other side of the hill there is a long beach, thronged with inhabitants of Chivirico and the outlying areas who arrive by splendid horse-drawn buggies to enjoy the weekend. These buggies are a feature of the southeast coastline and make a wonderful sight, all gaily painted, crowded with people, and visible from your yacht cruising just offshore.

If you have made an excursion to Chivirico from Santiago you will probably be glad to know that there's a gasoline station just a few hundred yards northwest of the onshore range-marks where you can exchange your coupons for fuel.

You'll be interested to see the firing-ranges alongside the road where the populace can shoot off their rounds at comic pictures of snarling Gringos in uniform. It's not personal, just that the revolution started here and they rather see themselves as still in the vanguard. Don't worry, everyone I've met has been almost overpoweringly friendly and would probably just die of embarrassment if it turned out you were a Norteamericano yourself.

ROUTE TO SANTIAGO
CHART NO. ICH 1136 (CUBAN)

Be careful not to foul the coral heads to the southeast as you leave the harbour, but once you're on your way and past the grotesque beige hotel on the coast at Quiebra Seca (5 miles) you'll have another great run. There is a promising looking entrance there but it's shrouded by fish-nets strung across, and further along this stretch of the coast the few rivers that make it down to the sea have bars at their mouths.

It's another 45-mile run to Santiago, cruising alongside an equally splendid seashore, sometimes so close you can hear the kids whistling over at you, and the buggy passengers will point in fascination from the roads cut along the water's edge. Then suddenly, above the surface in the **Asseradero** harbour at 076° 08.5W is another Spanish-American war wreck. This time with the turret and cannon pointing skyward! This sad sight, the cruiser *Viscaya*, brings to mind the whole wretched history of a war agitated by a newspaper publisher who wanted to drum up sales, and a president who went along for the ride.

In 1898 the old Colonial empire was contracting and Spain was only too eager to save face while leaving Cuba, but the strange explosion which sank the American battleship *Maine* in Havana Harbour was the perfect excuse for low-risk slaughter, the making of reputations, and the expansion of U.S. influence in the Caribbean and the Pacific.

The modern American fleet totally outgunned the ancient Spanish cruisers holed up in Santiago harbour and when they broke out on July 3rd they were butchered in 4 hours by the eager gunners. When it was over, the death toll along the coastline here was 474 Spanish sailors to two American casualties.

By the time history had played out that particular hand, huge areas of Cuba had become exclusively North American property, the seeds were sown for further strife, and now the whole cycle seems set to renew itself once again.

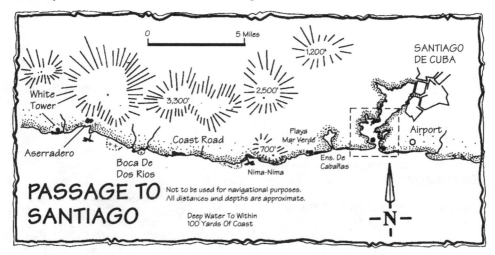

Further along, closer to Santiago, there is more war-wreckage in the shallow bay of Nima-Nima, but soon you will have other things to occupy your mind. The enormous harbour of Santiago is only 7 miles further and there may well be large commercial vessels proceeding through the narrow entrance, so in spite of the static prevalent on the VHF it is probably best to contact them with your intentions. In spite of my earlier advice, it is better in this instance to call the official harbour authorities direct.

Call **Morro Santiago** (the hill overlooking the entrance) on channel 16, and they will almost certainly reply with a speed and efficiency which makes you wonder if you've strayed into the wrong country! They use a working frequency of 10, and will liase with the marina at Punta Gorda inside the entrance so that by the time you've arrived all will be ready for your reception.

SANTIAGO DE CUBA
CHART NOS. ICH 1136, 1137, OR HARBOUR CHART NO.1805

Grandiosely called the "Ciudad Heroe" or the Hero City, it is regarded as second in importance only to Havana, but in many ways the inhabitants see themselves as first among equals.

Santiago was founded in 1514, considerably before Havana, and even had as its first mayor the famous conquistador Hernando Cortez (before he went off to do his thing further afield in Central America). The city grew rapidly, drawing its wealth as it still does from mining and agricultural regions surrounding it, and in spite of disaster following disaster, from pirates and pestilence to earthquakes and uprisings, it nevertheless continued to grow until during the revolution it became more or less the focus of the struggle.

Here, downtown at the Moncada barracks (now a museum and schoolhouse), the opening shots were fired in the battles to come and to this day it still retains a special place in Cuban spiritual heritage. July 26th (the anniversary of the unsuccessful 1953 attack) is presently celebrated all over Cuba as the major festival of the year.

It may not be everyone's cup of tea, but there is a certain vibrance to the place which sets it apart, and I admit that it's certainly *my* favorite Cuban city, with a flavor all of its own.

A SUPERB CITY LOCATION

The city is superbly located, standing amongst the eastern foothills of the Seirra Maestra and looking out onto an amazing bay guarded by a narrow entrance and a magnificent fort dating right back to the original days of its founding when it could be said to control the Caribbean. There is a wonderful cosmopolitan feeling too, reflected both in the architecture and the people who have variously come from Spain, Africa and France. The streets are consequently narrow and bustling with old houses pressing for space along pavements interspersed with tiny plazas where hustlers and Jineteros compete for your dollar.

The harbour authorities on the Morro will give entrance instructions, but if there has been no contact with them you're likely to be intercepted outside by a grey military patrol-boat or inside by a small boat shaped incongruously like a wooden-shoe (it brings the immigration authorities out from the main offices. In any case you're most likely to be sent to the dock at **Punta Gorda**, the original site of the oldest yacht club in Cuba.

EASILY IDENTIFIED ENTRANCE

The entrance to Santiago de Cuba is easily identified by the castle and lighthouse installations atop the steep hill on the eastern side of the mouth. There are a couple of large buoys immediately outside the entrance at a position of approximately 19°57.9N / 075°52.5W from which you can come in 34°M through the center of a deep channel some 200 yards wide, impressively guarded by the ancient castle and the more recent Spanish fortifications lower down.

Follow the line of buoys through the channel, pass the first inlet on your right and on your left you will see Cayo Granma, a key totally cut off from the mainland and accessible by the inhabitants only in small personal boats. A restaurant is situated here, its diners curiously looking on as you sail past, wrestling with your sails in the swirling entrance-vortex.

From here the marina is a couple of hundred yards north, a little to the left of the enclosed swimming area. It's easily identifiable by the low light blue buildings with their red roofs, and the dock with its reception committee waiting under the canopy at the outer end.

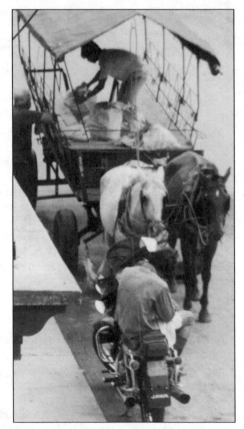

Horse-drawn carts have became a commonplace sight in Cuba. (Photo by George Halloran)

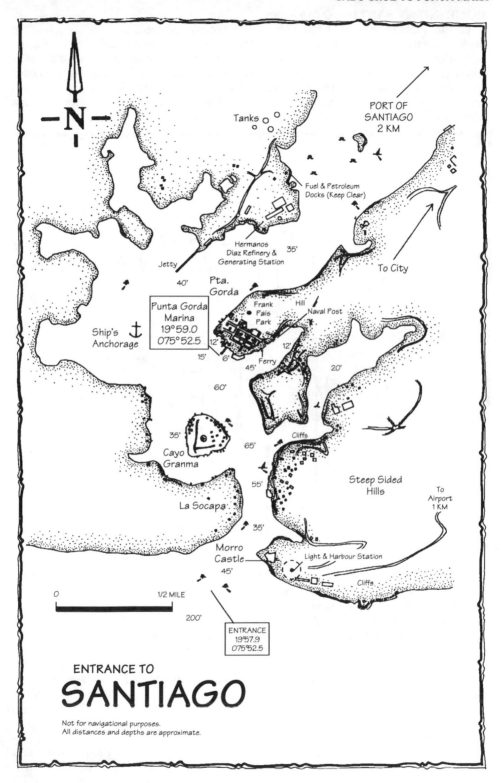

-N-

PORT OF
SANTIAGO
2 KM

Tanks

Fuel & Petroleum
Docks (Keep Clear)

Hermanos
Diaz Refinery &
Generating Station

Jetty

35'

To City

40'

Pta.
Gorda

Punta Gorda
Marina
19°59.0
075°52.5

Frank
Pais
Park

Hill

Naval Post

Ship's
Anchorage

12'

12'

15'

6'

45'

Ferry

20'

60'

35'

Cayo
Granma

65'

Cliffs

Steep Sided
Hills

To
Airport
1 KM

55'

La Socapa

35'

Morro
Castle

45'

Light & Harbour Station

Cliffs

0   1/2 MILE

200'

ENTRANCE
19°57.9
075°52.5

ENTRANCE TO
SANTIAGO

Not for navigational purposes.
All distances and depths are approximate.

203

DOCKING AT SANTIAGO MARINA

You are probably going to be the only yacht there, so if possible moor on the left of the dock where the water at 9 feet is adequate for all but the most impractical cruisers. On the right, the southeastern side, you are likely to be battered about somewhat by the swells filtering into the harbour. If you do have to moor there you should dinghy-out an anchor some 20 feet off, and by means of a taut line to that, you can keep off the dock while still remaining alongside. Whichever you choose, don't disembark until the immigration officers arrive and clear you in.

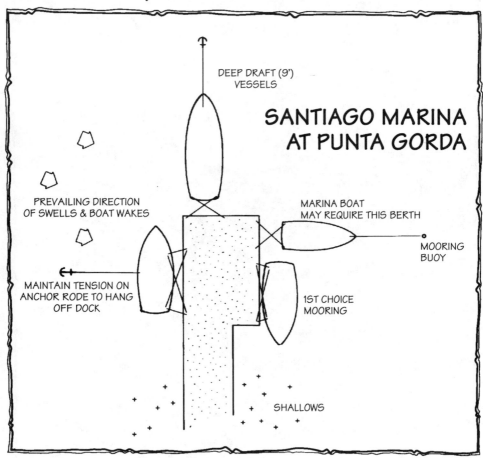

Even on the western side you are still liable to be tossed about by the wake from the multitude of turbine-powered military patrol-boats going to their nearby docks and the large vessels proceeding through the channel. Hang lots of fenders over the side and look out for the antenna getting crushed against the roof overhead when the boat rocks. Move as far as possible along the platform to leave room for the delightful Merino and his sportfishing boat which usually moors stern-on from the small orange buoy outboard of the dock. This cheerful young soul is responsible for casual tourist trips inside the harbour and for deep-sea fishing trips outside, and a more pleasant neighbor would be impossible to imagine.

A MAJOR PORT REQUIRING FORMAL ENTRY

Santiago is a major port and there is likely to be a more formal entry requirement than you've become accustomed to over the last few weeks, but you've also got more experience too, so things should still be fairly quick. If entering the country for the first time this is

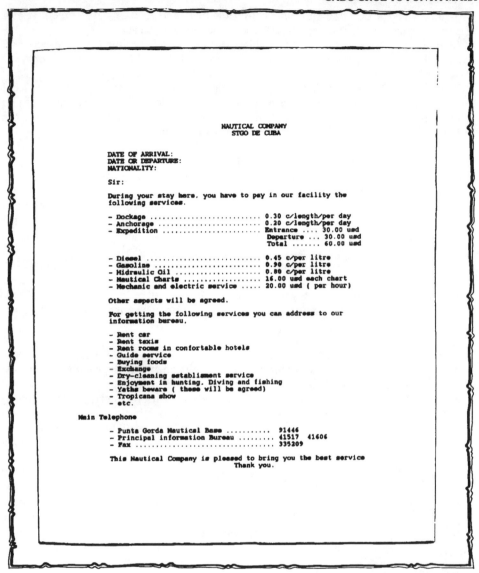

NAUTICAL COMPANY
STGO DE CUBA

DATE OF ARRIVAL:
DATE OR DEPARTURE:
NATIONALITY:

Sir:

During your stay here, you have to pay in our facility the
following services.

- Dockage .... 0.30 c/length/per day
- Anchorage .... 0.20 c/length/per day
- Expedition .... Entrance .... 30.00 usd
                                    Departure ... 30.00 usd
                                    Total .... 60.00 usd

- Diesel .... 0.45 c/per litre
- Gasoline .... 0.90 c/per litre
- Hidraulic Oil .... 0.80 c/per litre
- Nautical Charts .... 16.00 usd each chart
- Mechanic and electric service ... 20.00 usd (per hour)

Other aspects will be agreed.

For getting the following services you can address to our
information bureau.

- Rent car
- Rent taxis
- Rent rooms in confortable hotels
- Guide service
- Buying foods
- Exchange
- Dry-cleaning establisment service
- Enjoyment in hunting. Diving and fishing
- Yaths beware (these will be agreed)
- Tropicana show
- etc.

Main Telephone

- Punta Gorda Nautical Base 91446
- Principal information Bureau 41517 41606
- Fax 335209

This Nautical Company is pleased to bring you the best service
Thank you.

a good place as they've got lots of experience dealing with it, and this is where most of the Jamaican yachts arrive. I've never had much problems here and later on this will be the best place to sort out all further documentation; as far afield as Havana if that's where you're eventually going.

POWER IS AVAILABLE

Power is available alongside even if you have to improvise somewhat with the electricity connections, but the leaky water connections will fit standard U.S. fittings. If there is no water available at the time you will have to ask any of the workmen variously employed around the dock to turn on the pump (la turbina), as you will when requiring showers nominally available in a series of stalls ashore. There were plans to construct a small cafeteria at the base of the dock and upgrading work was underway when I last visited but how this has fared recently is anyone's guess.

The marina offices at the rear of the premises are contained in a wonderful ramshackle two-story wooden building surrounded by fruit trees and lounging watchmen. If you require anything, go up the steps onto the veranda in front and ask.

Available here are the normal services like calling taxis or arranging for rental-cars, and as usual the marina will sort out your documentation with the authorities. Remember to ask about this well in advance.

The marina at Punta Gorda handles general boatyard duties for a variety of smaller local vessels accommodating them both ashore and afloat in a couple of covered bays. If you require fuel or oil you will have to pull alongside one of the sagging wharves over to the left, easily identifiable by the oil-blackened workshop and depot.

ONE UNWELCOME MORNING CHORE

One unwelcome chore you're likely to be faced with is that of cleaning your boat every morning to remove the gritty deposits which rain out of the sky courtesy of the cement factory close by. There is also the black tarry deposit which washes out of the harbour daily and congeals along your waterline. This cleaning job may be postponed if you don't wish to take you chances in the water alongside but it should be attended to as soon as you have the chance further along the coast.

An additional point is that the water temperature in the harbour is some 90°F. (10-15° more than the outside waters) which encourages a heavy growth of barnacles or weeds.

This stuff quickly fouls your log impeller and coats the hull/prop in a week or so. Clear it off as soon as you have the opportunity to go underneath in cleaner waters and before it has time to harden.

THE GRAN PIEDRA PARK

From the marina it's a $10 ride to the centre of the city and you will probably find it best to put up with the rip-off prices and rent a car for a couple of days. At least this way you can get about the countryside and visit the inland cities or the prehistoric parks and resort areas to the east. Along here we find the Gran Piedra Park, with a huge stone which commands a wonderful view of the surrounding countryside, and further on there is the Siboney farmhouse-museum where the first action of the revolution was planned. At the side of the road there are macabre monuments every few hundred yards with the names and professions of those who later died in the fighting (but only on the winning side).

If you crave more naive amusement you can visit the prehistoric park where large concrete dinosaurs cavort in front of bemused tourists. And a short ride out of town along the same route east you can stop off at the hotel Buccanero to refill any scuba tanks you may have emptied along the way.

You may even find it rather fun to go back along the coast road in the direction you've just come from, towards Chivirico and the Sierras Maestra if you did not have the chance to do so previously.

Near to Santiago is the most religious site in Cuba, with a lovely church and a virgin who (significantly for you) has several times appeared before imperilled sailors and guided them to safety. You may visit the church by taking the Avenue de Las Americas and going 11 miles northwest through the mountains to the valley of El Cobre. The church is open daily and the faithful meet inside to worship in front of the statue (wheeled about town in procession on feast days) and to bring a strange variety of offerings which are displayed behind the altar.

A MULTITUDE OF DELIGHTS

The city of Santiago itself has a multitude of delights, and it's unlikely that you could exhaust them in a week so plan to stay some time. You might as well get it over with and start off at the Parque Céspedes where the Cathedral and Town Hall oppose each other in a neat if unconscious political statement. The first-floor restaurant balcony of the perennially under-repair hotel between the two is a good place to sip a cocktail and look out over the crowds in the square. On weekends little children promenade in their Sunday finest and even mount a train pulled by gaily-decorated goats, but at any time the square is a fascinating spectacle with a variety of human interest stories laid out for the entertainment of all.

Hustlers, for which the city is justly famous, intercept vague bespectacled camera-toting tourists from the nearby tour-buses and arm-in-arm parade them about like trophies... Meantime the plain-clothes Secret Police look on to make sure it all doesn't get out of hand, and to check on who's talking to whom.

With a few delightful exceptions the official guides in the hotel lobbies are usually not going to guide you anywhere except into the hands of the efficient money-extraction machine called the Tourist Industry, but sooner or later despite your healthiest doses of cynicism you are likely to be adopted by a Santiagero who "only wants to practice his English". Choose carefully, as the arrangement can be both to your benefit or detriment. On the one hand, you may be immediately touched for the price of a meal or two, a pair of shoes, a night on the town, someone's sister, someone's brother, or you may with better judgement find a friend who will guide you to places and experiences you could never find or hear about on your own.

In any case you are likely to encounter some of the most hospitable people anywhere, and a people who will unfailingly ask you back to share what little they have. I wish I could mention by name some of those who have shown me Cuban life as it is really lived. From whispered conversations in back-rooms at four a.m. (whispered, to avoid listeners next door), to gatherings attended by mothers, grandfathers, the pharmacist on the corner, students home on holiday, watchmen, and lovers. They know who they are, and if perchance they ever see this, I thank you from the bottom of my heart.

SOME NOTES ON THIS CITY

To avoid the danger of becoming a tour guide, I'm just going to end with a few quick notes about this fascinating city.

There are a couple of hard-currency shops where you can reprovision the boat. One, the Cubalse shop, north of the ugly and futuristic Hotel Santiago stocks everything you might need to continue your cruise (including a fascinating selection of tacky dry-goods), and another sometimes more convenient if less well-stocked Diplotienda is near the airport up by the Morro castle.

The best rum in Cuba is sold in Santiago so stock up here, but take due note of the sign prominently displayed above the road back to the marina, "Señor driver, drink is the enemy of the steering-wheel.".

And remember that the Spanish word for steering-wheel is also the word for "rudder" too!

The supply of reasonable restaurants within Santiago is remarkably limited, being confined to hotels and expensive places like La Maisón downtown where you have to watch yet another dreadful fashion-show with your meal. Mind you, the models there will sometimes accompany you later to the wild discotheque across at the Las Americas hotel nearby. Curiously enough, although Cubans and foreigners can mingle inside to the right of the disco floor, on the left there is an enclosed area supposedly reserved for the higher party-functionaries.

Just east of your dock at Punta Gorda however there is a large Cuban restaurant where you can sometimes persuade the staff to serve you for pesos... Good food, great value, and were there more of these in Cuba we might be persuaded to spend commensurately more ashore rather than being forced into eating on board to avoid the debtors prison.

Incidentally this is where the loud music comes from.

Across the bay, at the Granma Cay which you passed when you came in there is an excellent seafood place, El Cayo. Well worth the price, there's an inexpensive boat-service via a noisy Russian twin-cylindered dinghy from the marina to the dock in front of the restaurant. This fascinating cay is inaccessible by land and the only way onto the island is by personal boats which the inhabitants moor in small bays underneath the upper floors of the shorefront houses. There is a surprisingly highly regarded baseball team up the hill on the cay, and sometimes a helicopter can be seen using its playing field as a landing ground.

VISIT THE MUSEUMS AVAILABLE

Museums abound in Santiago even if the usual story is that they're under repair, but whatever your state of mind there is one place you should not miss, and that's the amazing castle you cruised past at the entrance to the harbour.

This nearly four-hundred year old building is accessible just ten minutes by car from your dock, turning right instead of left as you reach the main Santiago road. Go early and sit in silent wonder above the spectacular harbour, or sight along the cannons still looking out to sea for the approaching pirates who coveted the wealth they once guarded.

Again, take lots and lots of film. At least there's a half-decent restaurant nearby at the summit and if you beat the Dutch and German tour buses to it you can get a splendid meal with a view that only a sailor can really appreciate.

An equally wonderful view, in a more secluded environment is available near your dock from the Parque Frank Pais, so named after one of the original heroes of the guerilla war. The grounds are at the summit of the hill behind the marina, and a twenty minute climb will reward you with a welcome respite from the noise and bustle of the city.

A beautifully maintained park, this contemplative spot looks out onto the inner harbour of Santiago Bay, and is surveyed by a large statue of the revolutionary holding a U.S. M15 carbine at the ready.

OBTAIN AN EXTENSION TO STAY LONGER

Finally, if by now you have been seduced into staying longer than anticipated in Cuba you can get an extension (a Proroga) to your entry permit by taking your passports, pink slips, and $8.00 to the immigration offices at 412 Calle San Vacilio, between Carbarrio and Carniceria.

LEAVING SANTIAGO

No matter where you're going later, you should sort out all documentation here in Santiago.

The ports further along the coast are not used to private foreign boats, so if you're continuing on along the coast and west to Havana it's best to have arranged all subsequent documentation in advance. When filling in your Guia de Recala (the List of Ports) put in as many as you can find space for. You might not actually stop there, but it's as well to have the name down.

If you are leaving Cuba for foreign parts this is the only place along the coast that you can be legally cleared out, so you will likewise have to plan accordingly.

FEW OPPORTUNITIES FOR SHELTER

Between Santiago and the eastern tip of Cuba there won't be many opportunities to find good shelter overnight so you may choose to do it all in one go or to stop once along the way.

There is a Cuban port (Caimanera) situated inside the bay at Guantánamo behind the U.S. Naval Base, but entering can possibly involve you in unwelcome hassles further down the line so I'd give it a miss. You might instead go to Baitequirí 20 miles on, or merely seek shelter from the prevailing winds along the coast in a couple of shallow bays before rounding Punta Maisí.

The harbour officials will have to come to the dock in their boat to clear you, so make your arrangements in good time with the marina management and schedule their visit for early in the day. They are accustomed to handling foreign yachts, but this is still Latin America so don't fret too much when the whole process takes what seems to you to be an unnecessary length of time. Once the documentation is sorted out and the despacho and clearances handed over, you will not be allowed to go ashore, and in fact the immigration boat will accompany you to the mouth of the bay. Wave at them, toot your horn, and then turn left.

ROUTE TO PUNTA MAISÍ
CHART NOS. ICH 1135 & 1134 (CUBAN)

By now the wind is probably on-shore and the surge has gotten up, but as long as you feel up to it you may once again hug the coast as closely as you dare, passing steep cliffs deeply undercut by wave-action. The rock faces along here may be as high as 200 feet, but you will also come across little bays sprinkled with sand and set with tourist tables and umbrellas. If the wind is right and the surge is not too evident you may even pause by Siboncy where there is normally a bit of shelter in front of the public beach. A mile or so further there's the tiny cove in front of the Hotel Bucanero, but it's a bit surgey.

As you may have noticed by road, this is the main holiday area (both national and foreign) around Santiago and there are many hotels and beaches along the shore. The mountains are still evident all around but you get to see even more cliffs than along the western half of this coastline.

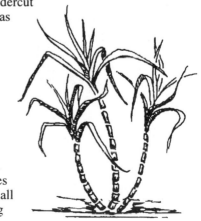

At longitude 075°13.9W we come across the great divide between U.S.-held territory and the rest of the country. This area at the mouth of the Guantánamo Bay was ceded to the U.S.A. at the beginning of the century and is still a bone of contention between the two

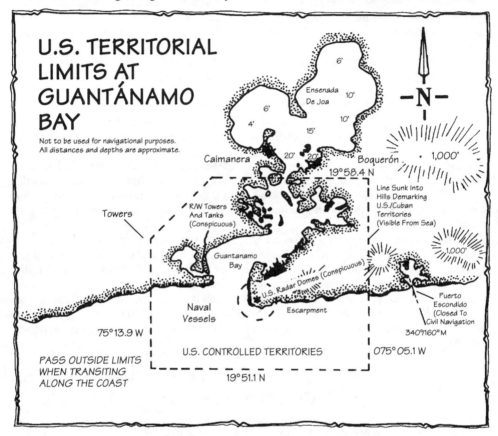

U.S. TERRITORIAL LIMITS AT GUANTÁNAMO BAY

Not to be used for navigational purposes. All distances and depths are approximate.

governments. It does seem a bit odd to see the U.S. positions and installations on either side of the entrance to the bay, with shiny well-appointed radar domes, tall pylons, and airstrips facing off against the rather more fundamental Cuban affairs you're now accustomed to.

If you do not intend to go in then make sure you aim well outside the southern limit, passing beyond latitude 19°51.1N .

You may in fact pass through the entrance north into Cuban territory again, so if you are going to the port of Caimanera hoist a U.S. courtesy-flag, contact Port Control on 12, and proceed on through. You will be subject to interrogation and possibly searches by the U.S. authorities on the way so have your documents ready. In any case you are not allowed to land at the naval base.

The entrance is well buoyed past the base as far as the southern section where the bay widens and the small town of Caimanera is situated round the corner on the left. There is a small boatyard here and there are road and rail links with the city of Guantánamo 20 miles away. On the right is the more major port of Boquerón where there is a large wharf set up for commercial vessels, and like its neighbor there are links with the inland. The bay offers good shelter in any weather, but there's not a lot to attract the cruiser and in light of potential problems it may be as well to give it a miss until the present unpleasantness dies away.

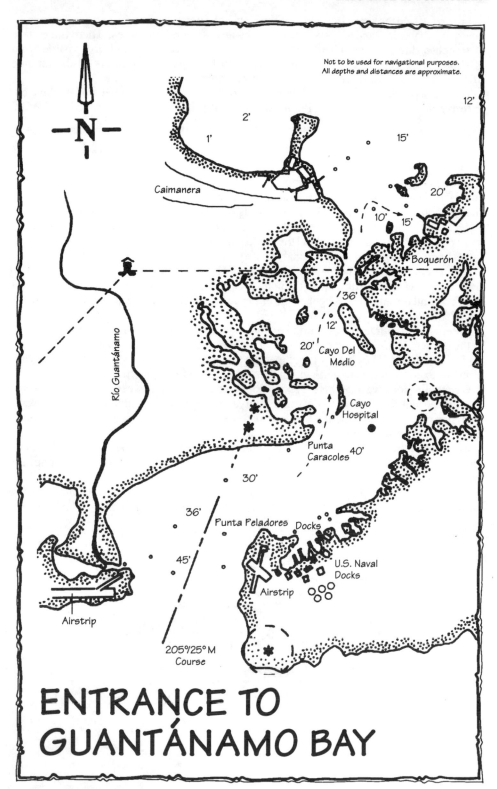

Not to be used for navigational purposes.
All depths and distances are approximate.

12'

-N-

2'

1'

15'

Caimanera

20'

10'

15'

Boquerón

36'

12'

20'

Cayo Del
Medio

Río Guantánamo

Cayo
Hospital

Punta
Caracoles

40'

30'

36'

Punta Peladores

Docks

45'

U.S. Naval
Docks

Airstrip

Airstrip

205°/25° M
Course

ENTRANCE TO
GUANTÁNAMO BAY

From outiside the scene is frankly fascinating, helicopters buzzing in and out, large coast guard or navy ships, and borders defended by watch-towers and fences. There is a system of trenches dug into the hillsides along the boundaries and these, clearly visible from offshore, are a good indication of just when you have passed the limits on the far side (075°05.1W) and can come back close inshore again.

There is a convenient habour at Puerto Escondido just past the Guantánamo enclave but unfortunately it is off-limits to civil traffic so we'll just have to go on towards the east.

BAITIQUIRÍ

If the growing swells in the afternoon have tired you out you might choose to come in at this harbour 20 miles past Guantánamo, with an extremely narrow entrance but a sheltered anchorage within. The coast here is relatively low and edged with mangroves except to the north of the bay where there is a small township of some 1,000 inhabitants, and a couple of small docks. Behind this there is a wide valley containing expanses of sugar fields and some agricultural buildings.

This small so-called Pocket-Bay (a feature of the east and northeast coasts) is situated some 3.5 miles west southwest of the point at Sabanalamar where the Pan de Azucar rises 800 feet, and is marked by a light on the eastern side of the entrance at position. 20°01.5N / 074°51.2W.

Enter along a course roughly northwest and, avoiding the reefs awash on either side, keep to the darker, deep-water center of the channel which shelves gradually from about 25-to-10 feet at the end. The channel is not marked and only some 50 feet wide at its narrowest point so exercise due care until within the wide bay and you can head across.

Over to the northwest there is a wooden dock some 50 feet long where fishing boats come alongside, and ashore there is a small boatyard and a white building which houses a freezing plant. East of the dock is a sunken barge and still further along a salt-works consisting of various yellow constructions and a dock.

The rest of the way to Punta Maisí is unremarkable except for the fact that there is no shelter available should you really need it, so it's best to wait up in Baitequirí until the weather is settled.

The remainder of this run should be no problem in anything but the most unwise circumstances, but it is as well to note that it's called the "Pass of the Winds" in Spanish.

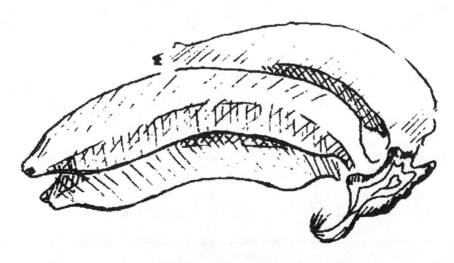

About 10 miles southwest of Punta Maisí, an outcrop called Nelson's Bank rises a couple of thousand feet from the depths to within 300 feet of the surface. This can cause a rather disquieting change in the motion of your boat if you are not aware of the cause, but apart from that there isn't much to worry about.

There is an **emergency-mooring** close to Punta Caleta near Maisí consisting of a buoy near the mouth of the River Caleta, but it is dubious that this could be available at short notice.

PUNTA MAISÍ
CHART NO ICH 1134 (CUBAN)

Just off the point the currents can be influenced somewhat by the winds, and we can get a strong westerly flow in winter. When the occasional summer southerly persists the current can reputably flow east against the trend, while just to be different the currents flow south if the winds come out of the north!

In spite of the above, the low coastline at this most extreme part of Cuba is usually subject to prevailing easterlies unaffected by any Kabatic effect, so once you're round the point you have the winds and current at your back. There is little to choose between making a daytime or night passage, so the final analysis it is probably down to when you actually departed from your last halt as to when you actually arrive round the corner in Baracoa. On principle, however, we always prefer to round such capes at night.

Along the way you will have the pleasure of listening on the VHF to the U.S. Coast Guard interrogating or even intercepting various vessels on the high seas. Whatever your position on the actual legality of this practice you should be aware of it, and if in international waters you may well be asked questions regarding the boat's name, captain, last port, flag, owner, and even your date of birth! A foreign-flagged vessel may refuse to answer, but (to twist the words of a famous poet) be aware of the fact that they have the Gatling gun and you in all likelihood have none.

Bicyclists cross a railroad track winding through the countryside. The bicycle is the most readily available and affordable means of transportation. (Photo by George Halloran)

213

An old cannon at Santiago's fortress castle is an interesting piece of history and art. (Photo by Simon Charles)

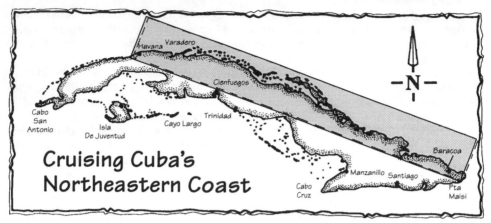

Cruising Cuba's
Northeastern Coast

BARACOA TO HAVANA

GENERAL

This gentle curve, stretching 520 miles northwest from the mountains near Punta Maisí to the lowlands of Havana is divided into two distinct sections. The first 220-mile stretch of coastline as far as Cayo Verde contains deep-water pocket-bays (a feature of eastern Cuba) neatly spaced along its length, while the next section, almost as far as Varadero, offers more in the way of cays and islets.

POCKETS PROVIDE HARBOURS

These pocket-bays provide harbours for all types of vessels, from tiny fishing boats with room for one man and his dog, all the way up to large ocean-going commercial ships. They are usually entered through a narrow channel, whereupon the bay widens out considerably into a deep expanse of water protected on all sides.

As the inner bays are so large, we will in general confine our remarks to entering and clearing in, leaving the question of where you might wish to moor within up to the individual skipper.

SHALLOW INNER SOUNDS

The cays on the other hand are similar to those on the south and northwest coasts, with the proviso that waters within the inner sounds here are usually quite shallow. You should check the depths carefully before venturing inside for a long run through.

Along the route, you are likely to see far more in the line of holiday development than elsewhere in Cuba. This still only means that you will come across maybe three or four international hotel complexes in the 460 miles before Varadero.

Elsewhere the cays are more or less deserted. By basing yourself in any of the inhabited stops along the way the cruiser can visit a multitude of inland towns and cities.

STRATEGY

Having rounded Punta Maisí, the prevailing winds and currents are with you all the way and the shelters are spread out along easy runs. With any good downwind rig, you should have an exhilarating run along the coast, surfing along at top speed if your vessel is fast enough. If the waves are small then you can pole-out the Genoa and gull-wing along, or even set a spinnaker if you have one. Exercise caution though if the wind is up and your boat is slow, as the swells can rise considerably and even swamp the vessel from behind. Under these conditions our lovely old trawler fishtails alarmingly as the swells overtake its 7-knot top speed and the autopilot clanks alarmingly trying to keep up with things. In this instance we find it best to hand-steer to ease the strain and to prevent any possible damage. A good helmsman *anticipates*, while an autopilot merely *reacts* and thus needs huge steering-changes as the stern gets pushed round.

Once again you may come in over the wall if there is room and depth, but be careful about uncharted shoals, or even islands. We once did this stretch with old U.S. charts and while they were more than adequate, there were a few notable errors calling for care just along the reef. If necessary, re-read the previous sections on navigating in coral.

Remember that a lot of the cays along here are quite shallow on the inside. There are lots of marked entrances and channels but check your charts well to be sure about the depths. There may be occasional medium to large fishing boats inside but most of these only draw about 3-4 feet so the water may not be enough for a deep keel.

Despite this there really isn't much to worry the prudent mariner (as they're always called in the official warnings) and we always like to moor inside the reef whenever possible.

Watch out for those northerly stretches, e.g., just west of the Bay of Nipe to Punta Lucrecia or around Cayo Romano where the current and prevailing winds strike more or less at right angles to the coast and the swells can roll you unmercifully. If you have to tack out then do it early in the day when the wind and waves are smaller.

CHARTS

Again the best charts to have are the Cuban Government ICH series, but if coming up from the islands it is unlikely that these are available to you. Luckily there are a multitude of U.S. or Admiralty charts dealing with the heavily passaged Old Bahama Channel, the Florida Straits, and the areas between Crooked Island and Inagua in the Bahamas down to Haiti and Punta Maisí in Cuba.

Almost any of these will serve perfectly well as they cover the Cuban coastline along their bottom edges, and as the U.S. charts are easily available on order to anywhere in the West Indies, I shall give the requisite numbers too.

BARACOA
CHART NOS. ICH 1134 OR 1133 (CUBAN) &
DMA 26240 (U.S.)

Having rounded Punta Maisí the motion of the swells is likely to abate somewhat, your boat-speed will pick up a bit and it's an easy coastal passage west northwest for the remaining 20 miles. Early morning views are pleasing, with mist pouring out of the valleys until you come to the escarpment covered with palms, and the bay of Miel (Honey Bay) opens up in front of you.

The bay is large and open with a good enclosed harbour to serve the city which sprawls across the hillside behind.

The city is recognizable from well out to sea by a peculiar flat-topped mountain further to the west. There is a modern stadium at the eastern end of the town, a long malecón (sea-wall), and a stately yellow ochre building looking out from the hillside near the harbour.

Enter the harbour at the west end of town, steering 245° M towards the inshore marker-light and remembering to keep to port closer to the large steel hulk moored on that side. The hulk in fact marks one side of the harbour mouth and to that end has a light mounted on its stern as shown in the drawing.

If passaging up the island chain from the West Indies, this may well be your first Cuban port so you will not be familiar with the procedure, but never mind, it's more or less the same for those coming round from Santiago and not so different from any other island.

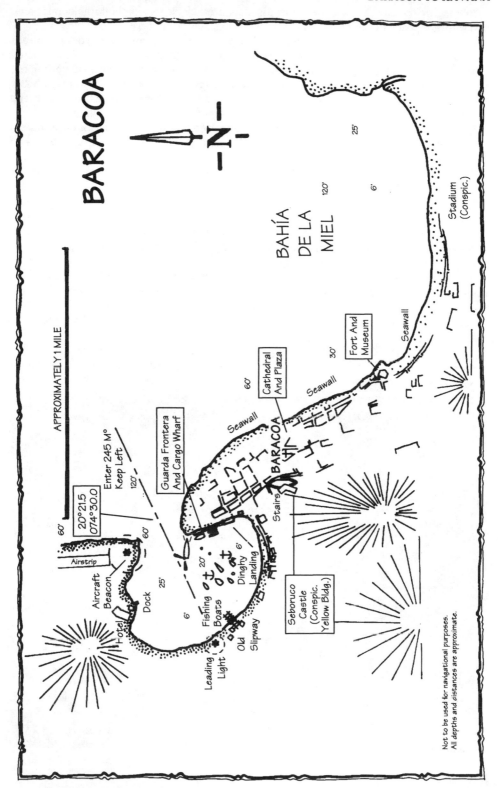

BARACOA

N

APPROXIMATELY 1 MILE

BAHÍA
DE LA
MIEL

25'

120'

6'

Stadium
(Conspic.)

Seawall

Fort And
Museum

30'

Cathedral
And Plaza

Seawall

60'

Seawall

BARACOA

Enter 245 M°
Keep Left

120'

Guarda Frontera
And Cargo Wharf

20°21.5
074°30.0

60'

60'

Airstrip

Aircraft
Beacon

Hotel

Dock

25'

6'

20'

Fishing
Boats

6'

Dinghy
Landing

Old
Slipway

6'

Leading
Light

Stairs

Seboruco
Castle
(Conspic.
Yellow Bldg.)

Not to be used for navigational purposes.
All depths and distances are approximate.

217

Just inside the mouth, on the left, there is a concrete dock serving both the commercial and military needs of the port with a mix of fishing and patrol boats.

Approach slowly, stopping close outboard the moored vessels and make your intentions clear by shouting over to the curious spectators. At this point there is likely to be a comedy of uniformed characters pulling shirts on, pointing in different directions, and calling out contradictory instructions. Unless obvious indications to the contrary, they are probably telling you to anchor somewhere close off the wharf and to await boarding by customs and immigration officers who will be brought out by a press-ganged fisherman in a skiff.

Formalities are much as anywhere else in Cuba (see previous sections on entry procedures), and as the port is used more often than most by foreign yachts there should be someone who has the requisite experience to keep things simple. As elsewhere, you should try to keep things light and stress that you are continuing on towards Havana after a day or two in town.

Your existing Guia de Recala should show your itinerary so there won't be a huge delay before you are requested to moor amongst the other fishing boats some 80 yards off in 20 feet of water. As the port is used by many small fishing boats they sometimes like you to hang a line back from your stern to another more tightly moored vessel to prevent you swinging too much at anchor.

To go ashore later you may leave your dinghy over by the steps on the inner end of the dock where swimming children will pester you with questions until chased off by the fishermen.

Entry into the tiny port area is restricted so don't worry, your dinghy will be safe while you set off up the hill directly in front of the gate. Don't forget to politely notify the officials at the post just outside that you are visiting their town. It isn't strictly necessary, but it makes a good impression on everyone and they'll just smile delightedly and give you directions to all the sites of interest.

A proud Cuban grandfather with his grandson. (Photo by George Halloran)

THE OLDEST COLONIAL AMERICAS TOWN

Baracoa was originally founded in 1510 by Diego Velasquez who established seven garrison towns to defend the coast of Cuba, but there is also some discussion that Columbus first landed here when he discovered Cuba in 1492. Whatever, it is still the oldest colonial town in the Americas and its relative isolation from the rest of the country has enabled it to retain a certain discreet charm and a style of its own.

The area surrounding the city specializes in the production of cocoa and coconuts, but although the town is supposedly famous for its chocolate you will be hard pressed to find any there.

The main vantage point in the city is the castle you saw when coming in (the yellow-ochre building on the hillside) and called at various times Santa Barbara or Seboruco Castle. Well worth a visit, this building was originally constructed in the 1700's, was restored early this century with the help of American engineers, and is now a dusty hotel following further restoration. The castle bar on the top floor is one of the most pleasant places in Cuba to spend a few hours and provides views of both the city and the mountains surrounding the bay. Over to the west you can see El Yunque, the flat-topped mountain which marks Baracoa. Also plainly visible is the exciting "Sleeping Beauty" or La Bella Durmiente, a remarkable formation of hills which look exactly like their description.

At night the local students gather near the main square in the lovely narrow streets to listen to music. Speakers are set up in windows and the sound reverberates off stone columns supporting the overhanging eaves. You'll have to help "practice my English" here too.

A walk east along the sea-front/malecón will take you to the town museum and fort. Nearby there is a statue of Columbus looking remarkably like Klaus Kinski, who himself acted as a conquistador during his distinguished film career (shame on you if you aren't familiar with his work).

In a rather grisly claim to fame, Hatuey, the Indian chieftain from Hispanola, who spearheaded the resistance to Spanish occupation was burned at the stake in Baracoa. Later they made up for this indignity by naming the national beer after him.

Across from your anchorage to the northwestern side of the harbour is the airstrip and a tourist hotel easily accessible by dinghy to the waterside bar. Here you may experience a rather undistinguished meal or the tepid delights of the disco. There is a hard-currency shop too, so if you need to reprovision you might be able to get a few of the more unnecessary items which have found their way down here.

DEPARTING FROM BARACOA

Departing Baracoa could not be more simple; If you have been suitably pleasant to all concerned at entry you will have received prior permission and it may not be necessary to do more than wave and set off. Otherwise it's probably simpler to row your documents over to the dock for inspection and to collect your despacho.

NORTHWESTWARD ROUTE
CHART NOS.ICH 1133 (CUBAN) & DMA 26240 (U.S.)

Between Baracoa and the nickel-mining port of Moa (30 miles) the course is purely visual and the coast is free of any dangers except where the reefs begin to extend offshore after Punta Guarica. Prior to that however there is a small cove at **Maraví** (enter 224° M from 20°26.3N/074°32.9W) which could provide an idle shallow anchorage if you so desired. Along this portion of the coast there are a multitude of little inlets generally accessible and accompanied by tiny beaches fringed with coconut trees and inviting slow passages. If you do enter, just be on the lookout for nets which are often strung across the entrances.

Another excellent bay is that of **Taco**: Enter obliquely along 255° M from 20°31.7N/ 074°39.8W to avoid the shallows then turn south southwest when just between the outer points of the entry channel.

Scuba dives along the coast here are interesting for the evidence they will provide of the rapid growth of barnacles acquired in Santiago harbour, and this is probably the first time you'll have the opportunity to clean them off the propeller or hull. My dive-logs also note persistent thermoclines, causing ripples in the visibility underwater as light is refracted by temperature changes at depth.

As you pass Punta Guarnica near the Bay of Moa you'll begin to notice wrecks and associated bits of steel strewn about so treat the reefs with caution and hang a bit further out. The lights along the coast are set back about a half-mile from the reef. At night keep away from them rather than being drawn to them like a moth to a flame. Large chimneys ashore on the other side of the reef will indicate the bay and nickel-processing facilities of Moa.

MOA

Note: Moa is a strange, oddly "sci-fi" place quite unlike the more normal Cuban ports, and with few casual visitors. Entering here with a private boat can perplex some officials and the unfamiliar procedures may sometimes lead to a more intrusive search than you are accustomed to along the same coast.

Remember that it is a tricky entrance with the harbour not obiously evident without some advice, a good local chart, or of course this guide. Once inside the bay, heading too far west towards the city itself is going to run you aground.

Do not approach the outer mark from due east as there is a reef (marked by a stake) close by on that side but enter from a position approximately 20°41.5N/074°52.1W well outside the green marker and go in along a course of around 217° M in along the line of the range marks.

About 4/10ths of a mile in past the green outer mark, or approximately 20°40.8N/ 074°52.5W, turn 248° M aiming between the two red/green marks marking the channel to the harbour and a mile on take up a course of 228° M into the enclosed docking area. Along the way you will notice that the waters have changed from a clean transparent blue to a foreboding satanic red, stained by the overflow from the nickel plants to the southeast within the bay.

Inside the narrow docks you will be expected to come alongside a rickety wooden affair usually used by pilot boats and close at hand to a disused seaman's club. Here you will be boarded by the local officials.

It is a fair distance into town so you will have to request a taxi from any of the officials or pilots. While you wait you can look over at the mosquito-plagued firing-range close by the ruined Seaman's Club. Boldly displayed is a message from the President (El Comandante) who lists among the prerequisites to be a good soldier, "Learn to shoot, and shoot well."

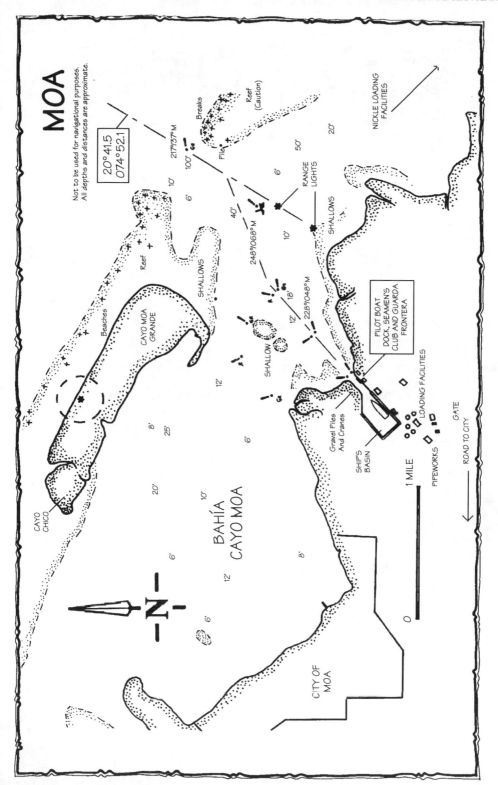

MOA

Not to be used for navigational purposes.
All depths and distances are approximate.

20° 41.5
074° 52.1

Breaks

Reef
(Caution)

217°/37° M

Pile

100'

50'

20'

6'

10'

Range Lights

40'

248°/068° M

10'

SHALLOWS

SHALLOWS

6'

10'

Reef

Beaches

CAYO MOA GRANDE

18'

228°/048° M

12'

SHALLOW

12'

NICKLE LOADING FACILITIES

PILOT BOAT DOCK, SEAMEN'S CLUB AND GUARDA FRONTERA

LOADING FACILITIES

GATE

ROAD TO CITY

Gravel Piles And Cranes

SHIP'S BASIN

PIPEWORKS

6'

12'

25'

8'

CAYO CHICO

20'

BAHÍA
CAYO MOA

10'

6'

12'

8'

N

6'

1 MILE

0

CITY OF MOA

If you have ever seen the classic film "Soylent Green" you will be familiar with the environment here. The city is based around the extraction of minerals, and the associated plumbing is a feature of the place. Huge leaking pipes along the roadsides hiss and bubble, oozing green slime and weird fumes from every joint all the way into town.

In the darkness around the gate, small groups of predatory girls await sailors from the ore-transports and the whole scene is one of unrelieved bleakness as the city itself looms ominously ahead, with dreary concrete apartment blocks and unlit streets. If tempted to the darkened hotel in town be careful about what you eat and stick to the vegetables at all costs.

If all this suggests a certain jaundiced view of the place, apparently I am not alone. I have later heard tales suggesting that Cuban engineers have been known to sacrifice their careers rather than serve time there!

Finally, just to make it worse, the Je-Jenes (no-see-ums) around your dock are the worst in Cuba and are particularly active at dawn as you hurry to clean your boat of the gritty crud that has dropped from the sky overnight. Use the hosepipe ashore to clean off the decks, get your papers, head 048° M dead center through the buoys (very important), and clear out of the dread place.

Of course, as a counterpoint, the pilots stationed there were extremely nice to us while we were there. They even went to the extent of establishing radio contact with us the first time we entered, preventing us from getting into trouble in the shallow bits after they noticed we had strayed too far westwards in the bay.

ROUTE TO BAHIA NIPE
CHART NOS ICH 1132 (CUBAN) & DMA 26240 (U.S.)

It's another 40 miles to the enormous bay of Nipe; You must remain well off land for the first 10 miles, but having cleared those reefs you can come in a little closer (about 3/4-mile offshore) along the edge of the reefs. This particular stretch of coastline seems to have claimed a fair share of wrecks, so don't let your guard drop. Fishermen in fact can sometimes be seen wading right out to the reefs where they cast their nets by hand.

You must also be aware of the nets which are usually strung along the shallow western gaps through the Moa reef (around 075°02.5W) or where the view changes to rolling countryside sometimes more reminiscent of England than Latin America.

The possibilities for diving along the wall here are endless and from the deck you can clearly see the bottom at 75 feet, so if you have time then take the opportunity. If you prefer to cruise uninterrupted you can remain about 100 yards off the reefs in about 30 feet while looking at the gorgeous beaches inside. It's a bit smoother too.

Before you reach the bay of Nipe there are a couple of other large bays worthy of note.

A Russian built patrol boat operated by the Cubans at Nuevitas Bay, resembles the "Batmobile", sporting the styling of a 1950's automobile. (Photo by Simon Charles)

TÁNAMO

About 14 miles east of Nipe is the bay of Tánamo, just as enclosed and well marked all the way inside. Pass west of the green mark to avoid the reef and its obligatory wreck. From 075°19.5W the range marks can be followed past the high watchtower and through the steepsided entrance into a large bay.

Once through the entrance channel and past the final cay on the left (Juanillo) the whole bay is now open to you with channels either side of the cay immediately in front. If you wish to go ashore at a dock then head 154° M towards a saddle-shaped cay 1.5 miles away whereupon a file of markers will take you further east towards Cayo Mambi serving the small sugar town of Frank Pais in the southeast. The dock here is in a state of ill-repair so if you prefer you may turn off to the right as you near the markers and approach the dock on the southern side of the bay off Punta Gorda.

LEVISA AND CABONICO BAYS

A distance of 9miles past the entrance to Tánamo and only 5 miles before Nipe is the common entrance (075°28.3W) to the bays of Levisa and Cabonico.

Having come in through the entrance, the channel forks. The right branch takes you southwest into the bay of Levisa with the town of Nicaro, and the left passage goes east into Cabonico.

Nicaro is situated 3 miles southwest of the entrance and has a couple of wharfs, but unfortunately navigation within the large bay outside of the port limits is limited regarding civilian vessels and you might have to argue with the Guarda Frontera at the entrance to move about freely.

The eastern part, Cabonico is somewhat encumbered by unmarked shallows and coral heads to within 7-8 feet of the surface but excellent shelter is nevertheless to be had. The coasts inside this bay are steep and rocky with yellow cliffs scattered about and the main evidence of inhabitation is along the entrance canal.

BAHÍA DE NIPE

This is a "must" stop along the way. Typical in its shape if not its sheer size, this is the biggest pocket-bay in Cuba and containing at least 50 square miles is easily large enough to have its own weather-system; My ship's log records the remark that if you can get into trouble coming in here you shouldn't have left home!

The entrance, 1.5 miles wide, is marked by a large light-pylon on the eastern side and there are range marks taking you through 206° M from approximately 20°48.5N/075°32.0W.

There is a dock and some tiki-huts forming a tourist complex along the beaches on the eastern side of the channel but you can visit these later.

First you have to clear in, so follow the marks round to the west, swing south past the patrol boats moored there, and come all the way round the corner to the dock at position (20°46.35N/075°34.64W) on the southern (inner) side of the promontory at Cayo Saetía.

Clearing in will take place here and should be a relatively painless process, assisted by staff from the tourist complex. After the formalities have been completed you may well be coaxed into an old Chinese army jeep and transported at breakneck speed up the hill.

The road will take you past a camp where Cuba's Young Pioneers come to learn farming techniques (looks rather fun, what with clay ovens and so on) and up to the complex of cabanas and the hotel-bar at the top of the hill.

Peculiarly, Cayo Saetía is stocked with exotic animals from Africa and the holiday resort there follows the same theme, with stuffed animals (even a shark) in the lobby. The buildings are deliberately rustic in style and the menu is the most varied and best cooked

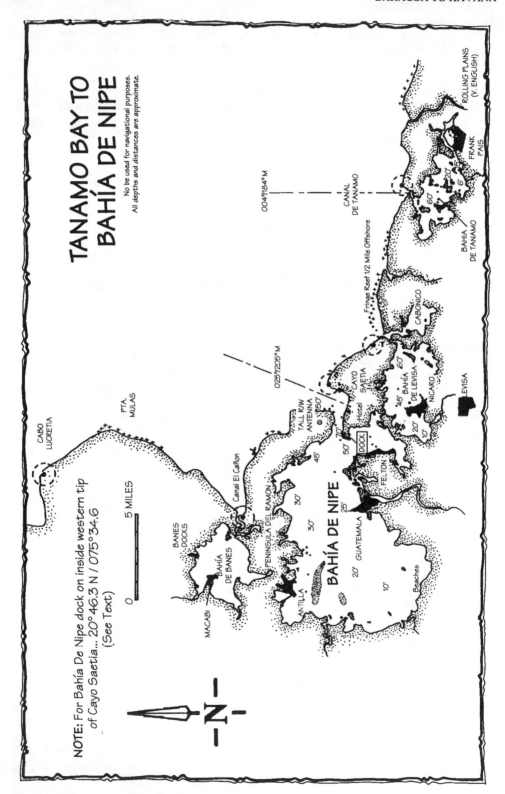

TANAMO BAY TO
BAHÍA DE NIPE

No to be used for navigational purposes.
All depths and distances are approximate.

NOTE: For Bahía De Nipe dock on inside western tip
of Cayo Saetía...20° 46.3 N / 075°34.6
(See Text)

0   5 MILES

CABO
LUCRETIA

PTA.
MULAS

BANES
DOCKS

BAHÍA
DE BANES

MACABI

MANTILLA

PENINSULA DEL RAMON

Canal El Cañon

30'

30'

20'

10'

Beaches

GUATEMALA

25'

FELTON

DOCK

50'

45'

70'

Hotel

150'

TALL R/W
ANTENNA

CAYO
SAETIA

025°/205° M

BAHÍA DE NIPE

60'

45'

BAHÍA
DE LEVISA

NICARO

20'

10'

LEVISA

CABONICO

Fringe Reef 1/2 Mile Offshore

CANAL
DE TANAMO

004°/184° M

BAHIA
DE TANAMO

60'

20'

6'

FRANK
PAIS

ROLLING PLAINS
(V. ENGLISH)

N

we've experienced in Cuba. With luck Riesel and Willy might still be there when you get in and the curse of officially decreed staff-turnover hasn't affected the wonderful atmosphere. All on board our vessel regard it as one of the nicest places to stop in the whole island.

TOUR THIS LARGE BAY AT YOUR LEISURE

This beautiful bay is far too large for me to give a thorough guide to the cruising areas within its boundaries, so use the docks as your base and wander as you see fit. By land, tours to all parts of the area are available here and they even go to the extent of arranging trips for the hunting, shooting, fishing set if that sort of thing is your bag.

When mooring alongside the various docks for any length of time remember that the tour-boats serving the area use them as well, so make arrangements accordingly.

I have read somewhere that sharks abound in the bay, but repeated questioning elicited only puzzled looks. Certainly apart from the dusty and rather unhappy-looking inhabitant of the lobby we've seen none while swimming in the crystal waters here.

ROUTE TO NARANJO (35 MILES)
CHART NOS. ICH 1132 (CUBAN) OR DMA 27040 (U.S.)

Leave early to lessen the effects of the winds which are going to be broadside to your northerly course for the first 20 miles. At Mulas point there is a large observation station rather like an airport control tower and an upturned iron wreck ashore, but the waves do tend to calm a bit as you come round at Cabo Lucretia. You can pass close to the picturesque lighthouse if the waves are calmed sufficiently, but take note of yet another wreck northwest of the light. A desperately sad sight this, bolt upright on the reef and pointing out to sea as if giving one last dying effort to get back home.

You can coast along some 200 yards offshore now in 300 feet of water, passing uninhabited wooded countryside, low green hills, and the delightful entrance to the Sama bay (075°46.2W) with its high escarpments to both sides and turquoise waters within.

You'll know when you are coming up on the bay of Naranjo when you see the hotel buildings along the beaches at 075°50.8W and the conspicuous flat-topped hill behind them.

NARANJO

Make a wide arc outside the light on the point and come in from coordinates of approximately 21°06.8N / 075°52.9W along 153° M. Pass between the red and green markers, but be careful of a strong current which can sometimes push you off to the right.

The channel passes east of the construction in the center of the channel where there were plans to establish a restaurant/aquarium complex, and is marked all the way to the end of the southeast branch at 21°05.7N/075°52.0W.

You will be required to clear in at the Base Nautica there, a somewhat dirty concrete wharf with corrugated iron roofs. Be careful coming alongside as the dock is used by a variety of local vessels from tugboats to fishing and scuba boats, but there will be plenty of willing hands to assist. Look out for the horrible black tires which are used as buffers.

The local Guarda Frontera representative will sort you out with a visit from the Provedor if you need any stores. Fuel, water, and ice are also available here. As the dock is so heavily used you will need to move off the dock after clearing in, so move over to the unobstructed area north northwest where you can anchor in 25 feet.

If you wish to visit the beaches or hotel it's a five-minute journey in a taxi called for you by the Guarda Frontera official on the dock. There you will be startled by the first international facilities since Santiago, with restaurants, bars and satellite televisions.

333°/153° M

DANGEROUS REEF
Go Wide... North

NOTE: Watch for
R & W Dive Moorings

Light
21° 06.8
075° 52.6

Punta
Sotavento

R

GR

70'

R

GR

ROCK FACE

Beaches And
Hotel Complexes

Low
Headlands

New Hotel
Construction

New Wharf
Construction
(Seaquarium)

40'
R

GR

APPROXIMATELY 1 MILE

R

20'

GR

Anchor
Here

GR

25'

30'

26'

Nets
Dock

R

R

Nets And
Oyster Beds

**BAHÍA
NARANJO**

Road North To
Hotel And
Beaches

-N-

0   1/2 MILE

Not to be used for navigational purposes.
All depths and distances are approximate.

The hotel, frequented by tanned Germans and Italians who lounge (startlingly, to a North American) topless on the beach, has phones, post offices, water sports, scuba diving, rental scooters and transport. Just don't assume that the DHL or other special delivery signs on the post office wall have any real significance.

ROUTE TO PUERTO PADRE
CHART NOS. ICH 1131 (CUBAN) & DMA 27040 (U.S.)

This is a 40-mile run and if you don't think you can make the bay at Puerta Padre then there are alternative shelters along the route at **Bahía Vita** (where there are plans to construct a new Base Nautica), Bahía Bariay, and the ancient city of **Gibara**.

600' 60' 20'
135°/315° M

Conspicuous Cliffs

White Lighthouse
(Conspicuous)
21°06.0
075°57.7

12'

25'

30'

–N–

BAHÍA VITA

Not to be used for navigational purposes.
All depths and distances are approximate.

Low
And Rocky

Fields

30'

12' Well Marked Channel

25'

8'

8'

6' .20'

30' Puerto
Vita

6'

8'

15'

18' 9'

8'

12'

Road To
Santa
Lucía

0   1 MILE

A cigar smoking gentleman poses beside a poster of the communist leader and Cuban hero Ché Guevara. (Photo by George Halloran)

Along the way you will see evidence of an officially encouraged paranoia (it encourages patriotism apparently) in the form of clusters of concrete machine-gun emplacements on the beaches. This inevitably leads one to wonder about what these crumbling pill-boxes were meant to repel. Modern warfare has long rendered them obsolete, and the threat of invasion may be less serious; but they remind us of a time the threat was very real.

PREPARE FOR STRONG WAVE ACTION

The Old Bahama Channel narrows here, squeezing the flow of water unmercifully and speeding it up with an accompanying strong wave-action. Consequently there are always the chances of higher swells coming in to Gibara on the west of the one mile wide bay. If you wish to enter then you should dock on the more sheltered east side, but as this isolates you somewhat it may be better to do your exploring by land from a halt either side of this historic city.

Far behind the impressive sea-front buildings and church cupolas marking the town you can see a flat-topped mountain. This was probably the hill noted by Columbus when he first landed in Cuba, an honor later confused with (or highjacked by) El Yunque at Baracoa (perhaps), and a point endlessly argued since then by the two cities. Mind you, there's one at Naranjo too, isn't there?

Once past Gibara, the terrain is dull and flat with little to note except lighthouses, and nothing in the way of refuge for the next 30 miles.

PUERTO PADRE BAY

Another large pocket-bay with an entrance well marked and free of any significant obstruction until well inside. Enter along a course of 200°M between the outer red and green buoys aiming towards a sandy area fringed with palms then follow the marked channel through the neck and into the bay.

If you do not intend to enter the bay, but rather merely need to shelter for the night, then clear in with the Guarda Frontera at the small community on the left as you come into the channel.

CLEAR AT THE SUGAR TERMINAL

All official clearance procedures in the bay itself are done at the sugar terminal, so if heading there the Guarda Frontera might come out in a boat from their dock to put one of their number aboard. He will accompany you the rest of the way into Carupano where you must officially clear in no matter where your final destination lies.

The Carupano sugar terminal is situated on Cayo Juan Claro some 2 miles south through the narrow channel and 3/4-mile southwest as you come out into the bay itself.

As with the other major international ports along the northeast the harbour authorities monitor channel 16 on the VHF.

In the absence of contrary instructions, go round to the western side of the island and proceed a little further south to the enormous concrete wharf docking alongside where space allows.

The sugar loading facility is well maintained with several huge mobile cranes set along a wharf some 250 yards long and 10 feet high. The large black rubber fenders hanging down are set a bit high for the average yacht, so be careful to make suitable arrangements to avoid damage to your superstructure.

FACILITIES FOR OCEAN-GOING VESSELS

The facilities here are really intended for large ocean going vessels so you may feel dwarfed by the praying mantis cranes looming overhead and the 150-foot deep concrete apron. Nevertheless the officials will have had enough experience with foreign ships to deal with your needs perfectly adequately, and any further cruising inside the bay can be cleared with them. The port of Puerto Padre (population 23,000) lies about 3.5 miles southwest of Carupano and counts on a couple of docks to handle the needs of passenger and fishing traffic. Note that there is always a stiff east northeast wind within the bay.

REMAIN AT DOCKSIDE

The terminal is connected with the mainland and the town of Puerto Padre via a causeway so you may find it convenient to remain at the dockside and communicate by road. If so, be careful to keep your windows and doors closed against the constant sand-storm blowing off the apron and over your boat. Note that the oily fenders will foul your topsides too.

There is a seamans club 200 yards away from the dockyard gates so it might fall to you to finally sample the dubious pleasures therein.

It consists of a small building with a bar, a small tacky hard-currency shop, and as is usual in such places, a few young ladies hanging out. They politely make their position quite clear from the start, but in fact are quite friendly even outside of their normal business relationships.

After the bar begins to pall, if you are especially interesting you may even get a lift across the causeway and into town; three to a motorbike! There you can continue carousing in special (and somewhat illegal) local restaurant-bars until the dawn comes up.

A final point to note here is that the port is really geared towards ships rather than boats, so when leaving request your clearance papers well in advance and don't fret if they are late.

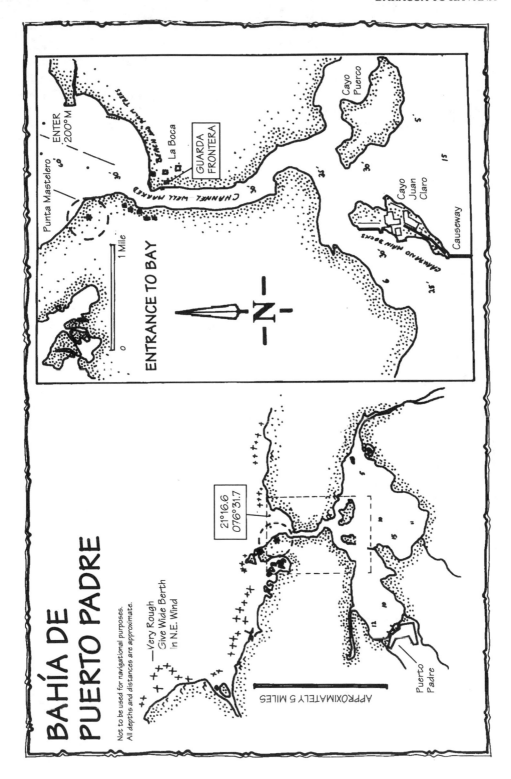

BAHÍA DE PUERTO PADRE

Not to be used for navigational purposes.
All depths and distances are approximate.

—Very Rough
Give Wide Berth
In N.E. Wind

21°16.6
076°31.7

APPROXIMATELY 5 MILES

Puerto Padre

ENTRANCE TO BAY

N

1 Mile

0

Punta Mastelero

ENTER
200°M

La Boca

GUARDA
FRONTERA

CHANNEL WELL MARKED

Cayo
Puerco

Cayo
Juan
Claro

CAMANAJO MAIN DOCKS

Causeway

ROUTE TO NUEVITAS (40 MILES)
CHART NOS. ICH 1131, 1130 (CUBAN) & DMA 27040 (U.S.)

Another long run made possible in daylight by the prevailing winds and the currents which are being thoroughly squeezed into a venturi by the Great Bahama Bank just to the north. The swells, however, heap up uncomfortably at times, so relax in port if there is a depression in the offing.

There is an offshore reef just six miles west of the entrance to Puerto Padre bay, so give it a suitable berth by staying well out. An additional advantage to going wide early is that it enables you to approach the entrance to Nuevitas from a more easterly direction rather than having to make a coastal passage broadside to the waves when they are at their height later on in the day.

MANATÍ

This bay, some 16 miles west of Puerto Padre makes for a handy refuge and might be worth a short visit if time is of no importance.

There is a lighthouse on the western point at the entrance and a lighted buoy at the head of the channel. There are few dangers inside and an approach should be made to the long dock on the eastern side 2 miles into the channel. The port serves the town of Manatí some 8-10 miles away and although it nominally handles sugar and molasses is not a very busy place.

There are customs and immigration facilities here as well as the usual communications by road and telephone.

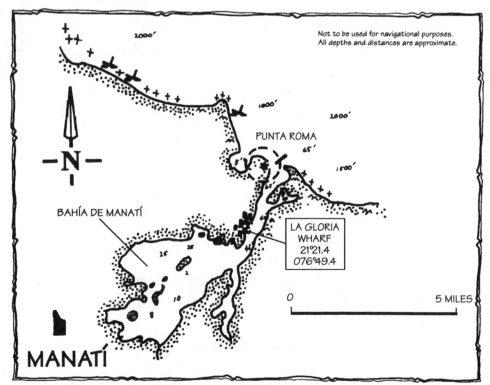

Not to be used for navigational purposes.
All depths and distances are approximate.

PUNTA ROMA

BAHÍA DE MANATÍ

LA GLORIA
WHARF
21°21.4
076°49.4

0   5 MILES

MANATÍ

Giant cranes at the Puerto Padre Bay harbour are designed to accommodate the cargos of large ocean-going vessels. The sugar loading facility is well-maintained with experienced officials. (Photo by Simon Charles)

NUEVITAS BAY

Another large bay with the usual feature of a long narrow neck and a wide bay. If you intend to enter be prepared for a 5-mile journey through the sheltered entrance channel before the enormous bay opens before you, and there's another seven miles after that.

BEWARE OF AN OFFSHORE REEF

If the multitude of protruding wreckage hasn't already tipped you off, be advised that there is an offshore reef extending some 10-15 miles east from the entrance. A stake (077°04.2 W) near the western end might tempt you through, but the entrance it marks is a bit shallow. If you are coming from the east, continue on northwest about 1.5 miles and come in 215° M from anywhere around 21°37.2N /077°05.7W towards the mark in the center of the channel. There are range-marks inside to guide you through, but you should remember to turn off to port (21°35.5N) where the Guarda Frontera have their dock. They will radio the port authorities inside Nuevitas if you are continuing in, and while awaiting permission to enter you can inspect the "Batmobile", a fast patrol-boat more reminiscent of a '57 Chevrolet, what with fins and things!

CONTINUING TO TARAFA

You will be continuing to the port of Tarafa on the promontory splitting the bay, so proceed through the serpentine channel following a combination of range-marks and standard red/green buoys for at least 4 more miles. Large sugar-transporters use this port, so give them a wide berth.

Once into the bay, do not be tempted to cut directly over to the west where the port lies unless you have an exceedingly shallow draft. Rather, follow the marks roughly southwest towards the ship's anchorage before making your cut, then come round north of the storage tanks and the jetty and continue two miles north northwest to the port itself.

At the northern end there are a series of quays pointing roughly NNE, with enough space between them to dock large ships. These wharfs can be rather crowded and if there is a large swell entering then they can become dangerous for a small boat, so give thought to your lines while awaiting the port authorities.

As with Puerto Padre, the officials here will deal with your papers quickly even though they don't get many (if any) private boats. Once you are cleared-in, ask if you can move to more sheltered conditions and go round to the far side of the dockyard or to a position of your own choosing elsewhere in the bay.

Note: Be careful of the shallows close in to the rear of the wharf on the northwestern side of the dock complex. You may be advised to go round there, and it is more sheltered, but do not approach the extreme southwestern end of the dock.

We once had the experience of a so-called harbour pilot leaping aboard with an offer to show us the way to a convenient mooring. True, he may have been a pilot but he certainly didn't know much about that side, and because he was aboard I must have shamefully lowered my guard. Before we knew it we were hard aground, being pushed sideways by the swells further into the rubble below the surface there.

Luckily some Cuban divers with whom we'd been chatting while awaiting our inward clearance saw our predicament and came to our assistance. With everyone cursing and swearing in the water, we waded anchors far outboard with lines attached, and when tension on these didn't work we moved *all* equipment and baggage forward.

Lightening the stern had the desired effect, and reversing hard while hauling on the lines finally got us off, but it was a close run thing.

As you may well imagine, everyone involved partied late into the night to the accompaniment of loud music and it was with serious hangovers that the next day was spent checking the hull below for damage.

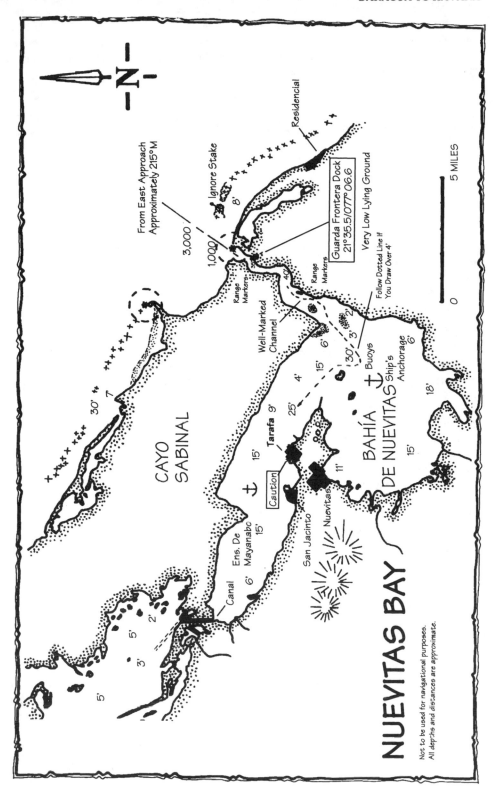

NUEVITAS BAY

From East Approach
Approximately 215°M

Ignore Stake

Residencial

8'

8'

3,000

1,000

Guarda Frontera Dock
21°35.5/077° 06.6

Very Low Lying Ground

Follow Dotted Line If
You Draw Over 4'

Range
Markers

Range
Markers

40'

Well-Marked
Channel

30'

Buoys

6'

3'

2'

6'

Ship's
Anchorage

6'

18'

15'

4'

Tarafa 9'

25'

15'

15'

BAHÍA
DE NUEVITAS

11'

Caution

San Jacinto

Nuevitas

CAYO
SABINAL

30'

7

15'

15'

Ens. De
Mayanabo

6'

6'

Canal

5'

3'

5'

2'

5'

5 MILES

0

Not to be used for navigational purposes.
All depths and distances are approximate.

As captain, needless to say, the fault was really mine for relaxing when someone supposedly "knew the way", and to this day I have been especially aware of the potential for this sort of thing happening again.

LOCATING THE HARBOUR AUTHORITIES

Ashore, you can find the harbour authorities by leaving the port through the gate and heading up the hill directly in front of you. In a most impressive columned building at the summit you will find customs, immigration, and all other functionaries whom you might need. As this is a major port all the normal dockyard facilities and services are available.

There is another less Bacchanalian seaman's club to the east near the harbour offices if you need to purchase any stocks for the boat.

Interestingly enough, apparently Soviet missiles and technicians came ashore here in 1962 and in the park at the foot of the hill there is a plaque dedicated to the missile crisis.

This bay is the last of the pocket-bays along the coast and continuing west will now take you immediately into the cays. There is a channel cut through the western side of the bay into the sound on that side, but the waters inside are rather shallow for general cruising so it may be better to take the outside route northwest.

At 50 miles, the next leg (to Cayo Confites) will require an early start if we are to have any chance of achieving our goal of a daylight run. To that end it is probably best to make arrangements with the Harbour Authorities to collect your despacho and clearance during the afternoon of the day before travelling. This way you can make the long journey out to the very entrance to the channel, rest up there, and depart at first light (or earlier) next day.

The need for this will be apparent when you realize that the authorities will probably be late in arriving with your papers, and the journey back across the bay is always into the teeth of a stiff east wind.

MOOR DOWNSTREAM NEAR THE MOUTH

Moor about 200 yards downstream (south) of the Guarda Frontera post near the mouth (first indicate what you will be doing) and well out of the way of any ships leaving at night. There are some rocky bits close inshore but you can easily find good anchorage in 12-14 feet.

The tremendous flow through the channel at rise and fall of the tides will cause your propeller to rotate all night so don't be alarmed if you hear a strange whirring sound from below, but despite this there is excellent snorkeling in the immediate area. As the floor is criss-crossed with old cables and such stuff you might also want to have a look at just where the anchor has come to rest if you want a quick getaway in the morning.

ROUTE TO CAYO COCO
CHART NOS. ICH 1130 & 1129 (CUBAN), DMA 27040 & 27060 (U.S.)

It is best to wait for winds less than 10-15 knots as the first stretch can be rough. The waves are not violent, but they heap up to alarming proportions as they sweep along and lift the stern in a sickening corkscrew motion. Never mind, further on there will once again be protection and the neck of the Bahama Channel will eventually widen to decrease the flow speed.

There is some danger of being pushed inside of your desired course too, so keep alert against the possibility, and as before try to go out wide early on.

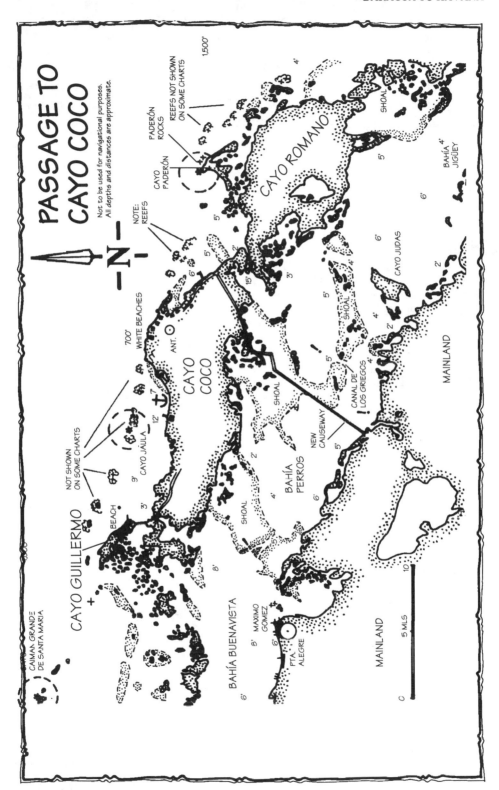

PASSAGE TO CAYO COCO

Not to be used for navigational purposes.
All depths and distances are approximate.

CAYO CONFITES

An interesting sidelight on Cayo Confites:
In 1947 an unknown young man called Fidel Castro joined an expedition based here with the intention of overthrowing President Trujillo of the Dominican Republic. That time, the attempt was successfully broken up by the Cuban government.

This is really not much more than an overnight stop, but handy enough while making the passage to Cayo Coco where better facilities exist. Come in due west through the stakes marking the reef at 22 °09.5 N, southeast of the small cay and turn due north when well inside. There is a small red buoy over to the north at 22 °10.8 N / 077 °39.8 W to which you may moor for a comfortable shelter just 400 yards inside the reef. You will not be protected in any way from the winds, but the waves are thoroughly broken-up and the motion of the boat at rest will assure you of a good night's sleep.

This is the eastern control station for the Cuban traffic-control scheme which monitors hazardous cargos through the narrows of the Old Bahama Channel. Ashore there is a complex of military/coast guard buildings with a small dock for the patrol boat there. They will not be too happy about your arrival if you come ashore but will certainly be helpful in giving you entrance instructions if you need them. They answer to "L E 60" (or in bad phonetics... "Estassion, elleh-eh sessenta") on VHF channel 16 and will speak English if you so desire.

They may suggest that you moor behind Cayo Verde about three miles south southeast at position 22°07.0N/077°38.8W and despite the vagueness of the charts this cay does in fact exist, so head on over there after entering through the reef as above.

LEAVING FOR THE NORTHWEST

When leaving for the northwest you will find there are also markers through the reef on that end of the cay. Use those to enter if making the long slog from that direction.

Once past Cayo Confites you can find room to come in over the wall at last for shelter from the incessant swells, but the current is at its maximum and you should still gain about a knot or two in the easterly direction. Despite the warnings on the U.S. charts the lights seem to be in excellent repair and it's fun to be hailed by the light stations along the coast here who inform each other of your progress. They inquire whether you are having a good time and wish you luck for the rest of your journey.

Be careful when coming up to the splendid yellow and black lighthouse on Cayo Paderon as there are some uncharted reefs just off to the east which could surprise you if you have begun to relax in the smoother water.

238

CAYO COCO

This is one of the largest cays in Cuba and is being developed along the lines of a tourist complex and nature reserve. It is important to realize that you should moor on the eastern half of the cay rather than continuing round to the more obvious harbour further on.

The cay contains a group of excellent foreign-operated hotels and there are plans to extend the docking facilities to cater to yachts, but in the interval proceed as shown below, or call in on VHF to "Servimar" (channel 16) for a boat to escort you in through the shallows.

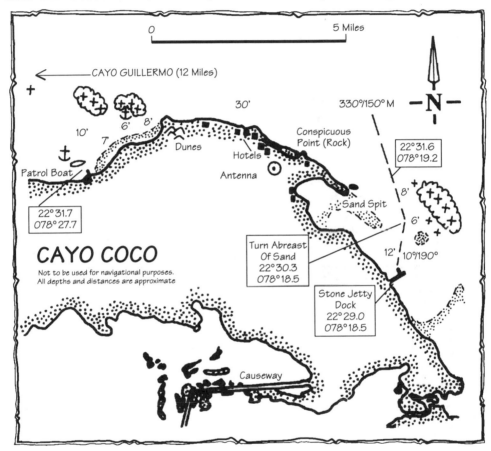

The spit of sand extending east from the promontory is easily seen through the water so come past it from the northwest and then curve round towards the long breakwater-wharf which points at you from land. There may be a crane and assorted machinery on the end, but behind these is a shelter where you may moor. If the dock space is occupied, then you can always raft alongside whatever vessel is there.

TRAVELING TO THE BEACHES OR HOTELS

Documents are unlikely to be required as there is no Guarda Frontera post on this side of the island, but there should be someone there who can call taxis if you wish to travel to the hotels or beaches spread along the northern edge of the cay.

The dusty stone dock is a fair distance to the hotel complex so plan your day accordingly, but there is a lot to do while in the area. The cay's natural resources are being aggressively managed by "Flor y Fauna," so there are many distinct varieties of wildlife to be seen and tours may be had from the hotel lobbies.

The Guitart (a Spanish group) hotels are large and not at all like the usually impersonal government managed affairs. The staff is Cuban but management functions are being controlled by foreign experts and the increased level of efficiency shows. They are clean and offer services the equivalent of anything on offer elsewhere in the world.

For the first time since leaving Santiago you will be able to change your travellers-cheques.

If you require fuel, water, or stores for the boat, the Servimar organization can help as their boat is normally moored alongside your dock and its intended function is to provide provisions for travelling boats.

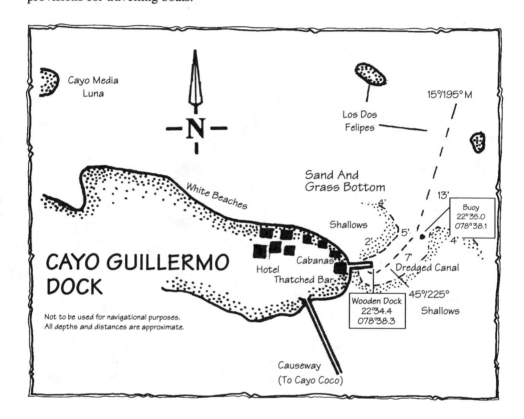

CAYO GUILLERMO DOCK

Not to be used for navigational purposes.
All depths and distances are approximate.

CAYO GUILLERMO

This short 20-mile run over to another group of hotels on the next cay can be accomplished most easily by visual courses along the outer reef. Once again, some of the obstructions following Cayo Coco do not show up on the charts but they're big enough to steer round on a course of 290-300° M from just off the tip.

There are two outer islets abreast of the eastern tip of Cayo Guillermo (itself recognizable by the large thatched hut, the wharf and the uncharted causeway linking the two cays). Once between them, take up a course of approximately 195° M to pass left of a red buoy at 22°35.0N / 078°38.1W.

Carefully proceed across the bar 225° M along a visible dredged channel to the narrow wooden dock. Be careful to pass 50-60 feet east of the end and only dock on the deeper **southern** side.

Note: At low tide you've only got 5-6 feet of water at the bar so be careful to look at the bottom colors for signs of the channel.

There is a small grey turbine-powered patrol-boat stationed at the dock, and it will come out to lead the way if you show any signs of uncertainty, so don't be worried.

A FOREIGN MANAGED HOTEL

Once again this is another foreign managed hotel complex and being guided by the principal of "No profit. No job," thus achieves a much better standard of service. It is perfectly amazing just how much better.

The staff here are personable Cubans who have been thoroughly trained (the waiters even have to take dancing-lessons!) and there is a constant effort to entertain the guests rather than to merely endure them.

As you are at the dock you'll have to be cleared in by the captain of the patrol-boat, but (if it's still Norbert) he shows an admirable efficiency and the whole process doesn't take more than ten minutes. Administration will also show up to let you know what you can expect here and despite it being somewhat out-of-the-way they will make a determined effort to assist in anything you require. We once rather optimistically requested propane gas of Sr. Manolito (the head of administration), and within 2 days our small bottle had been transported to a nearby town and via a soldered connection refilled from a larger one!

The guests here tend to be Italians or Spanish and a stylishly dressed lot they are, dancing wildly at night in the dockside disco-hut... pleasantly undressed too along the beaches.

ROUTE TO VARADERO
CHART NOS.ICH 1128, 1127, 1126 (CUBAN)
& DMA 27060, 27080 (U.S.)

Its still a long way to Varadero so we'll plan on stopping twice more along the route, first at **Cayo Francés** outside the channel to the port of Caibarién, and later at **Esquivel del Sur.**

Along the way the Santa María lighthouse at Cayo Caiman Grande (a beautiful compound looking like a set from Beau Geste) may call you up to wish you a happy trip and as the Bahamas Channel widens, so too will the current flow diminish.

CAYO FRANCÉS (40 MILES)

This cay is notable both for its shape and for the ship aground in the bight on the western side. The shape is rather like a Salvador Dali painting, and the ship is still used as a depot for molasses.

Come round the northwest tip giving the shallows a wide berth and moor in good water south of the Guarda Frontera post. The tides along the coast now are slowly becoming a factor again, so leave yourself a couple of feet below if necessary.

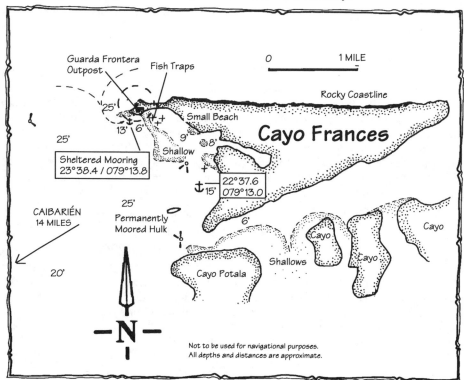

There are a couple of large buildings with a good-sized watchtower and a couple of antennae, but despite all this and the spectators along the roofs you may well have to swim ashore to clear in if they don't reply to transmissions. Of course, having done this, they'll say they don't need to see your papers and you can continue on without a despacho.

This is the first place on the coast that you're likely to be attacked by mosquitos, so review all those precautions which have lapsed into disuse, and pass the time snorkeling or dinghying.

Over to the south there is the large white ferro-cement hulk which has been there since World War II, and little fishing boats will wander in and out of the inlet leading into the cay. Beware of the shallow banks in the center of the bay.

The port of **Caibarién** lies to the southwest at the end of a well-marked channel.

It's a long way to the next stop, but there are alternate shelters along the way in any of the cays lining the latter stages of the route, and were you to come in through the Pasa Marcos you'd find a large sheltered bay with plenty of room and depth. Similarly the canal through the Boca de Maravíllas could take you through all the way to the large bay of Sagua La Grande and the city of La Isabela on the mainland. That channel is well marked along its length and can be entered southwards from the outer buoys at 23 °02.0 N / 079 °58.0 W. Nevertheless, making it all the way to Esquivel del Sur does allow a passage the following day to Varadero.

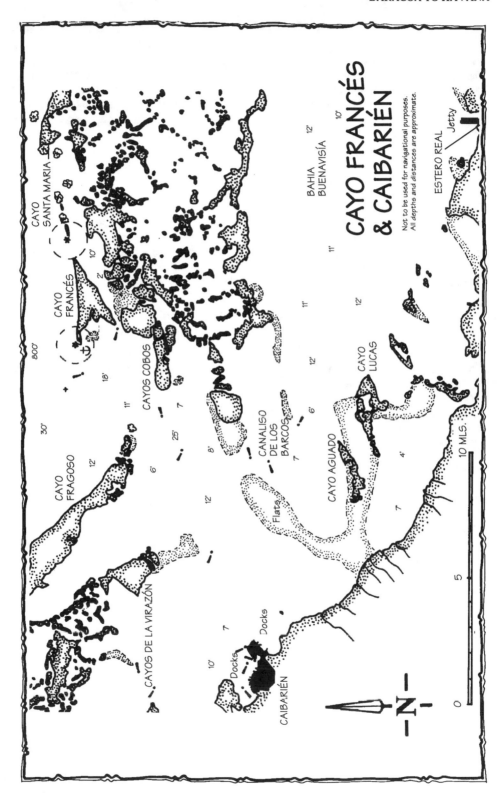

CAYO FRANCÉS
& CAIBARIÉN

Not to be used for navigational purposes.
All depths and distances are approximate.

CAYO SANTA MARIA

CAYO FRANCÉS

800'

30'

CAYOS COBOS

CAYO FRAGOSO

CAYOS DE LA VIRAZÓN

CANALISO DE LOS BARCOS

Flats

CAYO AGUADO

CAYO LUCAS

BAHIA BUENAVISÍA

ESTERO REAL

Jetty

Docks

Docks

CAIBARIÉN

10 MLS.

N

0   5

CAYO ESQUIVEL DEL SUR (55 MILES)

Go around to the west side of the cay to anchor 300 yards south of the light in 10-foot of water (approximately 23 °04.1 N / 080 °05.3 W) where you will be well protected from all likely winds . The area is deeper than shown on the charts and the anchor can be dropped into deep gullies in the turtle-grass for extra security. Leave before first light the next day, and once over the wall set a safe course (315 ° M) until it's light enough to steer visually (or a heading of 303 ° M).

ROUTE TO VARADERO

The water between this overnight halt and Varadero is startlingly clear. You would be able to actually see individual fish on the bottom at 35-40 feet if going slowly enough. Not a bad thing, as there are increasing signs of drift-nets strung across the surface from a haphazard mixture of polystyrene and cork floats. But in fact as the trip is something around 75 miles you may not want to delay.

Cut across the flats at the Pasa Falcones east of the Cayo Cadiz light to save a couple of miles, but if you can't do the journey in daylight then duck into the bay behind that same lighthouse to drop anchor at approximately 23°11.8 N / 080°29.4 W.

VARADERO AND THE BAY OF CARDENAS
CHART NO. ICH 1512 (CUBAN)

Sometimes not shown on charts as Varadero (which strictly speaking is merely the name of the beach area), this largest of the Cuban vacation areas is situated along the outer northwest corner of the Bay of Cárdenas.

The important thing to remember when coming in from the east is that the entrance to the marina where you will be expected to dock is both the **outside** and at the **eastern** end of the peninsula of Hicacos.

DESTINATION MARINA ACUA

Your destination will be the Marina Acua with which you should communicate in advance of arrival if possible. They monitor channel 68 on the VHF and will make all arrangements with the customs, immigration, and Guarda Frontera.

Do not enter the bay at the wonderful lighthouse in the middle as it marks the channel for the large commercial vessels which use the port of Cárdenas in the southwest corner. Instead, continue outside parallel to the crowded beaches and the enormous (comparatively) hotel developments, until you see the two large monolithic hotels at the base of the peninsula. Just past the most westerly hotel there are lights at 23°08.0 N / 081°18.8 W marking the end of the canal into Paso Malo and the marina.

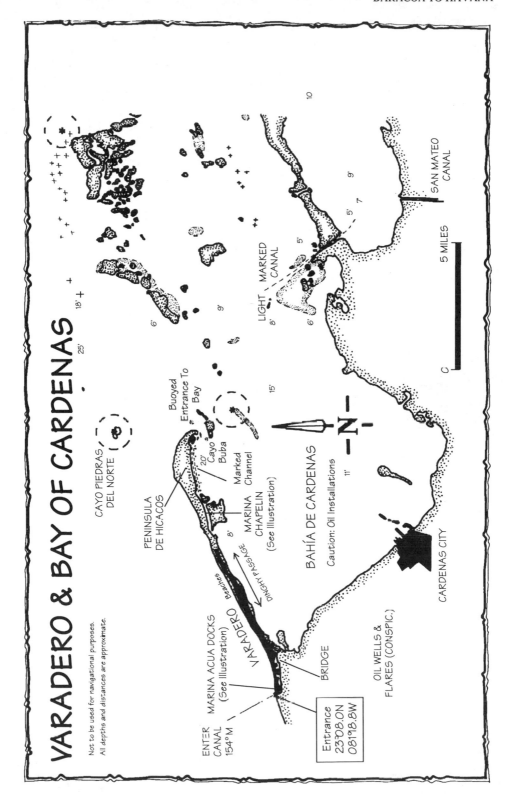

VARADERO & BAY OF CARDENAS

Not to be used for navigational purposes.
All depths and distances are approximate.

CAYO PIEDRAS
DEL NORTE

PENINSULA
DE HICACOS

Buoyed
Entrance To
Bay

Cayo
Buba

Marked
Channel

MARINA
CHAPELIN
(See Illustration)

BAHÍA DE CARDENAS

Caution: Oil Installations

DINGHY PASSAGE

Beaches

VARADERO

MARINA ACUA DOCKS
(See Illustration)

ENTER
CANAL
154°M

Entrance
23°08.0N
081°18.8W

BRIDGE

OIL WELLS &
FLARES (CONSPIC.)

CARDENAS CITY

SAN MATEO
CANAL

LIGHT   MARKED   CANAL

N

5 MILES

C

245

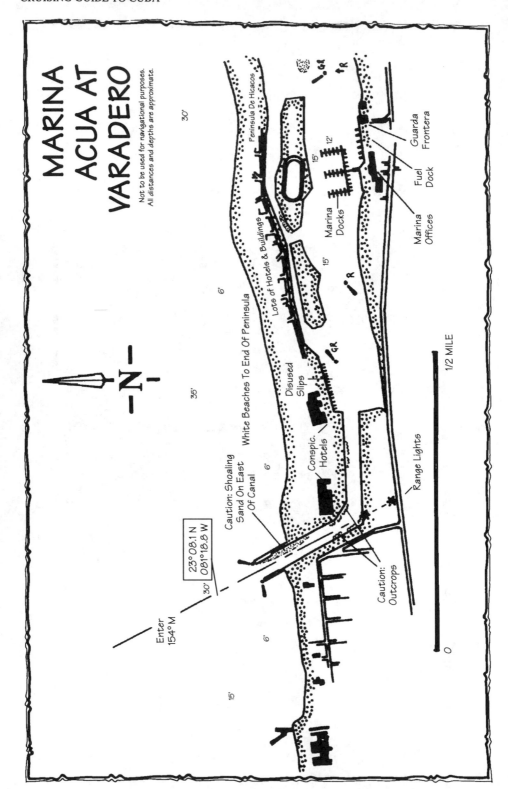

MARINA
ACUA AT
VARADERO

Not to be used for navigational purposes.
All distances and depths are approximate.

30'

Peninsula De Hicacos

Guarda
Frontera

12'

15'

Marina
Docks

Fuel
Dock

Marina
Offices

R

Lots of Hotels & Buildings

15'

6'

15'

N

35'

GR

White Beaches To End Of Peninsula

6'

Disused
Slips

Conspic.
Hotels

6'

Caution: Shoaling
Sand On East
Of Canal

23°08.1 N
081°18.8 W

30'

Enter
154° M

Caution:
Outcrops

Range Lights

1/2 MILE

0

15'

6'

There are range-lights to guide you, but in any case you can enter along a course heading of 154° M making sure you favor the **western side** of the canal as the other side is much shallower.

Follow the canal round to the left and through the large markers on either side of the channel until you arrive off the marina where you should dock as you see fit.

The marina counts on some 30-40 spaces so there is always going to be room, but in general it will be better to dock in one of the berths along the central spine as local vessels use the outer branches.

Avoid the extreme tip of the eastern dock too. That's where the naval patrol-boat docks.

HAVE YOUR DOCUMENTS READY

If you are coming in from abroad then you should read the appropriate chapter dealing with the subject and have your documents ready for customs and immigration, but we've never experienced any hassles. Looking back at our logbook, I note that clearing in from along the coast once took us all of five minutes while the Canadian couple who had arrived just that morning from Havana took over four hours!

As mentioned before, it's all a question of having the right bits ready at the right time.

For the local attractions of Varadero I would advise acquiring a suitable guidebook as there are countless diversions on offer. This is Cuba's premiere holiday resort and despite the general non-participation of U.S. citizens, thousands of European tourists arrive here to spend their time on the beaches and to use it as a base for further travel.

Any normal tourist facilities which you may have been denied while coasting offshore are now most certainly available by enquiring at the marina offices or in any of the hotel lobbies. On the other hand, the port of Cárdenas is also nearby with shipyard facilities there for any more specialized needs (within the constraints of parts-availability).

TOURISM ORIENTED BAY

The bay plays host to countless boat-trips with tourists of all descriptions crowding the decks of both foreign and local charters. If you have a large enough vessel and time to spare, then this is the one place in Cuba where there is the possibility of coming to some strange agreement with the government.

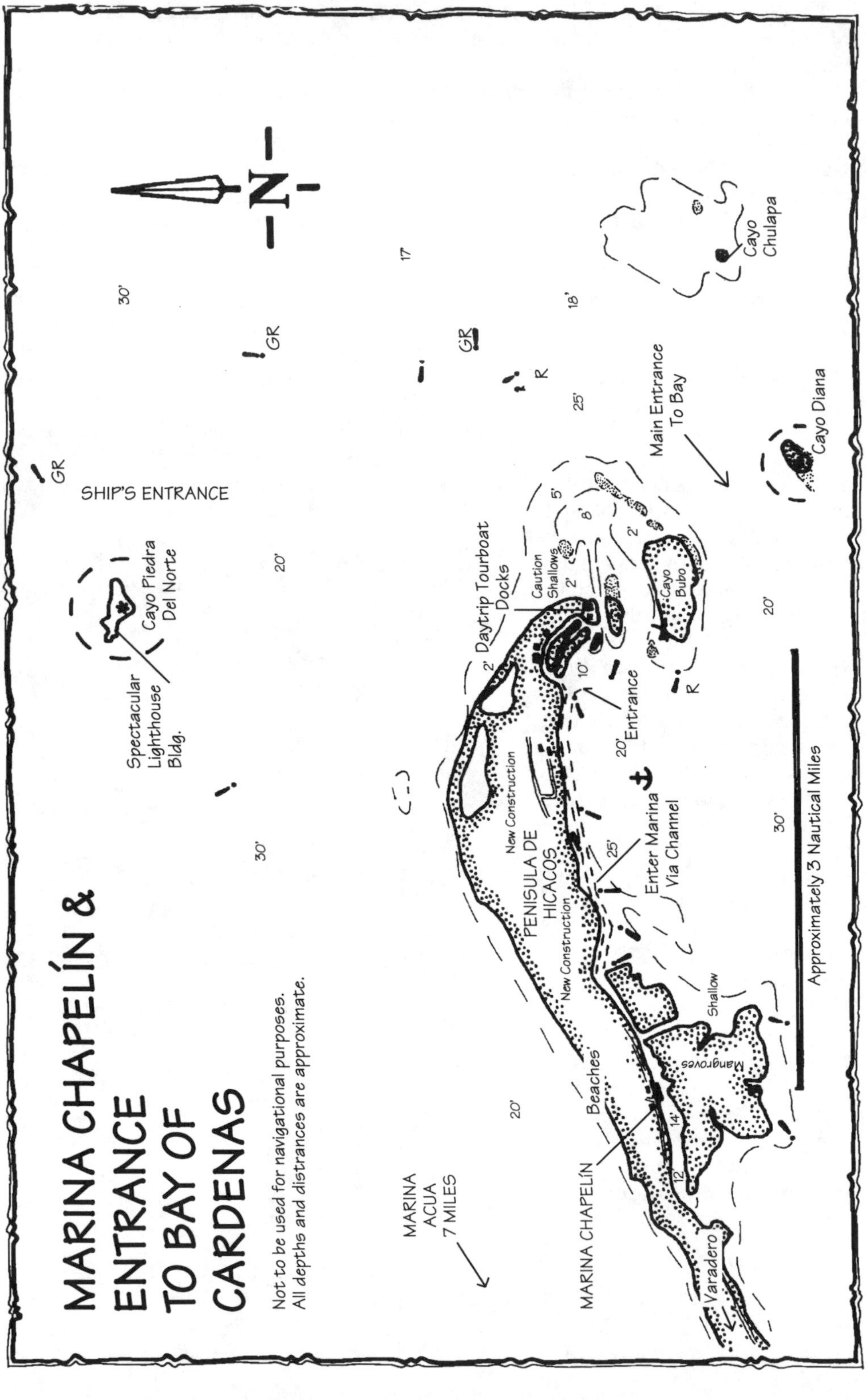

MARINA CHAPELÍN & ENTRANCE TO BAY OF CARDENAS

Not to be used for navigational purposes.
All depths and distances are approximate.

SHIP'S ENTRANCE

Spectacular Lighthouse Bldg.

Cayo Piedra Del Norte

GR

30'

20'

30'

17

18'

GR

25'

R

GR

Cayo Chulapa

Main Entrance To Bay

Cayo Diana

5'

8'

2'

2'

Daytrip Tourboat Docks

Caution Shallows

2'

10'

Cayo Bubo

R

20'

20' Entrance

New Construction

25'

Enter Marina Via Channel

30'

PENISULA DE HICACOS

New Construction

Shallow

Approximately 3 Nautical Miles

Mangroves

Beaches

14'

12'

MARINA ACUA 7 MILES

MARINA CHAPELIN

Varadero

20'

The most convenient base for day-cruising the bay itself is the **Marina Chapelín** half-way up the peninsula on the inside. This is where most of the tour-boats are based, and although the marina only occasionally has room for casual foreign yachts it may be worthwhile calling (channel 72) them to see if there is any possibility of overnight space.

There is an excellent restaurant alongside the docks at Chapelín too, and even though you may be based in Paso Malo (or Kawama) at the Marina Acua it is worthwhile taking the dinghy further east through the canal and northeast along the peninsula to visit it. Be prepared for a long trip if your dinghy can't plane, and look out for the current going under the bridge, but it's a fun trip.

To get there you will need to inform the Guarda Frontera over in the guard-house on your left ashore (just past the fuel dock), but a permit (a sort of mini-despacho) will be issued whenever you wish to take your dinghy out of the immediate area.

Once back at the Marina Acua, there is one extremely annoying feature you will possibly have to put up with. The broadcast of the news over crackling loudspeakers seemingly aimed directly at your boat.

There are few things less appealing than the heroic socialist achievements of the Youth Brigade or Cambodian current-affairs, at 6:30 a.m. In spite of everything else that is good about the place, the radio in Cuba lacks a certain something.

Luckily, if you need a break from the daily dose of exhortations, slogans, denunciations, and proclamations, you can pick up U.S. stations on AM (e.g. 940 WINZ). You can also sometimes pick up the odd stray FM signal from the Florida Keys. They may be equally biased, but at least you control the volume.

A lot of petroleum extraction takes place within the bay of Cárdenas, and the dire need for fuel supplies outweighs all other considerations such as tourism. The sulfuric fumes emitted at night from the flaring-off are deposited with the dew in the form of a weak acid all over your decks. It also dulls your fiberglass and will blacken and pit your stainless fittings in short order. The only way round this is to clean your boat scrupulously every morning while it is still damp, and to otherwise put up with the fumes.

Taxis are available through the marina offices to get you into town, but if you prefer you can walk or cycle as it is only a couple of miles.

A NIGHTCLUB AND FLOATING RESTAURANTS

On the bridge there is a nightclub which offers nightly cabaret. Just over the bridge and down to your left, there are a couple of floating restaurants. Personally, I would ignore them and head on another 200 yards to the excellent Club Alfredo overlooking the canal. This is an outpost of foreign enterprise, which gallantly tries to maintain decent standards of service and taste, in spite of the best efforts of Cuban tradition.

The club was originally founded as a dive-center, but the food-service aspect of the operation now has expanded to at least equal status. A surprising variety of pizzas are on offer. If by now you are not dying for something of this sort, then you've been at sea too long.

If you're interested in scuba, they keep their dive-boat at the Marina Acua, so it's only the work of a moment to board it for a trip along the coast with a proper dive-guide.

Before I leave the subject of Varadero there is one final feature of the resort which may be of interest. There are cheap, direct flights to Nassau from Matanzas just a couple of miles away.

The flight on an old Russian aircraft lasts only 40 minutes or less and can be a godsend if you have to acquire spares quickly.

When leaving Varadero, request early clearance and if necessary go over to the guard-hut to roust out the Guarda Frontera. The papers can be quickly prepared aboard with the help of coffee if it's before sunup, and cigarettes if the dreadful oil-well smell is too much.

The port of Matanzas is the first available port along the way, but it might be off-limits except in an emergency, therefore Havana is your final stop on the circumnavigation.

ROUTE TO HAVANA
CHART NOS. ICH 1125, 1124, OR 1106 (CUBAN) & DMA 27080 (U.S.)

As dealt with previously (chapter V), note that your destination is not in fact the port of Havana, but rather the Dársena de Barlovento 7 miles on from there. Being a major commercial harbour, Havana is off-limits to casual cruising yachts so schedule things accordingly for the extra distance involved.

You can cruise as close in as you care, but be on the lookout for the snorkelers who may be found up to a mile offshore. Sometimes you can even come across two small rubber-tire rafts lashed together and being used as a platform on which these snorkeling expeditions are based.

A PROTECTED INLET

There is a rather nice inlet at 081°46.8W which can be entered along 210° M, but this is one of the few protected spots worthy of note. In general the coastal character changes from wooded escarpments to electricity generating stations and rusting iron constructions, ending more or less in conglomerations of apartment blocks before Cojimar.

At Cojimar itself there is an impressive stadium overlooking the city while the old castle handles the defense along the western side of the seawall.

SIGHTING HAVANA'S SKYLINE

Havana makes for a wonderful sight as you come up on it at last, with ugly buildings and domed churches vying for your attention over to the far side, while the great castle at the entrance looks out across the river from the east. Along the famous seawall the decaying but still gaily colored facades only hint at their former glory, but it's nevertheless a wonderful sight as you come across the mouth of the harbour and parallel the city.

At this point it's a good idea to contact the Marina Hemingway on channel 72 with details of your arrival. They will contact the customs and immigration officials in advance, and by the time you arrive at the Guarda Frontera post at the marina entrance those officials should hopefully have had enough time to make their way out there.

Marina Hemingway is covered in chapter five and entry is the same whether arriving in Cuba for the first time or coming in from Varadero.

You will be able to make visual contact with the entrance buoy at 23 °05.4 N/082 °30.6W from some way off, and from there on it's 140° M through the reef, and just a matter of following the procedures you are already perfectly familiar with.

The Havana skyline. (Photo by Simon Charles)

APPENDIX AND GLOSSARY

This is a short, or not so short, list of useful words you might come across in dealing with the various aspects of your cruise. There are a couple of different headings, so if you vaguely know which subject you should be interested in then flick to it and search for what you need.

It is deliberately led-off by the Spanish term to encourage you to read the whole paragraph while searching, and hopefully something you don't need just right now will sink in. Maybe it will miraculously pop into your mind one day when you might need it in a hurry.

Incidentally, I've not bothered with the more obvious words everybody already knows.

GEOGRAPHIC AND HYDROGRAPHIC

(Terms you might see on a chart)

Acantilado	Cliff, steep
Alga	Kelp or turtle-grass
Altura	Height
Angosta	Narrow
Arcilla	Clay
Arena	Sand
Arroyo	Creek, brook
Bahia	Bay
Bajo	Shoal (or low)
Bajo fondo	Shallow water
Balneario	Seaside resort
Banco	Bank
Barra	Bar
Barro	Mud
Boca	Mouth
Bosque	Wood
Brazo	Arm, branch
Buque hundido	Sunken ship
Cabecería	Group of reefs
Cabeza	Head (of coral)
Cabezo	Outcrop (of rock)
Cabo	Cape, headland
Caleta	Inlet
Canal	Canal, channel
Canalizo	Narrow channel
Cascajo	Shingle
Cayo (Cy)	Key, cay
Cima	Top
Corriente	Current
Costa	Coast
Cuenca	Basin
Cueva	Cave
Curva de nivel	Contour line

Darsena (Dars)	Dock, harbour
Destello (Dest)	Flash (eg. bouys)
Duna	Dune
Ensenada (Ens)	Cove, anchorage
Entrada	Entrance
Escarpe	Escarpment
Estero	Creek
Estrecho	Strait
Estuario	Estuary
Fango	Mud
Faro	Lighthouse
Farallón	Cliff, high rock
Fondo	Bottom
Fondeadero	Anchorage
Golfo	Gulf
Isla	Island
Islote	Islet
Isobata	Depth contour
Laberinto	Labyrinth
Laguna	Lagoon
Lengua	Tongue (of sand)
Loma	Hill
Mangle	Mangrove
Medano	Sandbank
Morro	Headland
Orilla	Shore
Paredón	Wall
Pasa	Pass
Paso	Passage

Pena	Rock		Restinga	Ledge
Pico	Peak		Rio	River
Piedra	Stone		Roca	Rock
Pilote	Pile		Rompeolas	Breakwater
Placer	Large sandbank		Rompiente	Rough
Playa	Beach			
Poco profunda	Shallow		Salina	Salt pan
Profunda	Deep		Sargazo	Sagasso
Profundidad	Depth		Sierra	Mountain range
Promontorio	Promontory		Silla	Saddle
Punta (Pta)	Point		Surgidero	Ancorage (shelterless)
Quebrado	Break (in reef)		Valle	Valley

WEATHER AND SEA CONDITIONS
(Sorry about most of these, the fault lies in the pessimism of human nature)

Aire	Air		Inundacíon	Flood
Aire frío	Cold air			
Aire húmedo	Moist air		Lluvia	Rain
Aire seco	Dry air			
Altura	Height		Marea	Tide
Aviso	Warning			
			Neblina	Mist
Baja	Low		Niebla	Fog
Barlovento	Windward		Nivel del mar	Sea level
Borrascoso	Stormy		Nube	Cloud
Bravo	Rough, angry		Nubosidad	Cloudiness
Brisa	Breeze		Núcleo	Core
Brisa marina	Sea breeze			
Buen tiempo	Good weather		Ola	Wave
			Onda	Wave
Calma	Calm			
Ciclon	Cyclone		Pendiente	Coming
Cielo	Sky (or heaven)		Picada (mar)	Rough
Clima	Climate		Pronóstico	Forecast
Chubasco	Shower			
Crepusculo	Twilight		Relámpago	Lightning
Disperso	Dispersed		Severa	Severe
Disturbio	Disturbance			
			Tempeste	Storm
Frente	Front		Terral	Land breeze
			Turbido	Turbulent, rough
Galerna	Gale		Viento	Wind
			Visibilidad	Visibility
Hondonada	Trough			
Humedad	Humidity		Zona	Zone
Huracán	Hurricane			

NAVIGATION AND MANEUVERS
(Terms you might hear)

A bordar	Board		Embalizado	Marked
A la deriva!	Adrift!		Embarcar	Embark
A popa	Astern		Embarcadero	Wharf
A proa	Ahead		Encallar	Run aground
A babor	Go to port		Enfilacion	Leading line,
A estribor	Go to starboard			range marks
Acerase	Approach (request)		Enfilar	Aim
Aguas	Waters		Escala	Scale
Alcance	Range, reach		Estima	Estimate
Altura	Height		Estribor	Starboard
Amarrar	Moor, tie up			
Anclar	Anchor (verb)		Faro	Lighthouse
Autonomía	Range, self-sufficiency		Fondear	Anchor (verb)
Approximarse	Close-in (verb)			
Arribar	Arrive		Jalar (halar)	Haul
Atracar	Come alongside			
Aviso	Warning or notice		Luces	Lights
Babor	Port, left		Marcación	Bearing
Baliza ciega	Unlit beacon		Metro	Metre
Baliza luminosa	Lighted beacon			
Boya	Bouy		Naufragio	Wreck
Braza	Fathom (armspan)		Nudo	Knot (both types)
Buque	Ship			
			Remolcar	Tow (verb)
Cable	Cable (1/10th mile)		Rumbo	Course
Carta nautica	Chart		Ruta	Route
Cuaderno	Notebook			
			Tendero	Holding (anchor)
Deriva	Drift		Tirar	Pull
Destino	Destination		Tome	Take
Diario de			Toda máquina	Full speed
navigacion	Logbook			

DIRECTIONS
(Just where am I...?)

Norte	North		Babor	Port
Sur	South		Tribor	Starboard
Este	East			
Oeste	West		En frente	In front
			Por atras	Behind
Septentrional	Northern		Al lado	To the side
Meridional	Southern			
Oriental	Eastern			
Occidental	Western			

PORT TERMS, OFFICIALS, PAPERS ETC.

(You'll need these ashore)

Acopio	Storage facility		Inmigración	Immigration
Administrador	Administrator			
Aduanas	Customs		Lancha	Launch
Agente	Agent		Leyes	Laws
Amarradero	Mooring berth			
Astillero	Shipyard		Malecón	Waterfront road
			Muelle	Wharf, mole
Bodega	Storeroom			
Buque	Ship		Nave	Vessel
Calado	Draft		Pasarela	Small pier
Capitán del			Patana	Barge
puerto	Port Captain		Pedraplén	Stone causeway
Capitanía	Harbour master's office		Práctico	Pilotage
Consignatario	Ship's agent		Ponton	Pontoon, hulk
Cuarentena	Quarentine			
			Remolcador	Tugboat
Darsena	Dock, harbour		Revisar	Search
Despacho	Clearance, dispatch			
Destino	Destination		Salvamento	Rescue
Dragado	Dredged, dredging		Senalizacion	Signals
			Sondeo	Search
Embarcadero	Wharf, landing			
Entrada	Entrance		Tuberia	Pipework
Espigón	Jetty, pier			
Fecha	Date		Varadero	Slipway
Fondeadero	Anchorage		Viaje	Voyage
Grua	Crane		Zarpe	Foreign clearance
Grada	Slipway			

YOU AND YOUR BOAT

(Simple words you may need to describe your boat over the radio
are grouped together first)

Achay Pay	HP		Procedencia de	Coming from
Ancho	Width		Tonnelada	Tonnage
Bandera	Flag, nationality		Tripulantes	Crew
Barco turistico	Tourist vessel (yours)		Velero	Sailboat
Caballos	Horses (horsepower)		Yate	Yacht
Calado	Draft			
Casco	Hull		Aleta	Fin, centerboard
Eslora	LOA		Ancla	Anchor
Fibra	Fibreglass		Alternador	Alternator
Lancha	Motorboat		Arboladura	Rigging
Nombre	Name		Arrancador	Starter motor

Balsa	Raft, dinghy
Bandera	Flag
Bay Achay	
Effe	VHF (radio)
Bita	Bollard
Bodega	Hold
Bomba	Pump
Bote	Boat
Brujula	Compass
Cabo	Line, rope
Cadena	Chain
Caja	Gearbox
Cambios	Gears
Combustible	Fuel
Contenedor	Container
Cornamusa	Cleat
Cubierta	Deck
Cuerda	Cord
Defensa	Fender
Ecosonda	Echo-sounder
Embarcación	Vessel
Escala	Stair, ladder
Escape	Exhaust
Francobordo	Freeboard
Gasolina	Gasoline, petrol
Guia	Keel
Guinche	Winch
Gaz	Gas

Helice	Propellor
Lastres	Stores
Manga	Width, beam, hose
Manguera	Hose, pipe
Mareado	Seasick
Mastelero	Topmast
Mástil	Mast
Motonave	Motor vessel
Petroleo	Diesel fuel
Popa	Poop, stern
Proa	Prow, bow
Puente	Bridge
Roto	Broken
Quilla	Keel
Salvavida	Lifejacket
Tanque	Tank (fuel, water, air)
Toma	Supply hose, tube
Timón	Helm, rudder
Tripulación	Crew
Tripulante	Crewmember
Vela	Sail

SCUBA TERMS

Aletas	Fins
Atmósferas	Atmospheres (14.7 lbs/in)
Buceo	Scuba
Careta	Mask
Chaleca	Jacket
Licencia	Dive card
Plomos	Weights
Presion	Pressure
Profundimetro	Depth guage
Regulador	Regulator
Superficia	Surface
Tanque	Cylinder

INCIDENTALS
(Add your own as you go)

Carpeta	Front desk (hotel)
Congrís	Rice and beans
Divisa	Foreign currency
Je Jene	No-see-um
Jinetero	Neer-do-well, hustler (literally cowboy/jockey)
Jutia	Delicious rodent
Mojito	Rum, spearmint, sugar, soda and ice.
Mosca	Fly
Mosquito	Mosquito
Pesca	Fish
Turbina	Pump (landside)